STARS FELL ON STOCKTON

The story of the Denvers: a memoir of life in a rock band in the 1960s

By

Brian K. Ashcroft

Grosvenor House
Publishing Limited

All rights reserved
Copyright © Brian K. Ashcroft, 2018

The right of Brian K. Ashcroft to be identified as the author of this
work has been asserted in accordance with Section 78
of the Copyright, Designs and Patents Act 1988

The book cover picture is copyright to Brian K. Ashcroft

This book is published by
Grosvenor House Publishing Ltd
Link House
140 The Broadway, Tolworth, Surrey, KT6 7HT.
www.grosvenorhousepublishing.co.uk

This book is sold subject to the conditions that it shall not, by way of
trade or otherwise, be lent, resold, hired out or otherwise circulated
without the author's or publisher's prior consent in any form of binding or
cover other than that in which it is published and
without a similar condition including this condition being imposed
on the subsequent purchaser.

A CIP record for this book
is available from the British Library

ISBN 978-1-78623-306-6

CONTENTS

		Page
	Prologue	v
Ch. 1	In the land of the Prince Bishops	1
Ch. 2	Growing up on Teesside	7
Ch. 3	Musical Awakenings	27
Ch. 4	Pedro and Burdon's	43
Ch. 5	The Denvers	62
Ch. 6	Sam Curtis and the French Connection	104
Ch. 7	Guests of Uncle Sam	115
Ch. 8	From TFAD to DEFCON-2	145
Ch. 9	Out of the Shadows	179
Ch.10	Enter Jimmy English	212
Ch. 11	A Taste of Paris	241
Ch. 12	Liverpool Party	264
Ch. 13	Coming of age	282
Ch. 14	Moving On	302
	Epilogue	314
	Acknowledgements	318

PROLOGUE

I was thirteen when I started to go to dance halls in Billingham, Stockton and Middlesbrough. At that time, 1960, the traditional dance fare served up on Teesside was fast withering away. In the 1930s and the war years Stockton was well served by several bands and large dance halls: the Palais de Danse with Jack O'Boyle, the Maison de Dance with Jack Marwood and his band and the Jubilee and Corporation Halls. The locus of my mother and father's courtship traversed midweek visits to the Cinema in Stockton High Street and a dance at the 'Maison' on a Saturday night. Jack Marwood, resplendent in tuxedo, would front his similarly dressed band of daytime clerks, railway and shipyard workers, draughtsmen and other assorted occupations as they tried to capture the magic of the latest Ambrose, Henry Hall, Jack Hylton, Joe Loss, or Roy Fox recording. But as the evening wore on the music began to drift more and more across the Atlantic. Foxtrot and quickstep became more energetic as the couples and singles - many fortified by a break for alcoholic sustenance at the Theatre Hotel, known to many in the 1950s as "Jocker Brown`s" - embraced the swing of Marwood versions of Count Basie, Tommy Dorsey, Duke Ellington, Benny Goodman, Woody Herman, Harry James, Glen Miller, and Artie Shaw. Indeed, Jack Marwood's dance band had reigned supreme over the Maison de Danse and Stockton's popular culture right from the twenties down to the late fifties[1]. But by the early 1960s the band was a shadow of its former self, its reputation having declined almost inversely as Jack's own corpulence grew[2].

My early teenage visits to the Teesside dance halls in 1960 and 1961 were altogether a more introverted activity than the dance focused exuberance of my parents' courtship years. Indeed, I wasn't interested in dance at all. And if I was keen to meet girls, I didn't see how my nascent sexual longings could be met by squirming unrhythmically 18 inches away from some unknown girl with my face flushed red reflecting the 45 minutes of anxiety that I took to pluck up the courage to ask for the dance. No, what drew me to the 'Maison' and the Jubilee Ballroom in Stockton, the Bellasis Hall in Billingham and the Astoria in Middlesbrough was the band. But not the middle-aged, tuxedoed players of the Marwood ensemble, rather the young, sharp-suited pop bands such as the Johnny Taylor Five and the Midnighters who were gaining local ascendancy over the dance bands. Sadly, the heyday of these bands was to be much shorter than the reign of Jack Marwood and his contemporaries. They were eventually superseded from the late 1960s in

---

[1] Jack Marwood and his band are reputed to have held the longest British band residency from around 1917 to Marwood's retirement in1968

[2] In case this is interpreted as being unfair to Jack Marwood, I should make it clear that Marwood was well aware of the changing trends in modern music and increasingly promoted the appearance of new pop and rock bands at the *Maison*. One of these bands was the Denvers.

PROLOGUE

Stockton as everywhere else by the disco. Modern record production quality and powerful electrical amplification meant that the recorded sound of popular singers, groups and dance favourites became preferred to the 'covers' of local live bands.

Without doubt, the principal stimulus to these local bands was the success of the Shadows. As Roger Taylor, of Queen, writes

> "Around the year 1960 there existed in Britain a curious epidemic of about 39,000 instrumental beat groups. With a peculiar regularity they would tend to consist of four youths in identical shiny suits - one would play drums, the other three would wield salmon-pink Fender (or cheaper look-alike) guitars in choreographed poses, whilst executing a curious synchronized "dance-walk". The lead guitarist would often wear horn-rimmed spectacles and the electric bass player would tend to be a swept back bleached blond. The bass player would usually get the girls. All these groups would play almost exclusively covers of Shadows tunes. In many cases they would actually imagine themselves to be Hank, Bruce, Jet or Tony. These groups were The Shadows clones. I know - I was that group!"[3]

And Teesside's Midnighters were another. To a thirteen year old with musical aspirations, the Shadows

---

[3] His testimonial to the Shadows is on their official website at http://www.theshadowsofficial.com/

were like Greek gods, to be glimpsed on the pedestals of hazy black and white television screens and, if you were lucky, on their occasional appearances at Stockton's Globe theatre. As it happened, Stockton was more favoured by the Shadows than I appreciated at the time and it was indirectly through their connection with Stockton that I was given the opportunity to become a professional musician. But more of that later.

The Midnighters were Roger Taylor's archetypical Shadows clones. But to my untutored ears they were no pale imitation. They played more frequently to the south of the River Tees, with occasional forays to Stockton's Maison de Danse. So, to hear them on a regular basis I would have to travel by bus from Billingham to Middlesbrough. A regular venue was the Astoria, which was not cheap to get in and when bus fares, entrance fee and costs of a solitary orange juice were added together my week's pocket money would be exhausted on this one outing. But what a return for my investment.

The Astoria was a refurbished theatre with pretensions and could be seen as a precursor of the nightclubs for the masses that began to spring up on Teesside in the middle to late 1960s. Its pretensions were realised by dimmed lighting, the large revolving crystal ball floating over the dance floor reflecting directed light in thousands of different directions and the spotlit, canopied dais at the end of the floor under which the artists of the evening performed. The Midnighters stood on the dais, three guitarists up front and drummer behind. At the right of the dais stood the lead guitarist. The improbably named Granville B. Leacy *was* Hank Marvin in everything but name: horn-rimmed glasses, slimly built in shiny suit with a red Fender Stratocaster hanging

PROLOGUE

from his neck and an ability to play and sound like Hank that made me salivate with envy. At the other side of the stage stood the bass player: Ray Hudson. Ray was tall, handsome and sported a sunburst Fender Precision bass. But Ray's talents extended beyond rhythmic bass riffs and Shadows' covers. He had a voice to die for. A voice that stilled the dancers as they listened in awe to his rendition of Roy Orbison's 'Only the Lonely', which had risen to number one in the New Musical Express singles charts in October 1960.

One night, as a single spotlight picked out Ray, his head thrown back, voice rising effortlessly to the peak of Orbison's legendary three-octave range, and a clutch of girls describing a longing semi-circle around and below him, I knew that I had to be a member of a pop band. Remembering my fumbling difficulties in meeting and asking girls to dance, with that scene of a group of adoring females surrounding Ray etched into my mind in a preview of Roger Taylor's own reminiscence, I also knew that I had to become a bass player. And, as something of an afterthought, I reminded myself that perhaps I'd better learn to play the bass guitar!

CHAPTER 1

IN THE LAND OF THE PRINCE BISHOPS

My early life was spent in Stockton-on-Tees. Stockton was and is a market town. Situated on the north bank of the Tees, Stockton[4] lies 38 miles south of Newcastle, 257 miles north of London and 186 miles to the south east of Glasgow, where I have spent most of my working life since 1974. The roots of present day Stockton go back to the creation of the Manor of Stockton in 1138, but in 1189 Bishop Pudsey purchased it and the local economy functioned largely to serve the Bishops of Durham for many years thereafter. The Prince Bishops did much for the town, including freeing the serfs, making the village into a borough at an unknown date in the thirteenth century, and the granting of a market charter by Bishop Bek in 1310, which greatly facilitated

---

[4] My main sources for historical information about Stockton include *"A Brief History of Stockton –on –Tees" by Tim Lambert* http://www.localhistories.org/stockton.html; *"Teesside Online"* http://www.teessideonline.net/kb.php?mode=article&k=21; *"Wikipedia, the free encyclopedia"* http://en.wikipedia.org/wiki/Stockton-On-Tees; *"Picture Stockton" http://picture.stockton.gov.uk/default.aspx* Books by David Simpson and North East Timeline http://www.thenortheast.fsnet.co.uk/page88.htm

trade. Taxes were collected from the southern end of Durham county by the Prince Bishops of Durham, who when they were in the area were based in a fortified manor house in the south of the town, which became known as Stockton Castle. While much of this was beneficial, the monopoly position of the Bishops began to limit the growth of trade. So, in the 1500s, the ties to the Bishops were reduced, allowing the growing population to trade with areas outside Durham and, through the developing port, much further afield.

By the mid seventeenth century the Stockton economy was booming. Exports were a key driving force with local agricultural products such as wool, bacon and butter, and others such as lead, passing through the port by sea to places such as London and beyond. The port also served as an entry point to a growing flow of imports, which included raisins, wine, coal, glass, and household goods. Hence, the town became something of a prize and in the turbulent times of the 1640s the town was occupied by the Scottish army between 1644 and 1646. At the end of the Civil War, Oliver Cromwell ordered the castle to be destroyed to prevent it ever again falling into royalist hands and so effectively ending the power of the Prince Bishops in the town.

Along with economic growth came urban development. By the mid 1700s Stockton had developed into a bustling Hanoverian town with a population of more than 2000. It was during this period that the distinctive face of Stockton, still evident today, was fashioned. A long, broad, High Street was constructed, which continues to be Stockton's pride, leading to claims that it is the widest high street in England and even in Europe! To the east, two or three streets paralleled the High Street and three or four streets led down to the river and quays. In 1735, in the centre of the High Street, on the site of an old tollbooth and cells, a Town House or Town Hall was built in the Dutch style. The Town Hall was further extended in 1744 becoming a landmark and focal point of the town. The Town Hall was complemented by an impressive church located at the northern end of the High Street. With spiritual needs satisfied, cultural demands were met by the construction of Stockton's first theatre in 1766, a notable example of Georgian architecture still evident today in other parts of the town. And, the River Tees ceased to be a barrier to land travel southwards when a stone bridge was built in 1769.

The industrial revolution further accelerated Stockton's economic development. Shipbuilding, which had begun to develop earlier with its associated trades of sail and rope making, began to prosper. An iron working industry developed in the late eighteenth century. Then, during the first half of the nineteenth century a large engineering industry grew up, one of the fruits of which led to international recognition and Stockton's great hubris. The first passenger railway, hauled by George Stephenson's engine Locomotion No. 1, opened between Stockton and Darlington in 1825. The railway opened up the hinterland to Stockton's industry and port allowing, for example, coal to be brought to Stockton's factories, which further encouraged the growth of industry. But just as Stockton's port had superseded Yarm, which was a little further up river, so Middlesbrough began its rise as the principal port of the Tees largely at Stockton's expense. Further, the discovery in the 1850s of ironstone in the Cleveland hills to the south of Stockton led to the rapid growth of an iron and steel industry on both the north and south banks of the Tees. This development, along with the continued growth of shipbuilding, worked to the benefit of Stockton so that by the final quarter of the nineteenth century the town was transformed from the quiet market town of hundred years before to a flourishing centre of industry. And, as the economy expanded so did Stockton's population, which rose rapidly, through both natural growth and in-migration, from 8,562 in 1801 to 86,073 in 1901[5]. Population growth in turn led to public investments in social infrastructure, with the first hospital built in 1862, a public library in 1877, street trams in 1881 and a public park – Ropner Park[6] – in 1883.

Engineering continued to dominate the local economy until the 1920s and 1930s when the chemicals industry began to develop initially on the north bank of the Tees at Billingham, a few miles to the north of Stockton. In 1932 around 5,000 workers were employed in the chemical industry at Billingham. During the 1930s my father's family migrated from Tyneside to Billingham, with my grandfather transferring as a process worker to ICI Billingham. The further growth of the railway had also encouraged my mother's family to migrate during the

---

[5] Source: *A Vision of Britain through Time:* http://www.visionof britain.org.uk/data_theme_page.jsp?u_id=10095086&c_id=10001043&data_theme=T_WK

[6] The park was named after local shipbuilder Robert Ropner, who made a significant fortune from shipbuilding. Preston Hall, which lies between Stockton and Yarm was Ropner's palatial home. Today it is a popular museum and country park, owned and managed by the local authority.

CHAPTER 1

second decade of the twentieth century from the Yorkshire dales to Stockton, where my maternal grandfather transferred jobs as a signalman moving to a new post in charge of a signal box just south of the town.

When my parent's courtship began in the late 1930s, Stockton's economy was just beginning to recover from the ravages of the Depression. Shipbuilding and shipping in Stockton were badly hit and had almost disappeared. In 1931, the male unemployment rate in Stockton stood at 27.2%, compared to the British rate of 12.7%. As the local MP for Stockton in the twenties and thirties, Harold Macmillan[7] was so moved by the experience of high unemployment that it coloured his attitude to economic policy when he became Chancellor of the Exchequer and subsequently Prime Minister in 1957[8]. But with the growth of the chemical industry and the impact of war preparations on local industry, jobs were increasingly available on Teesside. My father, William Kemp Ashcroft, was completing an apprenticeship as a fitter and turner at ICI Billingham, while my mother, Phyllis May Hardwick, had found secretarial work in Stockton.

The start of World War II had a profound impact on many lives in Stockton as well as elsewhere in Britain. My father joined the RAF as an aircraft fitter, and so before the anticipated overseas posting my parents were married in Stockton in March 1940. They spent some of

---

[7] He was MP for Stockton from 1924 to 1929, then from 1931 to 1945 losing his seat under the Labour 'landslide' General Election victory of that year.
[8] S. Brittan, *The Treasury Under the Tories, 1951-1964*, Harmondsworth, 1964.

the war together on various RAF postings in places such as Peterborough, Cumberland and Northern Ireland. But the anticipated overseas posting duly arrived and my father went off around the world, primarily working as a fitter maintaining Sunderland flying boats. With my mother back in the wartime austerity of Stockton, living with her parents, it is probably with mixed feelings that she received my father's military censored letters and photographs from such seemingly exotic locations as Kenya, India, and Ceylon.

Both my parents got through the War unscathed, although not without domestic tragedy (see below). Indeed, my father was never close to enemy action. Although, when once flying over the Mediterranean a US warship opened up on them with its anti-aircraft guns. Fortunately for my father, the rest of the aircrew, and I guess for me, any 'friendly fire' fatalities were avoided. My father returned to work at ICI Billingham, taking my mother to live with him and his parents on By-pass Road Billingham, which was closer to his work. By mid 1946 my mother had fallen pregnant with me and I was born in March 1947, one of the countless births that constituted the post-War 'baby boom'.

CHAPTER 2

GROWING UP ON TEESSIDE

Within eighteen months of my birth my parents moved out of my grandparents' home to take up residence in a new council house, two miles away, close to Wolviston and just west of the A19 in the north of Billingham. The grandly named Matlock Gardens was part of the Monkseaton estate, which was one of the first local housing estates in the post-War flurry of council house building. If it was not meant to live up to the 'homes fit for heroes' concept of post World War I aspiration, the estate certainly offered to its largely skilled working-class residents new, even aristocratic, possibilities with street names such as Matlock, Chatsworth, Belmont, and Queens.

Number 17 Matlock gardens, our home, was typical of the other semi-detached houses on the estate: two spacious bedrooms, a small bedroom, living room and dining room – divided by an alcove – kitchen, bathroom and separate toilet. Outside there was a fairly large garden, which as my father's fingers became greener, evolved into a small lawn and flower/shrub border at the front, a sizeable vegetable plot at the side running well past the house, and a large lawn and flower/shrub border at the rear. A small semi-detached outhouse, containing a 'wash-house', coal bunker and storage room, completed the facilities. It is difficult perhaps for us today to appreciate what a change such living conditions offered from the shared rooms and often cramped urban living conditions that my parents and others like them of their generation were subject to in the 1930s and 1940s. With fairly spacious, modern accommodation and almost no unemployment – down to just 2% in Stockton in 1951 – the young families on the estate must have entered the 1950s with much hope for the future.

For my own parents, mam[9] and dad to me, the 1950s brought mixed fortunes. My mother stayed at home to look after me for the first years of my life until I went to school, while my father worked at his trade at ICI Billingham. There is much that could be written about my early childhood but I shall not detain the reader with such personal details. What should be said is that from apparently happy beginnings my parents' relationship began to deteriorate. Although they never split up, or separated even temporarily, the growing tension and conflict between them during the first ten years of my life did, I have no doubt, induce in me a growing desire to escape. Yet, paradoxically, I was not psychologically very well equipped to 'flee the coup' as early as I eventually did.

My father was personable, imaginative and bright but brought up by a domineering mother and in awe of

---

[9] Alan Bennett's revelation that in Leeds one's mother was always known as 'mam' rather than the 'mum' of midland and southern England, also applied elsewhere in the north of England and especially on Teesside. Although I tended to use 'mum' more and 'mam' less as I grew older.

CHAPTER 2

his father he appeared to suffer from low self-esteem. As the 1950s wore on he began to drink more and spend less and less time with my mother and myself. This happened despite initial successes in his work life, valuable service as a local councillor, and a flair for gardening that won him several prizes for one of the best kept gardens in the locality. Such prizes were clearly considered by the local council as a key inducement to tenants to keep their gardens neat and tidy, an incentive that I fear would be little prized today. His insecurities worsened after my mother went back to work. She took up an office job, first on a part-time basis, allowing her to take me to and pick me up from the village school in Wolviston, and then full-time after I'd reached the age of six or seven and could take myself from and to school. It wasn't long after her return that my father's insecurities turned first into resentment and then into drink-fuelled jealousy of my mother's increasing involvement with her work.

My mother was hard working and very single-minded yet she was flexible and more willing to embrace change than my father. While she was no feminist in the strict sense, she certainly didn't view herself as my father's chattel. Not for her the anonymous title of Mrs W. K. Ashcroft. If not seeking to continue to use her maiden name, she insisted that her own initials P. M. should precede her married name; unexceptional today, but I remember listening to the strident complaints of my paternal grandmother, Alice Ashcroft, as she berated my father for allowing my mother to style herself so in some *vox pop* in which my mother featured in the local paper. Worse, the august columns of the Billingham Express featured a photograph of my windswept and clearly wayward mother with the caption *Mrs P. M. Ashcroft* in large type underneath. But that wasn't the end of my mother's revolutionary tendencies. She believed that women should be able to support themselves, and not rely on their husband's income. This wasn't simply an abstract point of principle, I believe, but a prudent necessity in case my father's drinking became too much for her. So, along with the increasing numbers of women of her generation she went back to work after having children. But not until I could effectively fend for myself, since the option of hiring a childminder was not financially feasible.

She bonded strongly with me and was fearful for me. Her fearfulness was clearly engendered by the loss of my brother, whom I never saw. He was born on 14 October in 1944, but died of a defective heart valve two days later on October 16th. His birth certificate contains no first or Christian name and is simply shown in the public records as 'Boy' Ashcroft. I first found out that he had not been officially named while researching this book and I must say that it saddened me greatly. My mother spoke little of this traumatic event in her life. For many years, I believed that they had intended to call him Ronnie but the news about the birth certificate was disquieting. However, when leafing through some personal papers left by mother after her death in 1997, I found copies of the Evening Gazette – the main evening paper on Teesside - for October 17th and 19th. In the former his birth is announced, even though he had been dead one day by then. The latter contains the death notice but also gives his name as Ronald. I am happy to use this book to correct the bald anonymity of my brother's birth certificate.

CHAPTER 2

One can only guess at the impact of Ronnie's infant death on my mother and her relationships both with my father and with me. I became close to my mother. But there was always an implicit barrier in her behaviour towards me, which helped fuel my own half conscious insecurities as to whether I was truly loved by her. While it is dangerous to play the amateur psychoanalyst, I eventually came to the conclusion that the loss of her first child made her fearful that the same might happen to me. But, the desire to avoid again the terrible pain that she experienced following the loss of Ronnie must have led her to ring fence her emotions towards me so at times she appeared to be holding something back.

At primary school I was a bright but self-conscious boy. Not surprisingly, I had a strong desire to be liked by my fellow pupils. This manifested itself in a conformist tendency, which sat uneasily with that other side of my personality, which hoped that I was smarter, surer, swifter than anyone else, and wanted others to know it. The conformist side invariably dominated. So, one morning in 1954 I turned up at Wolviston village school led by my mother, who in turn was being dragged by 'Sooty' the mongrel puppy dog I'd been given the previous Christmas. No other boys being visible, I said goodbye to dog and mother, passing over to her my rubber tomahawk, knife and headdress having concluded that 'Cowboys and Indians' was not on the day's play agenda. Dog and mother had just disappeared around the corner, when a series of ever louder whooping noises could be heard resulting in a gaggle of Red Indian braves storming into view from the rear of the school. The fear that I was about to be exposed and then massacred as the day's only cowboy had a galvanising effect. I turned on my heel and ran like mad eventually catching up with mam and dog, rubber knife in its mouth, to demand the return of my Red Indian gear, and through tearful eyes indignantly berate her for allowing me to make such a dreadful public mistake. There's little wonder that my mother was keen to get back to work.

The Victorian built school of about 70 pupils, mainly the sons and daughters of local farmers, farm workers and shopkeepers, was divided into two, lower and upper. The lower school of 4 to 7 year-olds contained about 20 pupils in one class taught by a Miss Bateman. Miss Bateman was the classic spinster teacher. To my young eyes she was of indeterminate age, that is, she was either very old or extremely old. In reality she probably would have been about forty. She ruled us literally with a rod. The rod was a large wooden blackboard ruler one yard in length. The ruler helped draw straight chalk lines on the blackboard, served as a pointer to indicate whose turn it was to read the next passage, or recite the eight times table, but above all it was in our eyes her weapon of mass destruction. If you paid insufficient attention, talked in class or, heaven forbid, started a fight with your neighbour, you would be hauled out to the front of the class. Then with your classmates cowering in anticipation one to six strikes of the ruler were applied to your backside. As far as I remember only the boys were 'given the ruler' even though not all the girls were angels. The thought of girls having to bare their knickers to the on-looking class was probably too much for Miss Bateman's sensitivities, so a stern look was her main weapon of control over the female gender. Knickers or not, I too managed to escape the dreaded ruler, an outcome no doubt of a complex

CHAPTER 2

mix of my cowardice, a desire to please and some success at convincing Miss Bateman of my worth. However, my infant efforts to get her to appreciate me must only have been partially successful. One day on a class nature walk we visited the back garden of her house a few hundred yards from the school situated in front of Wolviston duck pond. As we sat on the grass making daisy chains I realised that I was sitting on, and had crushed, a bird's egg. I immediately burst into tears at the thought of the dreadful thing I'd done. Miss Bateman gave me a withering look, said that it wasn't much to be crying about and gave me the impression that she felt I was an insipid wimp. And she was probably correct!

Whatever Miss Bateman's idiosyncrasies, I moved to the upper school when I was seven with good reading and arithmetic ability, which was a tribute to her rigorous approach to teaching. The upper school was eventually split into intermediate and higher groups, with the new Mrs Pottage coming in to take the former. But in those early days around 50 of us sat, arranged roughly by age, in five columns of desks facing the Headmaster, Mr George Fleming. Mr Fleming was probably in his late forties and looked quite distinguished with thinning, sandy hair slicked back over his head behind a forehead that had clearly grown some compared to his younger self. Being faced with 50 kids of varying ages must have posed several pedagogical problems for my new teacher. First, there were at least 4 or 5 age groups that each had different teaching needs. The ten year olds were preparing for their Eleven Plus exams, while at the other extreme seven year olds such as myself had to be taught to do real or joined-up writing, develop their vocabulary and be introduced to the mysteries of sums. Secondly, there was the sheer amount of energy required to control 50 kids and keep them focused on the work in hand. Fleming, navigated through most of his problems by affability and good humour, but if he thought his good nature was being abused he soon lost his temper. The loss of temper was frequently followed by the introduction of his own weapon of mass destruction: a leather tawse.

I must have received 'the strap' as we called it about three times during the 4 to 5 years that I was in Fleming's charge. By the standards of my male classmates this was pretty reasonable. But the trauma I went through on each occasion was not trivial. Typically, having being caught trading blows with my neighbour, I would be marched to the front and told to wait while he searched for the weapon in his desk. Once the strap was retrieved, he would instruct me to stand still and put the palm of one hand straight out in front of me. I would wait with trepidation hand outstretched. Then, with the sun invariably blazing through gothic windows over Fleming's shoulder, hand and strap would rise, followed by a whoosh of leather and an eye watering crack as the tawse connected with my hand. This would be repeated on alternate hands up to six times. One of these occasions took on even greater import when I found out that Mr Fleming and his wife had been invited to our house for dinner just a couple of days after I'd been given the strap. Dinner parties were not something that I associate with my parents and I do not remember them having anyone else for dinner during the whole of my childhood. This may, though, be a reflection of a faulty memory on my part but, even so, such events were not frequent. However, it is likely that the dinner in question was an outcome of my father's political activities.

CHAPTER 2

At the time he was a local councillor and was Chairman of the school's Board of Governors, and dining the headmaster was probably a politic thing to do. In any event, my father's position as Chairman of the Governor's had not saved me from the recent strapping and so my greatest fear was that Mr Fleming would tell my dad that I'd been naughty enough to have been given the strap. What I thought my father would do to me if he found out I don't know. My dad was at that stage not drinking too much but even when he started to drink more I don't remember him hitting or beating me. Nevertheless, I lay awake in my bed upstairs, trembling in fear as the low buzz of their conversation and the clink of cutlery on plates drifted up to my room. But nothing appears to have been said. No recriminations were made. And, thereafter, my admiration and respect for Mr Fleming rose dramatically for exercising such forbearance. The cynic in me later reasoned that either the event was so insignificant to him that he didn't remember it, or, even more cynically, to raise the issue with my father, the Chairman of his Board of Governors, would be to reveal his own failing in controlling the class. I would like to think it was neither of these and that he did me a favour.

Wolviston School was not all fear and whooshing tawse. Indeed, Mr Fleming's philosophy of education evidently emphasised the value of leisure pursuits. While school activities involved much of the usual academic work there was also quite a lot of play. This ranged from sports days, through helping in the school garden, to country dancing, and the staging of theatrical events – comedy and musical sketches - for parents and visitors.

Country dancing was fun because even in those pre-pubescent years it was exciting - to me at least – to get the chance to be close to, and put your arms around, a member of the opposite sex. It was during these close encounters that I fell in love for the first time with a girl called Jetta Yuill, who was the eldest child of a professional couple who lived in the village. My yearning for Jetta went unspoken and unrequited for the three subsequent years that I remained at the school. Being shy and verbally inarticulate, the closest I got to declaring my intentions was in sneaking a kiss onto her cheek while in the main corridor of the school. How I managed to achieve this, or how I got away with it without response, favourable or unfavourable, still exercises me to this day. I would work hard at getting Jetta to be my partner for the 'Dashing White Sergeant' or 'Strip the Willow'. And as the recorded music played on the school Dansette – no school piano – I would luxuriate in the exquisite aroma of Jetta's unperfumed body and thrill to the rustle of her dress. How hard it was to concentrate my mind on 'problems' or a 'spelling' test in the teaching period immediately after the country dancing session!

Our dancing activities were not simply confined to the school. On summer days, we would troop out on to the village green, which lay in a semi-circle surrounded by bungalows and small houses before the school. In the centre of the green a maypole would be erected, with red, white and blue ribbons streaming from it. Miss Bateman, or Mrs Pottage, I can't remember which, but certainly not Mr Fleming, would then take us through the various steps that would result in different intricate patterns appearing down the pole according to the particular steps of the dance. Maypole dancing is not something

CHAPTER 2

that I remember featuring much in Stockton or anywhere else on Teesside for that matter, so its introduction at our village school says something for the imagination and initiative of the teaching staff. Of course, the actual outcomes of the dances only occasionally conformed to the idyllic setting described above. Often I would forget whether I should go right or left of the approaching dancer, or straining to catch sight of Jetta's flashing heels I would fail to take my position in the inner ring. The result of my terpsichorean stumbles would invariably be the growth of a large knotty tumour on the side of the pole completely at odds with the expected pattern. Soon frenetic shouting would emerge from Miss Bateman or Mrs Pottage and we would have to re-wind until the offending missteps and perpetrator were discovered. This would inevitably result in exhortations to concentrate on what I should be doing and not to daydream. And perhaps if I watched Jetta closely I might get the steps right. If you say so, Miss Bateman!

My memories of Wolviston primary School are suffused with a warm glow. This is no doubt because such recollections are filtered through the prism of age. As I look back across 60 years discrete images float into my mind. Images of a day when Mr Fleming marches us outside to stand in the small playground at the front of the school and urges us to look skywards. After a short while we hear the sound of an aeroplane the drumming of its propellers getting louder and louder. Then we see it. A twin-engine monoplane, a shiny dark green colour with an RAF roundel on its side and on top of the fuselage near the front of the 'plane two figures can be seen. The 'plane comes lower and closer until the figure at the front starts to wave madly at us. Mr Fleming, thin sandy hair lifting gently from his head, starts to wave back in large semi-circular arcs. And we all join in. Waving and shouting at the top of our voices to Gerald the headmaster's son, who is flying the 'plane as part of his RAF pilot training on their way back to the RAF station at Thornaby. Heads appear out of windows around the village green. The local postman gets off his bike, shades his eyes and looks up. We continue to cheer, until after completing a circuit low over the school, and no doubt breaking every rule in the book, the plane steers south for Thornaby, and disappears over our heads with the drumming of its propellers fading gradually away. Chattering excitedly we all troop back into the school.

A military context for my childhood memories surfaces again in November 1956. It is 8am, Monday November 5th. I am nine years old. My mother marches in to my room – she never did knock – and rubbing the sleep from my eyes I exclaim "Goody, it's bonfire night . . . ." She rewards my enthusiasm with a stern look and then says "You'd better make the most of it, because it could be the last for some time." Puzzled, I follow her down stairs. There on the kitchen table is a copy of the *Daily Sketch* I read bits about Budapest radio asking the world for help and then silence. Our own radio is droning away in the background, a pan of porridge bubbles on top of the gas oven. I am asking mam what it all means when she urges me to be quiet. The programme is being interrupted to give further information on earlier reports that British and French paratroopers had landed at Port Said in Egypt in an attempt to gain control of the Suez Canal. I learn later that this was in response to President Nasser's recent

CHAPTER 2

unilateral nationalisation of the Canal. Mam packs me off to school. Curiously I am excited, a sensation to be repeated in the future when I am confronted by major news events. But as I walked to school that day I had a vague sense that something in my world had changed. A sense that there were powerful, even malign forces beyond the boundaries of mam, dad and school that could change my life forever. I was beginning to lose my childhood innocence.

The influence of external forces was also soon to be felt at my school. Mr Fleming took pride in the school's theatrical productions, which were invariably a mixture of short sketches with some music and singing rather than full-length plays. We all loved to participate in these activities. But one day I returned with others to the classroom to find jotters and sundry bits and pieces piled on top of my desk. Mr Fleming sat scowling at his desk and upon noticing me he launched into a tirade about my failure to keep my desk tidy – a habit that is still evident today as I raise my eyes above the computer and gaze at the surrounding clutter of papers and books[10]. Gradually,

---

[10] Of course in self-justification mode I have been known to argue that a tidy mind - and desk - isn't necessarily a creative mind. And certainly academic success does not require a tidy desk. A quite distinguished economics professor colleague of mine had a legendary untidy desk and room. It was contended, perhaps apocryphally, that when the year drew to a close he covered the assorted scatter with newspaper and wrote "198x". He also gained a fame of sorts outside his particular specialism as a result of the University Safety Officer photographing his room and then circulating to the whole University and no doubt beyond as an example of a significant fire risk and general safety hazard, previous occurrences of which no doubt had led to the decline

we understood that school inspectors had visited the school, presumably unexpectedly, and amongst other things he had wanted to show them some example of my work, which he'd been unable to find. I realise now, and probably did so then, that I was one of the school's better pupils. My untidiness had let him down. But what became clear was that the inspectors thought that the balance between 'work' and 'play' in the school was weighted too much towards 'play'. Things were going to change. And, with sad eyes Mr Fleming warned us that the school's theatrical activities would have to cease.

While I didn't think so at the time, this probably would have been viewed by Sellar & Yeatman[11] as a 'good thing' in my personal history. It was now 1957. Within a year I would be sitting Part 1 of the Eleven Plus examination. Part 1 had to be negotiated before Part II and only if that were passed would a place at grammar school be available. During the year before the first exam, we worked hard at past papers and with Mr Fleming's help I tried to remedy my problem with 'problems'. You know the type:

> "Tim runs a mile at a constant speed of 5 yards per second. John runs the first half mile at 1 yard per second slower than Tim, and the second half mile at 1 yard per second faster than John. Who will win, and by how many seconds?"[12]

---

and fall of Rome, the British Empire and the source of the road towards BREXIT today!

[11] W. C. Sellar and R. J. Yeatman *1066 and All That*, Methuen, 1930.

[12] Tim wins by fourteen and two third seconds. I think!

CHAPTER 2

While I was pretty good at mental arithmetic and the speedy manipulation of numbers, when it came to boys running around tracks or men digging ditches, I would frequently run around in circles or dig a ditch for myself. Now, if it had been Jetta dancing around the maypole . . . . . . ! Mr Fleming said that I 'made mountains out of molehills'. As it happens, this was a very perceptive comment on at least one aspect of my personality. Yet it wasn't simply that I saw difficulties where none existed. Rather, concern at my slow progress in solving a problem, produced in me such terror and fear of failure that I almost entered a catatonic state. We spent time trying to scale down the mountains and my performance improved. But whether this would be sufficient to keep my brain from seizing up during the actual exam only time would tell.

The first part of the 'Scholarship', as my parent's called it, was scheduled for a day in February 1958. That month is etched into my memory not just because of the Eleven Plus exam. On February 6th seven members of Matt Busby's first great Manchester United football team were killed as their 'plane was attempting to take off in slushy conditions from Munich airport after touching down to refuel following a flight from Belgrade where they were playing a European fixture[13]. The horror of the deaths[14] had a big effect on me, producing an echo almost exactly one year later when Buddy

---

[13] Twenty-three of the 43 people on the aircraft died in the crash.
[14] Seven players – Roger Byrne, Mark Jones, Eddie Colman, Tommy Taylor, Liam Whelan, David Pegg and Geoff Bent – died immediately, with the young England centre-half Duncan Edwards finally giving up his struggle for life 15 days later.

Holly, another childhood hero, died also in a snow affected air crash. My personal sorrow at the massacre of the "Busby babes" was not just because I was an impressionable ten-year old, but also probably because I had had the privilege of seeing the team play just over a year before the crash. My father had taken me the forty miles by bus and train to see that great team play Newcastle United[15] at St James' Park in September 1956. The match was billed as "Busby's Babes versus Mitten's Kittens" – Charlie Mitten was Newcastle's Manager at the time. The match ended in 1-1 draw, with the equalising goal for Newcastle scored by the legendary Jackie Milburn, then 32 years of age at the end of his career, and as unlikely a "kitten" as there could be.

A few days after the crash came the exam. The morning of the dreaded day was dark, cold and wet as eight of us trooped into the main classroom of the school. (Where all the other pupils were I have no idea, although I assume they must have been given the morning or day off.) Mr Fleming had arranged for extra heating to be available in the room. So, in that dark, eerily lit but warm room the exam began. I remember that it was a Maths exam and assume that there was an English exam later in the morning. But I have no

---

[15] Following my father, I have, for my sins, been a life-long supporter of Newcastle United, a preoccupation that caused me much grief during my youth on Teesside where every other person appeared to be a Middlesbrough supporter. Little was I to know as I watched that match that, to date, May 2018, (hope still lives on!) Newcastle would never again win a major domestic trophy after the club's victory in the FA Cup Final in 1955, 16 months *before* the match discussed here!

CHAPTER 2

memory of the second exam, probably because it was the fear of maths and 'problems' that dominated my thoughts. In the evening, I made the mistake of going over the maths exam paper with my parents, which ended in floods of tears and my mother hugging me as I became convinced that I had not passed the exam. I would be consigned to Billingham Secondary Modern School, a failure at eleven. This was not idle fancy. The fear was real, although no doubt conditioned by my parents' views and expectations.

Yet, I passed the exam. In fact four of us passed: the gorgeous Jetta, her friend Barbara Benson, Graham Scott and myself. Graham a quiet, secretive character was the nearest to a friend I had at the school. His elder brother Neil who had moved on to secondary school two years earlier had overshadowed him. But since his brother's departure Graham had begun to display more of an identity of his own. The Scott's lived almost opposite the school on the corner of the village green. Neil described his mother to us as 'an author', although it was never clear to me whether she wrote novels, cookery books, or car manuals. Anyway, whether in the pursuit of her authorial commitments or some other employment, she was out of the house most of the time. And there was no sign at all of a Mr Scott, whose whereabouts constituted a mystery. I think we were meant to believe that he was 'working away'. But that didn't seem exactly right. Despite their middle-class aura the family were not well off. Neil and Graham had appeared regularly at school, winter and summer, dressed identically in Nordic looking woollen cardigans that fastened up to the throat with metal buttons and alternated grey and white horizontal stripes. Suffice to say that even in the farmyards of Wolviston such garments were not viewed as the epitome of cool. With parents absent Neil, Graham and I, and then after Neil's departure just Graham and myself, were able to spend our dinner break at their house. I cannot resist the temptation to say that we spent the break 'fiddling with our flies'. However, this is not an admission of pubescent awakening and nascent homosexual attraction. The reality was more mundane. Following Neil's example, we spent our time making flies for fishing. Pins were bent. Fine cord was wrapped around metal, and different colours used to distinguish body from wings. Why we did this I have no idea. Any fishing that I had done previously was with a net in rock pools, although when I was in my early teens I graduated to hook, line and sinker but never to a fishing rod and certainly not to fly-fishing. So, all of this remains a mystery to me. Perhaps we did it because we could.

The second half of the 'scholarship' exam was held at Grangefield Grammar School in Stockton on March 13. Children were bussed to the school from all over the Stockton and Billingham area. Everything about Grangefield seemed to be on a different scale from our school: playgrounds, playing fields, classrooms and buildings. Then there was the gym, tennis court and swimming pool that we never dreamed could be part of a school. But above all was the sheer number of children: running in and out of the cloakrooms, charging around the playgrounds, and squeezing past one another along linoleum corridors and stairs. Order was imposed on the mayhem by assigning us to classrooms according to the first letter of our surnames. I therefore found myself in a roomful of 'A's. Soon the incessant chatter

CHAPTER 2

of excited ten and eleven year olds was stilled as the ordeal began. I drifted off into my solipsistic world and as the morning passed by I began to feel that that I was doing quite well. The anxieties of the first exam seemed a distant memory. Even 'problems' seemed to be less life threatening than the previous month's trial. By this time we were on to the mental arithmetic paper and I breezed easily to the end of the paper with ten to fifteen minutes to spare. So, being the dutiful student, I returned to the beginning to check my answers. After about five minutes checking for some reason I moved to the final page of the question paper. There at the bottom of the page I noticed for the first time the words 'PLEASE TURN OVER'! I was sure that hadn't been there before. Gingerly I raised the question paper then flipped it over. Rows and rows of questions swam into view. Twenty to be exact. Twenty questions and less than ten minutes to complete them. My heart sank. Of course, I didn't finish them managing only about five. Was I to be denied a place at Grammar School because I'd failed to read three simple words?

Two months later on a bright spring morning an envelope lies on the mat at the front door. Mam whispers quietly in my ear: 'Go on, open it.' The brown envelope is resistant to my fumblings. Mam produces a knife. A white sheet of paper is withdrawn. And there, in what today would be called Courier font, I read the words: 'You have been awarded a place at Stockton Grammar School.' Later that day I learn that only Jetta and myself had passed. Barbara and Graham were to go to Billingham Secondary Modern. Jetta would attend Grangefield Grammar, scene of our examination ordeal. I find out in September that in opting, in the event of a pass, for Stockton Grammar, I would be one of 35 boys entering that year to the direct grant Church of England Grammar School for boys. And, as a reward from my parents for becoming the first member of our family to attain Grammar School status, I am presented with an acoustic guitar.

CHAPTER 3

MUSICAL AWAKENINGS

The guitar was a second-hand acoustic with metal strings, a neck of darkened mahogany, and a body of varnished wood, polished so highly that at certain angles one's own reflection was visible. Finally, the guitar was embellished with a feint white line around the upper, outer rim of the sound box. The metal strings indicated that the guitar did not have a classical provenance, while the scuffs and marks on the plectrum guard below the opening to the sound box suggested professional use perhaps in the rhythm section of a jazz or dance band. Had it seen service with Jack Marwood's band at the Maison de Danse? I never pursued the matter with my parents for fear of a more mundane history.

I loved the look of the guitar. One reason was that it reminded me of Gene Autry. When I was about eight, I was a big fan of Roy Rogers and Gene Autry and their respective horses Trigger and Champion. On balance I favoured Autry because of his singing and supportive guitar playing. My paternal grandparents encouraged this interest and I would often be given press cuttings of Autry's exploits when I visited them. The cutting that sticks in my mind describes his collection of cowboy boots, a collection that would make Imelda Marcos blush. An accompanying photograph shows Gene with several lines of boots arranged in regimental fashion snaking away from him and out of the picture. But it was his relaxed cowboy musical style that enthused me. Perhaps with my new guitar something of Autry's glamorous world would rub off on me.

Sitting with hands around the guitar trying to pick out the melody line of Duane Eddy's *Rebel Rouser* my dad would urge me to listen to the records of the jazz guitarist Django Reinhardt and his violinist collaborator, Stephan Grappelli. According to dad, Reinhardt was a 'proper' guitarist, whereas Eddy was juvenile in comparison. I would object and suggest that my father didn't fully appreciate the twenty year-old Eddy's talents. For me, the seduction of cool American rock guitar playing was preferable to the rustic and seemingly archaic European musical sounds of what my father called the 'Hot Club de Paris'[16]. I imagined musicians with berets pulled across their heads, riding bicycles carrying guitars strung across their shoulders like Mexican bandoliers. This was clearly a somewhat restricted view of French musical culture, coloured as it was by my sole contact with mainland Europeans, namely the annual visit of the 'French Onion Men'. They would appear in Matlock Gardens, cycling from door to door bedecked in berets, and Guernsey sweaters, with multicoloured kerchiefs knotted around their

---

[16] Actually Reinhardt's quintet played at the Hot Club Of France in 1934 and was an immediate hit. As they became more famous they became known as *The Quintet of the Hot Club of France*.

CHAPTER 3

necks. Multiple strings of brown onions that looped over shoulders and across chests completed their regalia. Little is known about their musical propensities, although their onions were much in demand.

In a short time I would realise how right my father had been about the respective merits of the two guitarists. Indeed, I was forgetting just how much my growing interest in music was a product of stimuli from my family.

As a small child of three or four, I was introduced to recorded music on visits to my paternal grandparents house on Bypass Road Billingham. Situated in a corner of their living room was a deluxe electric radiogram. This wood panelled box on legs towered over me. At its front, about half way up, there was a semi-circular glass or Perspex window. Occasionally an orange glow emanated from this orifice, and voices could be heard coming from a rough cloth square, criss-crossed by fine lathes of polished wood, which was about level with my chest. I became aware that this was the 'wireless' part of the contraption and that I should be quiet when the glow and voices were present. But on other occasions, when the glow was absent I would on occasion be invited to listen to a record. There appeared to be only two options, for me at least: *Run Rabbit Run* and *Teddy Bears' Picnic*. I loved both. The lid of the radiogram would be raised, a shiny 78 taken out of its brown paper sleeve, inspected and then placed carefully on the felt disc that covered the turntable. Occasionally, my grandfather would take a needle out of a small brass box and insert it at the end of the arm that lay on a rest by the side of the turntable. Once the needle was in, a lever would be moved, the turntable would gather speed and the arm lifted and then tentatively lowered onto the spinning disc. As sounds became audible my grandmother's voice could be heard alongside the music as she encouraged me to go down to the woods and join the teddy bears' picnic. At first I enjoyed this ritual and became excited as I was transported into the imaginative possibilities of a real teddy bears' picnic. But it didn't take me long to get bored. However, the thought that I might be putting at risk my grandmother's frequent present of a half-pound box of Cadbury's Milk Tray encouraged me to participate. I was right to appreciate the significance of this gift but at the time I would not have understood its true significance. In the early 1950s chocolate was still rationed and would continue to be so until 1953. My grandparents would have had to use all of their ration coupons to keep me in the chocolate habit to which I was rapidly becoming accustomed.

Sing-alongs were not confined to my grandparent's house. On certain high days and holidays, such as Boxing Day or New Year, visitors to 17 Matlock Gardens would be encouraged to participate in a communal singsong. The availability of small quantities of alcohol – at Christmas time my mother's ginger wine was gaining legendary status – and the presence of a piano in our living room assisted the process. Then, to my initial amazement, my father would step up to the piano, and cigarette in mouth play the chords of a song that would embolden my mother to lead the singsong. My father's piano playing talents were largely confined to 'vamping' chords, which he could fit to most popular songs. Yet, to have the singing accompanied by a musical instrument turned the whole event into a much more glamorous affair.

CHAPTER 3

As I remember it, the songs were mainly wartime and traditional, or local, favourites such as: *We'll Meet Again, Danny Boy, She'll be Coming Round the Mountains, My Bonnie (lies over the ocean)*, *Blaydon Races*, augmented by some Bing Crosby – a particular favourite of mam and dad – and Frank Sinatra songs. I was allowed to stay up and watch and listen to the proceedings provided I kept quiet and made myself inconspicuous. This compact suited both my parents and me. They could enjoy themselves while still keeping an eye on me and I could delay going to bed until finally 'discovered', which would be much later than usual. But as the piano played on and song followed song, the sounds drifted away and the next I knew I was in my father's arms as he carried me up the stairs to bed.

At other times music played a not insignificant part in our lives. Sunday lunchtimes were spent listening to the radio, or 'wireless' to my mother, with *Forces Choice* or *Family Favourites*, and the *Billy Cotton Band Show* being particular favourites. And from 1954 when we acquired an *Eko* television – financed by the sale of the latest batch of ICI shares that my father had received through the ICI's employee share ownership scheme – certain musical shows such as the *Black and White Minstrels*, or *Sing Something Simple* would be watched and listened to avidly. My mother would often continue singing one or more of the numbers that took her fancy long after the programmes had ended. For reasons that I still don't understand, the sound of her soprano voice echoing down the stairs as she Hoovered or, worse, sat on the toilet, used to irritate me intensely. It wasn't that my mother was a bad singer. She would soon be accepted into a local amateur choir, along with her sister Winnie.

And I remember attending with my dad a performance of *Pagliacci* and *Cavalleria Rusticana* with mam and Winnie dressed in regulation white stoles and black dresses performing stoically in the chorus. But her voice irritated me nonetheless, and when she sang alone on a sustained basis I would rush to turn the radio or television on to drown her out.

However, my mother's love of singing and her Christian inclination were to have significant consequences for me. We attended services regularly at St Peter's Anglican church in Wolviston. On Sundays, my parents and I attended morning and evening services, while I returned in the afternoon for Sunday school in the church hall. Dad's attendance at the Sunday morning service was less frequent. He liked a Sunday lunchtime pint, or two, and since my mother always insisted that lunch should be as soon after 12 o'clock as possible he preferred to skip church for his pint. But despite that, our visits to church were not taken lightly. 'Sunday best' would be worn and for one or two key services in the Church calendar, such as Easter, new clothes would be purchased. So, the first occasion that I was allowed to wear long trousers was on Easter Sunday in my tenth year after my mother had taken me one Saturday a couple of weeks earlier to buy a jacket and trousers from *Maxwell's* at the top of Stockton High Street.

Dressed in our Sunday best we would tackle the hymns with gusto, listen to Reverend Harrington's sermon and then chat with the minister for a few seconds after the service. One Sunday, my mother's conversation with Reverend Harrington was longer than usual as I stood back from her on my own – one of my dad's pub

CHAPTER 3

Sunday's. On the short bus ride from Wolviston back to Billingham, my mother announced to me with a look that sanctioned no refusal that Rev Harrington had agreed that I should join the choir and that I was to report to Mr Hudson, the organist and choir master, for choir practice at 6pm on Wednesday evening!

Joining the church choir was a big step forward in my musical education. In effect, I became a producer – of sorts – as well as a consumer of music: a boy soprano, or treble, in the most junior ranks of the twenty-strong choir. Dressed in white surplices over black cassocks, we marched – actually, ambled – up the nave of the church each Sunday behind a curate holding aloft a large brass cross. The procession ended as we filed into parallel choir stalls on each side of the church before the chancel with boys at the front and the adult female sopranos and male bass and tenors seated behind us. There we would lead the congregation in the singing of hymns and occasionally we would perform on our own works that ranged in scale from ballads such as Maybrick and Weatherly's *Holy City* to large oratorios such as Stainer's *Crucifixion*. The larger works required much rehearsal and our Wednesday evening choir practice would mainly be devoted to the current choral project once we had run through the next Sunday's hymns. But choir practice wasn't simply confined to singing. Before practice and sometimes after, we, that is four or five of the other boys and myself, would play 'hide and seek' amongst the gravestones. Little thought was given to the sacred nature of our playground. Indeed, our main consideration was to know which headstones provided the most cover. The prospect of a good game of 'hide and seek' and the threepenny bag of chips on the way home made choir practice a weekly event that I looked forward to. Added to this was the comparative status of being able to swan about in cassock and surplice on Sunday mornings and evenings, while mam, dad and others were relegated to the ranks of the congregation. I gave little thought to the singing that was meant to be the purpose of it all until one day the axe fell. Turning up for choir practice, and before we could disperse amongst the gravestones, four of us were summoned to see the Choir Master. We trudged up the aisle to be confronted by a clearly nervous Mr Hudson seated at the organ but facing outwards in the direction of the choir stalls. He mumbled something about things not progressing as well as he had hoped, and before I could understand what it all meant, we were told that we were out. I was sacked from the choir.

My mother was incredulous. A cross-examination began, which ranged from queries about dodging choir practice to the unthinkable: "have you had your hands in the collection box?" Satisfied that I was neither deserter nor thief, she announced that she would speak to Mr Hudson on Sunday. The next few days were not easy as I worried what my mother would say to Mr Hudson and, more scarily, what Mr Hudson would say to my mother!

As mam and I enter the church on Sunday morning – dad having prudently chosen to take one of his pub Sunday's – I smile sheepishly at my three sacked pals who are sitting with their parents in the congregation. Mam walks right to the front and we sit down in a pew with a direct sightline to Mr Hudson when he turns from the organ to the choir. The service drags on. Reverend

CHAPTER 3

Harrington speaks about understanding and compassion in his sermon. My mother nods vigorously. The final hymn is sung. The Benediction is given. Then the choir departs to a voluntary played by Mr Hudson. The congregation begins to drift out except for my mother and me, who under her prompting retain our seats. As the last bars of the voluntary echo around the now empty church, mam rises from her seat, indicating that I remain seated, and approaches the organ. I hear nothing except mumbled conversation and certainly no argument or raised voices. After a while, Mr Hudson moves in the direction of the vestry, while my mother turns on her heel, collects me and we walk out of the church together. Once outside she announces, with raised eyebrows and just a hint of a smile that Mr Hudson has agreed that I can report for choir practice as usual next Wednesday. No reasons, either for sacking, or reinstatement, are given. I am back in the choir.

My singing career, for what it was, can really be said to have taken off from this point. Once reinstalled in the choir I suffer no discrimination from Mr Hudson, to his credit. I process up the aisle each Sunday morning glancing guiltily at my still sacked pals, who appear less and less frequently in the congregation. Within a couple of years I am made Head Choirboy, much to my Mother's pleasure. In this role I am allowed to wear a diamond-shaped bronze medallion or pendant, which hangs around my neck dropping to mid chest over my surplice from a one and a half inch ribbon of rough dark red cotton. A bronze medal position in the choir Olympics almost certainly flattered my capabilities. Two additional perks accrued to the post of Head Choirboy. First, I got to lead the choir up the aisle each

Sunday following close behind the cross bearing curate. And, secondly, I took all the principal treble solos. This was something of a mixed blessing. So, one Christmas, I stood at the head of the choir at the bottom of the church waiting for the organ to strike the first chords of *Once in Royal David's City* and begin the traditional solo soprano/treble rendering of the first verse of the carol. As the chords are struck I start into the first line realising too late that I am singing at least a semitone flat. I struggle to retrieve the situation only managing to get back on key by the fourth line of the six-line verse. With the full choir launching into "He came down to earth from heaven", the first line of the second verse, we all process up the aisle. My face at this point is as red as the ribbon around my neck. I feel that I have let my parents down who are singing away dutifully eyes fixed straight ahead as I pass them in our journey up the aisle. But above all, I fear that I have made a public tit of myself. I have disgraced myself in front of a congregation containing some, I suspect, who believe that I am only in the choir because of the force of my mother's personality rather than any intrinsic singing talent on my part. Fortunately, any thoughts that Mr Hudson has on the matter are kept to himself.

By this time I was a member of the cubs and soon to become a scout, although not a very distinguished scout. I managed to gain my Tenderfoot but did not acquire any more badges before post-pubescent interests, Grammar school homework, television and rock n' roll began to divert me away from both choir and scouts. But my boyhood singing career had not yet come to an end. The scout troops in Wolviston and Billingham had decided to hold a Gang Show and

CHAPTER 3

were in the process of putting together the acts for the event. I found myself asked to perform a solo song and we settled on *Bless This House*, for reasons which now escape me, although I suspect my mother had a strong influence on the choice. This religious song was first published in 1927 as *Bless The House*. The famous Irish Tenor John McCormack began to sing it in the 1930s, changing the title to "Bless This House," along with minor revisions to some of the lyrics and made a best selling recording of it. While the song oozed religious sentimentality, it was clearly a good choice to tug at the heartstrings of the anticipated rows of mums and dads.

The show was to be held at Stockton and Billingham Technical College in the auditorium on the Billingham site. The auditorium seated over one thousand people. And so on a warm May evening, I walked out from a group of around fifty boys to the front of the stage, the lights dimmed, a spotlight picked me out and to piano accompaniment I sang the song to a full house. As the song ended with the house duly blessed, a wave of cheers and applause washed over me. Such attention and acclaim had a powerful, even cathartic, effect on me. I had sniffed the smell of the greasepaint and heard the roar of the crowd and I wanted more. But my future as a treble singer was distinctly limited, with my voice expected to break at, or soon after, puberty. If I couldn't be a singer, I sensed that my only route into show business would have to be through music[17]. But what to do?

---

[17] My later existence as a university lecturer and economics professor might, with hindsight, be seen as another means of satisfying my desire to 'play to the gallery' and for public acclamation!

My parents' gift of a guitar as a reward for passing the eleven plus perhaps offered a solution.

But, with a new school to attend, competing attractions and distractions meant that time for guitar practice was limited.

Each weekday I took the 24 United bus on a four and a half mile journey into Stockton dressed in a regulation navy blue blazer with the school badge on the breast pocket, a grey shirt with school tie and school cap. The school cap was the most contentious item because even sixth formers had to wear one when I first arrived in September 1958. During my first year this was changed so that wearing a cap became optional after the third form. This decision was greeted ecstatically and celebrated by the older boys with a cap burning ceremony in the toilets at the back of the school out of sight of masters and prefects. In our grammar school uniforms we were subject to much ridicule from other boys. Various strategies would be adopted to hide the fact that we were at the grammar, such as only putting your cap on a short distance from the school when within likely sight of the masters. By my second year I had taken this subterfuge further by donning a leather - actually pvc – jacket over my blazer presenting myself as a pale, spotty imitation of Marlon Brando: a contender on the Tees waterfront! The image was further rounded out by trying to get your mother to agree to a narrowing of your trouser bottoms from the eighteen inches favoured by the school authorities. I managed to get mine down to fourteen inches. But Peter "Pedro" Thompson, a friend in the year above me (see below), shocked the school one morning by turning up in

CHAPTER 3

12 inch bottoms, which verged on the Max Wall[18]. This was in the days before Lycra, which would no doubt have allowed a more shocking outcome.

All generations believe themselves to be different. We were no exception. It appeared to us that the strong effort we were making to assert our individuality against the drab uniformity demanded of us by the school authorities was more than the school had been used to, at least in recent years. For me, grammar school was a liberating experience, realised in a struggle for identity amidst conformity. But it was also a frightening experience: physically for fear of intimidation from bigger and older boys, intellectually because of the more rigorous demands of a grammar school education. So, my rebellion was as much a survival strategy as a principled assertion of my individuality. In effect I became a 'rebel without a cause' and a bit of a 'hard man'. But the hardness was based on a thin carapace that concealed a soft centre. Whether my state of mind was ultimately a reflection of a subconscious wish that my father stand up to my dominating mother, as James Dean's character in the movie reputedly desired, is anybody's guess.

My opposition to conformity should not, however, be overstated. I worked hard and fretted about the

---

[18] For those of later vintage, Max Wall (1908-1990) was an individualistic comedian whose "most famous comic creation was Professor Wallofski, the weird spidery travesty of the old masters of music walks. Dressed in larger-than-life boots, white socks and black tights, the professor spawned a veritable 'chameleon' of impersonators who number among them, John Cleese. (Cleese, in a magazine article, confessed it was after watching Max that the idea for 'The Ministry of Silly Walks' was born)." Source: http://www.tales.ndirect.co.uk/MAX2.HTML

extensive homework that we were given. I wanted to do well in class. I valued the approval of the masters. And, I feared punishment, a fear that limited how far I would go in seeking to challenge authority. This did not stop me from hating the prefect system, which appeared to me to legitimate the exercise of arbitrary power by a select bunch of psychopaths. With prefects you never knew when the hand of divine wrath would descend upon you, literally, since I remember one day in the playground being slapped hard across the face by the Deputy Head Prefect – perhaps pushing for the top job – for reasons that to this day remain unclear to me. I think he thought that he saw me bullying one of my classmates, when in fact what had occurred was just a playful shove in which we were both complicit. In any event, no master would have meted out such summary punishment. The rule of law held in the staffroom if not in the Upper Sixth.

While today I can start to become nostalgic when thinking about Stockton Grammar School, I know that objectivity demands that I should not go far down that route. Our school was a cramped Victorian slum located at the corner of Garbutt Street and Norton Road, which led into Stockton High Street. We were cramped for space and had few facilities on site. Lunch required a fifteen-minute orderly march down and across Norton Road, past the gasworks to a church hall, where the food would arrive in metal containers having been cooked – a euphemism – off site. Swimming, was a five minute trek to Stockton Baths, made ludicrous by the assignment of only one thirty-five minute period for the practice. We had twenty minutes maximum in the water, the remaining time being taken up by undressing and dressing. My classmates were invariably much faster at

CHAPTER 3

changing their clothes than I was as I struggled in a stiff-backed way to get feet out of, or into, my underpants and trousers. This meant that I had even less time in the water and would turn up for the next class more dishevelled than usual, with hair still wet and water leaching down my backside and legs. Finally, sports such as football, cricket and athletics could only be played following a thirty-minute bus journey to playing fields on the outskirts of the town, a trip that was fortunately confined solely to Friday afternoons for the younger boys and Wednesday afternoons for the Fourth Form and above.

The main problem was a lack of investment in equipment and buildings. This I suspect was the consequence of the school being a Church of England Grammar funded by direct grant from the local authority to take 'scholarship' students. It was starved of resources because the state funding probably barely covered running costs and the school had long ago ceased to take in paying pupils. The poor quality of the facilities stood in marked contrast to those available at the fully state funded Grangefield Grammar School where we had taken the second half of the eleven plus exam. Yet, despite these archaic conditions the masters worked heroically to teach us, and the academic record of the school was good, with a reasonable proportion going on to university education and a select few to Oxbridge. Fortunately, the governors managed to secure the funds for a new building in Fairfield, a western suburb of Stockton, which opened in 1963 a year after I had left the school. Under normal circumstances I would have still been at the school in the fifth or lower sixth form. But my fate was to be otherwise.

My parents had found someone to give me guitar lessons, a Mr Evamy who lived less than a mile from the school. Mr Evamy was a kindly man who would reminisce about playing jazz guitar in Jack Marwood's band at the Maison de Danse. I would turn up at his house with guitar in carrying case. His wife would let me in. The guitar would be unpacked and I would wait for Mr Evamy to enter the room with his banjo. A banjo? Yes, a banjo! I thought it rather strange myself. Yet that is what he did. He gave me guitar lessons on his banjo. I can't say that I suffered significantly because of it, but it would have been nice to see a guitar other than mine in his house. He taught me the basic chords and I managed to excel in accompaniment to songs such as *Camptown Races,* and *Oh Susanna*. Songs that, I was only dimly aware at the time were essentially for banjo accompaniment. I guess I thought that this is what you had to do to learn to play the guitar properly. But it did seem a world away from my then musical interests.

CHAPTER 4

PEDRO AND BURDON'S

In my eleventh and twelfth years, 1958 and 1959, my main musical enthusiasms were for American rock music that featured electric guitar. I'd had a passing interest in skiffle and Lonnie Donegan in particular, with *Rock Island Line* being a particular favourite in 1956. But, despite my tender years, Bill Haley and the Comets left me cold, with John Lennon's comment that "There was just this fat man in a tartan jacket with a kiss curl on his forehead"[19] effectively summing up my own feelings. I'd also had a passing flirtation with Tommy Steele and the Steelmen, which was rewarded by a 1956 Christmas present from my parents – the myth of Santa Claus long since dissolved - of a small plastic guitar. The guitar had plastic strings and a coloured transfer drawing of Tommy Steele on the sound box. Similar Elvis Presley guitars sold in the shops but neither could be classified as 'real' guitars. The marketing of the guitar was appropriately timed, coinciding with Steele's hit *Singing the Blues*,

---

[19] Quoted in Philip Norman *Shout! The True Story of the Beatles* (London, 1981), page 21.

which had reached number one in the New Musical Express (NME) chart in the middle of that month. But Steele's cover was soon to be swept aside by the American Guy Mitchell's original version, which reached number one in the UK charts at the beginning of January 1957. And, as if to emphasise the boy from Bermondsey's cockney resilience and the fickle taste of the British record buying public, Steele's cover climbed back to number one in the week following only to be supplanted again by Guy Mitchell the next week.

Elvis Presley was of course an attraction. But in those early days, when his more polished RCA records were being heavily marketed rather than his earlier, and perhaps more authentic, Sun records for Sam Phillips, such as *That's All Right (Mama), I'm Left You're Right She's Gone* and *I Don't care If The Sun Don't Shine*, he was only of passing interest. We wanted more Scotty Moore and Bill Black! Much the same could be said for the Platters who we knew were a great vocal group, with magnificent songs such as *The Great Pretender, Only You* and *My Prayer*. But there was nothing for us to emulate: we weren't black and couldn't really sing, at least the way the Platters could! And what of the vast majority of artistes that populated the "Hit Parade" and variety shows of the time, such as Alma Cogan ("the girl with the laughter in her voice"), Ronnie Hilton, David Whitfield, Dickie Valentine, Ronnie Carroll, Gracie Fields, Petula Clark, the Beverly Sisters, Mantovani (he of the cascading string sounds), Vera Lynn, (who once was: "the forces sweetheart!") Perry Como, Dean Martin, Eddie Calvert ("and his golden trumpet!"), Russ Conway, Winifred Atwell ("the Queen of the Ivories"), Frankie Vaughan, Lord Rockingham's XI (*Hoots Mon*

CHAPTER 4

"there's a moose loose about this hoose!!") and so on? Nice people and talented artists they may have been. But since our mother's liked them, we definitely did not.

The "we", "us" and "our" in the above paragraph refer to the people I used to hang out with at this time. The most important of these was Peter "Pedro" Thompson, whom we first met in his Max Wall look-alike, 12-inch trouser bottoms. Pedro was a one off. Looking like the comedian Frankie Howard on a bad day, he could not be characterised as one of life's beautiful people. But what he lacked in looks he made up for in personality. In the Form above me at Stockton Grammar, he was more than a year my senior. Despite his seniority and the convention that boys from a higher Form did not mix with those from a lower Form, we became friends. We discovered that we had similar musical tastes and that we both possessed guitars. So, it wasn't long before we were visiting each other's houses to have jam sessions of sorts.

More often than not we would go by bus from school to his house in Beaconsfield Road, Norton, about half way between Stockton and Billingham. I would then get a later bus home. On these occasions an older boy Chris would sometimes join us. Chris was a glamorous character who being sixteen had a provisional licence to ride a motorbike and would turn up at Pedro's house in his brand new 250cc Royal Enfield Crusader. The earnings from his apprenticeship, while small, were much in excess of our schoolboy pocket money and sufficient with parental help to enable him to meet the hire purchase payments on the bike. Much of our sessions would then be about motorbikes as well as music. When we weren't arguing the merits of the Crusader against Ariel's Arrow, Chris would play a snare drum and cymbal – eventually augmented by a bass drum – in rhythmic support of Pedro and myself on guitars. Frequently, the volume of the "music" would begin to rise until the door of the front room was thrown open by Pedro's elder brother demanding that we turn it down. This we usually did immediately because his brother looked really scary. The best comparison I can come up with is Charles Laughton's portrayal of Quasimodo and even that doesn't fully capture the image that confronted us as we rushed for volume controls and switches. The comfort for Pedro was that compared to his brother he looked positively Olympian, which reminded me of the danger in dealing in absolutes: almost everything is relative.

Jam sessions fuelled by jam sandwiches saw us turn our hands to imperfect covers of Duane Eddy instrumentals, and the songs of Eddie Cochran, Gene Vincent and Buddy Holly. By mid 1960 both Holly and Cochran were dead: Holly dying in a snow affected 'plane crash – along with Ritchie Valens and J. P. "The Big Bopper" Richardson – on 3 February 1959; and Cochran dying on 17 April 1960 in a taxi accident at the end of his first British tour as he travelled through Chippenham on his way to Heathrow airport.[20] For a while Holly and his Crickets were our idols. The song *That'll be the day* was a particular favourite, which had topped both the US and UK charts in September 1957, followed by *Peggy Sue* in early December, a number 6 chart hit, and *Oh*

---

[20] Gene Vincent and Cochran's fiancee' Sharon Sheeley survived the crash.

CHAPTER 4

Boy, which reached number 3 in the UK charts in late December. The group had arrived in Britain to begin an arduous tour on 1 March 1958. On March 2nd they appeared live on ATV's Sunday Night at the London Palladium, which went out at 8pm in the evening. Bob Hope headlined the show, but although the Crickets had second billing they performed last.

So on that Sunday, I sat with my parents at a card table covered with a tablecloth eating our Sunday supper – usually a fry-up of the Sunday lunch: fried mashed potatoes, re-heated vegetables, or a tin of peas, and cold meat – peering at our 15 inch black and white television. Eventually, after what seemed like an interminable wait, the group took the stage. The memory of Bob Hope, and the preceding "variety" acts that were the bane of live "rock shows" in those days, thankfully receded as the band moved quickly into the first of their three hits. But it wasn't the music, great though it was, that grabbed my attention. It was Buddy Holly's guitar. A guitar unlike any that I'd seen before. Gone was the large, bulbous sound box that had covered half of Gene Autry or Bill Haley's body. In its place there was a small, thin, curved plate of seemingly shiny plastic from which the string and neck of the guitar emerged to finish in a curved head of wood resembling a treble clef. I would learn later that this was a Fender Stratocaster and the first to be seen publicly in the UK. This iconic guitar became the staple of the beat scene in the UK after Hank Marvin of the Shadows became the first UK owner of the instrument in March 1959.[21]

---

[21] Cliff Richard imported the guitar from the Fender factory in Santa Anna California as a gift for Hank. It is currently owned by Bruce Welsh of the Shadows.

Three days after, on my eleventh birthday, Holly and the Crickets would play at the Globe Stockton. I would have been too young at just eleven to attend on my own and it is not clear that my parents would have thought it worth the expenditure on the two tickets to take me. Significantly, I was unaware of their visit until after the event. And the Second Half of the Eleven Plus was looming. Two years later as we sat jamming in Pedro's house it is inconceivable that we would have missed seeing them live. But by then rock music had become a much greater part of my life.

I was now playing a Vox solid electric guitar, which my parents had bought for me, along with a small amplifier, the previous Christmas. The Vox was no Fender Stratocaster. But it was red and it was electric. The three of us could now whip up quite a storm in Pedro's living room, which was sufficient to attract interested friends and neighbours who were mostly sympathetic. One of these was Franc Roddam. To us Franc was trendy and slightly aloof. He exuded a certain arty sophistication, which was less Beaconsfield Road, Norton and more Kings Road, Chelsea. I am sure this was as much a problem of our self-conscious perception as Franc's behaviour. But we were clearly not part of his set and he soon disappeared from our lives. An interesting footnote occurred nearly 20 years later when I discovered that the movie of the Who's rock opera *Quadrophenia* was adapted and directed by him. The theme of the movie of alienated working class youth and conflict between 'mods' and 'rockers' was clearly close to Franc's heart. For me he was the archetypical 'mod' and I guess for him Pedro and I came closer to the 'rocker' stereotype. It perhaps threw a little more light

CHAPTER 4

on why we failed to hit it off so many years before. Franc pursued a distinguished career in film and television and if he reads these words he should know that I remember him with affection.

As I trudged through the dimly lit streets of Middlesbrough following my epiphany watching Ray Hudson of the Midnighters at the Astoria, I resolved to trade in my Vox six-string electric guitar for a four-string electric bass. At a musical level this made sense since a lead guitar – Pedro – and a bass, plus drums offered a better balance than two six-string guitars. But where was the extra money required to fund the exchange to come from? Our band had no evening engagements. We were, quite frankly, not good enough. My pocket money, though generous, would not be up to the task. And I couldn't expect my mother to bankroll me as she did so frequently in my early life. But if my mother didn't bankroll me directly she did provide the solution: a labouring job during the forthcoming Christmas holidays at the company that she worked. She clearly pulled strings to deliver this since I was only 13 years old and most heavy labouring tasks would have been beyond me.

So early in 1961, just before my fourteenth birthday, I became the proud owner of a Burns electric bass guitar. This was soon followed by a red and cream, "blood and custard", Truvoice Professional amplifier made by Selmer. The 8 watt amp with a 12 inch speaker pales into insignificance against modern amplifiers but it was more than respectable at the time. The 'gear' was purchased from John Burdon and Sons (Pianos) of Yarm Lane, Stockton.

Burdon's became an increasingly important part of our lives. The shop had for many years enjoyed a respectable trade in pianos and in band instruments. Indeed the store can be seen on photographs of Yarm Lane dating back to 1900. With Jack Marwood's band playing at the Maison de Danse about 100 yards further down on the other side of Yarm Lane, Burdon's was almost provided with a ready market. Yet Burdon's had to move with the times as demand began to shift away from traditional, live, dance-band music to pop and rock bands and the improved record playback technology offered by 45rpm singles and 33rpm LPs. The shop installed listening booths for records, employed a young female sales assistant and generally made itself friendlier to the new, more youth focused, music culture. It put a greater emphasis on guitar and drum-kit sales and began to hire out amplifiers and PA systems to bands that couldn't afford to purchase such expensive equipment. As part of this policy it did not object to a few nascent pop musicians and band members 'hanging out' at the store on Saturday afternoons, and I soon became part of this scene.

It was clear to me that Pedro, Chris and myself were not going to go further than our Beaconsfield Road jam sessions. All three of us had much to learn musically and we had no idea how to move from the living room to paid engagements at pubs and clubs. I was also not certain that Pedro and Chris were that keen to go further and so concluded that the best solution for me would be to join an established band[22]. Burdon's on a Saturday afternoon provided the opportunity of

---

[22] This was arrogance and also a mistake on my part because Pedro later became a successful and popular bass player with the Bluecaps.

CHAPTER 4

meeting, and making myself known to, like-minded others who were interested in pop, rock, blues and country music. I knew that several of these people were band members and maybe, just maybe, something would turn up.

On most Saturday mornings I would go for the customary weekend lie-in but my mother would be loath to let me lie after 10am. And this turned out to be no bad thing since it allowed me to hear the radio show *Saturday Club* on the BBC's Light Programme hosted by Brian Matthew. The programme ran for 2 hours from 10am to 12pm and consisted mainly of original pre-recorded sets performed by the most popular artists and bands of the time. The emphasis on "live" pre-recorded music was due to the restrictions on the amounts of "Needle Time" (record playing) that were then current[23]. Most programmes had four live acts and only contained around six record requests and three new releases. The programme for 14 January 1961 reveals the fairly eclectic mix at that time with: Cliff Richard and the Shadows, riding that week at number 2 in the NME charts with *I Love You*; the pop/rock roll hybrid trio the Viscounts, hits such as *Short'nin' Bread*, and later in 1961 *Who Put the Bomp*; the early rock n' roller Don Lang and His Frantic Five – hit *Witch Doctor* – and a touch of world music in the form of Dorita y Pepe.[24]

Saturday morning was also when I had to help my mother with the household chores. But often this

---

[23] For further information about *Saturday Club* including programme content see http://www.saturdayclub.info/
[24] Sourced from http://www.saturdayclub.info/

reduced to trying to convince her not to use the vacuum cleaner – she called it "Hoovering" – while *Saturday Club* was on.

Once the programme was over I would jump on my bike to pedal, or occasionally walk, the mile to Smith's fish and chip shop, which sat in a row of about 5 shops opposite the Swan Hotel across the A19. Family tradition decreed that we had fish and chips twice a week: for Saturday lunch and Thursday supper. I would hope to arrive at the shop just after the fish and chips had been taken out of the fryer and certainly not after a new batch had just been put into the fryer, since that would mean an extended wait. As soon as the fish and chips were ready and paid for I would emerge from the steamy "chippy" clutching the warm newspaper parcel, clamber back on my bike and pedal furiously home. Usually, my mother would have the small table in the kitchen set with knives and forks, a pot of tea, bread and butter, salt and pepper and tomato ketchup on the red formica top. We would sit opposite one another my mother reading the *Daily Sketch* propped up against the teapot as she ate, while I perused the *New Musical Express* with one hand and used a fork to guide ketchup-doused chips and chunks of battered fish into my mouth with the other. Snippets of information drawn from our reading material would occasionally be exchanged across the table.

I remember little of my father on these occasions so I assume that most likely he would be at work at his job in the Nylon plant at ICI Billingham. Many non-shift work employees other than office staff tended to work Saturday mornings and my father was no exception. Although it is probably more accurate to say that as my

CHAPTER 4

mother and I ate our fish and chips my father was about to sit down to his first pint of Newcastle Exhibition ale as he stopped off at the Kings Arms on his way home from work.

But all this was a preamble to the then highlight of my Saturday: the afternoon trip to Burdon's. I would take a United bus from the Swan Hotel bus stop to Stockton. The four and half mile trip on the red double-decker would take about 25 minutes with stops at Billingham village green, then on to Norton, first Beaconsfield Road, then the Modern cinema, soon to become the Fiesta nightclub. After a couple of further stops the bus would enter Stockton on Norton Road passing my school, Stockton Grammar on the corner of Garbutt street. A few minutes later I would get off just past the Town Hall in the central area of the High Street, opposite the Shambles and outside the building and chemist shop, long since gone, where John Walker invented the friction match in 1826. There then followed a five minute walk south down the High Street, first passing the Vane Arms and in a few further steps the Black Lion Hotel[25]. Continuing parallel to the market stalls – some of the *circa* 120 stalls that lined the centre of the High Street almost from Maxwell's corner to Barry's corner on Saturday and Wednesday market days – passing Doggarts department store, to

---

[25] Both would disappear along with many traditional shops, such as Wilson's and Doggarts, in the 1970s redevelopment of the south eastern side of the High Street that for many represented thoughtless destruction of an aesthetic and cultural heritage that could never be replaced.

Rossi's ice cream parlour crossing just up from the Empire cinema on the east side to just down from the Odeon cinema on the opposite side, and rounding the Grey Horse pub into Yarm Lane. Another couple of hundred yards passing the Theatre Hotel, or "Jocker Brown`s" and the Maison de Danse, on the other side of the road, before coming to Amos Hintons grocery shop, after which and just before the Green Bushes hotel I would walk into John Burdon's (Pianos) music store on 52 Yarm Lane.

On entering the shop there was little initial indication that this was a hotbed of Teesside rhythm groups.[26] The front of the store was mainly devoted to pianos and traditional band instruments. However, walking further in and up a couple of steps as the store narrowed you would be confronted by a couple of record listening booths to your left and to your right a small glass counter where the records were stored and sold. Further on from this, the store widened again to some degree where there would be guitars hanging on the wall, amplifiers and the occasional echo chamber on the floor with manufacturers catalogues available. Here there would be several people, sometimes as many as ten to fifteen on a Saturday afternoon, who were mostly talking amongst themselves. Some would be trying out guitars, others would be looking at catalogues but for the most part this was less a bazaar of records and musical instruments and more a market of musical

---

[26] I use the term 'rhythm' group because it was very common in the early 1960s and many bands described themselves as such rather than 'pop' or 'rock' group. The term 'beat' group was also more commonly used than the latter two.

CHAPTER 4

information and ideas: which groups were doing which gigs, who was looking for a lead guitarist, what money venue x was offering, which strings were wearing better than others, who had bought a Fender Stratocaster, whether the new echo chambers with magnetic discs were a better bet than the older loop-tape machines, and so on.

And amidst such chatter one might spot one or two celebrities from the top local bands of the day: Mick Kemp, Charlie Peacock and Eric Whitehouse of the Blue Caps; Brian Taylor, and Gordon Valentine of the Johnny Taylor 5; George Hart and John Rogan[27] of the Hartbeats; Alan Coverdale of the Zephyrs; and Roy Smith of the Denvers. Members of groups from Middlesbrough such as Tommy Gibson of the Midnighters, Alan Ludley of the Denmen, and George Kitching of the Tempests, the Victors, then the Kalvins joining Dennis Trowbridge and Terry Popple[28], were less frequently sighted since they had their own haven: Hamilton's music shop in Middlesbrough. Micky Moody of the Road Runners, then Tramline and later the super group Whitesnake describes the role played by Hamilton's in the early 1960s Middlesbrough music scene in his excellent book *Playing with Trumpets*.[29]

---

[27] Later bass player of the Roulettes, Adam Faith's backing group from 1963 to 1965.

[28] Terry went on to much greater success with Middlesbrough band Tramline formed by John McCoy (vocals, harmonica),with Mick Moody (guitar), Terry Sidgwick (bass, vocals), and Popple (drums). Popple subsequently worked with Snafu, Matthew Fisher and Alan Hull, and Radiator.

[29] Page 46 in Micky Moody (2006) *Playing with Trumpets: A Rock'n'Roll Apprenticeship*, SAF Publishing.

I moved uneasily into this milieu. I had no experience of playing in a group on live gigs. I could hardly play the bass guitar. Yet, my intuition suggested that if I made myself visible and acceptable to the key band members of the local group scene then something might turn up. I began to hit it off with Roy Smith and we had several in-store conversations about music in general, country music in particular, and the experiences of the Denvers on the local pub and club scene. But Roy was by no means the only person I warmed to. Alan Coverdale was an unassuming but genuinely "nice guy". Mick Kemp could be described as something of a 'card', a larger than life character, perhaps a bit of lad, but someone who was a great drummer, a natural leader and moulder of musicians and for whom you would, if it came to it, be prepared to go that extra mile. I drank in the atmosphere and would drift away from Burdon's through the descending gloom at about 5pm, finding my way back to the High Street and a United bus home after straining to see the flickering black and white televisions in Barry's electrical store in an attempt to catch Newcastle United's result.

As the early weeks and months of 1961 moved one into the other, I settled into my third-form school routines: regular homework, football on Friday afternoons, cross-country runs to be avoided, participation in the school choir, and fleeting involvement in the school debating society. Family life was less than satisfactory. My parents were clearly drifting further apart and while my mother devoted more and more of her energies to her clerical job at Tennets, including secretary of the firm's social club, my father preferred to spend more time at the pub only appearing after 9pm each evening.

CHAPTER 4

In my free moments, if not practising with Pedro and Chris, I would be at home trying to improve my skill at the bass guitar. An endless series of 45rpm singles would be put on the record player as I tried first to hear and then to play the bass line in accompaniment. The Shadows second hit *FBI* had reached number 6 in the UK charts in February and then their next release *Frightened City* reached number 3 in the charts in May. Elvis Presley numbers were even more popular and demanded to be studied and the bass lines learnt: *Are You Lonesome Tonight* reached the top of the UK charts in January and stayed their for four weeks; *Wooden Heart* attained number 1 in March holding that position for six weeks; and then *Surrender* hit the charts in June remaining at the top for four weeks. Despite some of these songs not being my personal favourites, I knew I had to expand my repertoire if I was to offer myself as a plausible candidate for membership in a local band. Needless to say all this activity in our front living room did not meet with the wholehearted approval of my parents and may not have been an insignificant factor in my father's preference for the Kings Arms over domestic bliss!

Our family life was by no means focussed solely on domestic matters. Television was more and more becoming a bridge to the wider world, imagined or real. On some evenings I would watch TV both before and after our 'supper'. In 1961, we saw *Coronation Street* for the first time and also a new, slightly surreal, detective programme: *The Avengers*. The most popular TV programme in the 1950s was *Wagon Train* with nearly fourteen million people in the UK watching the US made 'Western' on 30 November 1959[30]. The show continued to be popular in the early 1960s and my mother and I, occasionally joined by my father, watched the Monday screenings on ITV with much expectation. The 'cowboy' movie veteran Ward Bond[31], playing wagon master Major Seth Adams, and Robert Horton, playing the dashing scout Flint McCullough, led the cast. I suspect that my mother's enthusiasm for the show was perhaps driven more by the attractions of Robert Horton than any intrinsic interest in the 'Western' genre.

The 'real' world entered our home through the nightly TV news bulletins, with a tendency for the BBC to be preferred to ITN News on ITV - the opposite of our entertainment preferences. Both my mother and father shared a strong interest in keeping abreast of the news, and perhaps because of their influence I too shared that interest. My father, as befitted an ex independent councillor with strong right-wing Tory sympathies, was a fervent anti-communist and a strong believer in the use of force to sustain British and US political objectives in the international arena. He had stopped buying the *Sunday Times* in 1956 at the time of the Suez crisis because of its hostility to the British, French, Israeli invasion of Egypt! In 1961, he believed that the US should deal firmly with Cuba and resist strongly the threatened Soviet aggression against Berlin. The US aided invasion of Cuba at the Bay of Pigs by anti Castro exiles in April met with his

---

[30] Source: http://www.bfi.org.uk/features/mostwatched/1950s.html
[31] Ward Bond sadly died of a heart attack whilst on location in Texas on 5th November 1960, and John McIntire, already playing Chris Hale in the show replaced him. McIntire later went on to star in 'The Virginian'.

CHAPTER 4

approval, while the failure of that ill-judged exercise led him to roundly condemn a lack of US resolve.

As a fourteen-year old my political sympathies were fairly fluid but I had a strong sense that my father's views were somewhat extreme and, perhaps echoing my mother, that a more conciliatory approach to international politics might achieve better results. Cuba would play an important role in my life, as in the lives of many others, some eighteen months later during the so-called Cuban missile – see Chapter 8 – but in 1961 I was more interested in other items of news. For example, the death of George Formby[32] in March and the obvious distress that might cause Mr Evamy, Yuri Gagarin's first manned space flight in April of that year, and amazingly the BBC's decision in March to ban 'rock' versions of the classics, with its refusal to air *In the Hall of the Mountain King* - Edvard Grieg's final piece of the Peer Gynt, Suite No. 1, Op. 46. - recorded by the band Nero and the Gladiators.

But not every evening was spent practising bass guitar or watching television. There were dance halls to visit and bands to watch, subject to the limits of my pocket money, school homework and parental edict. Often I would take a United bus to Billingham Green

---

[32] From http://www.biography.com/search/article.do?id=9298994 "Formby, George (1904–61) Entertainer, born in Wigan, Greater Manchester, NW England, UK. He developed an act in music halls throughout England that was subsequently transferred to film. In a series of low-budget, slapstick comedies he portrayed a shy young man with an irrepressible grin and ever-ready ukelele to accompany his risqué songs. From Boots Boots (1934) to George in Civvy Street (1946) he was one of Britain's most popular film stars." For ukelele read 'banjo'!

and then walk the mile to Billingham Synthonia Social Club on Belasis Avenue where bands such as the Johnny Taylor Five and the Bluecaps would play in mid-week as well as weekends. On one Saturday I remember turning up at the club in a three-quarter length white mac with diagonal zip breast and side pockets, which I had persuaded my mother to let me buy and in which I felt terribly 'cool'. Later that evening metaphor turned into reality when on presenting myself at the cloakroom I found that my new coat had been taken by somebody else. I trudged away from the club, shivering in anger, having missed the last bus home and fearing what my mother and father would say on my return.

Yet, if I thought that the gods had turned against me that night another evening at the Synthonia club a little later in 1961 had a very different conclusion. That night I left the club quite early, got on the bus at the Green jumping off at Hillcrest bus stop on the A19 just before the road – in those days – swept on past the Kings Arms, then briefly through open country before entering Wolviston. I dodged past the barrier at the bottom of the 'cut' that led up into Matlock Gardens. This barrier is worthy of mention because my father claimed it as one of his political achievements as a councillor. It stood at the bottom of the fairly steep 'cut', an obstacle to preoccupied children who might dash out on to the busy A19 a few short steps away. With hindsight I can see why my father viewed this simple piece of fencing as a lifesaver and worthy of pride. With the 'cut' soon navigated I passed the end of Queens Drive and up into Matlock Gardens, my thoughts drifting back to the girls that I had failed to ask to dance at the Synthonia. My reverie was then rudely disturbed by the noise of the

CHAPTER 4

engine of a van, which first slowed, drew parallel and came to a halt a few yards ahead of me. Out of the van from the right stepped a large, balding, middle-aged man; from the left came a much shorter, younger guy. The younger man seemed familiar through the gloom of the streetlights as he turned to his left and said, " This is my father Jack, our manager. We were wondering if you would like to join us". Recognition began slowly to dawn but not before Jack interjected "what Roy is trying to say is that we sacked our bass guitarist this evening and we would like you to replace him in the Denvers." I do not remember my reply.

CHAPTER 5

THE DENVERS

The Denvers were the brainchild of Roy Smith from Billingham who started the band in the late 1950s while still a pupil at Grangefield Grammar School in Stockton. By 1960 the band had acquired a drummer from Middlesbrough, Ron Telford, and Roy had replaced his Grammar school colleagues with more experienced musicians: John Maunder on rhythm guitar and Johnny Hebb on bass, both from West Hartlepool. The cosmopolitan trans-Tees line-up was completed when Ronald Porter – stage name Johnny Rocco – joined the band as lead singer and another "Smoggie", or Middlesbrough, resident.

Roy, or to give him his full name, Godfrey Le Roy Smith, was the musical, intellectual and commercial driving force behind the group. He had built up a reputation at Grangefield as both a smart, articulate, young man and a talented guitarist with diverse musical interests beyond the current pop scene. An example, of the former was his decision to stand as the Conservative candidate in a mock election held at the school and winning the contest comprehensively against formidable opposition from older, and perhaps more traditionally academic, schoolboys representing the other mainstream political parties. His success in the school election was even more impressive when it is remembered that Stockton had become a Labour stronghold. Although it might also be the case that the intake to Grangefield Grammar did not constitute an unbiased sample of Stockton's voting population! In the October 1959 general election, which Roy's school election was meant to shadow, George Chetwynd was returned as the MP winning 54% of the vote compared to Labour's national share of 44%. The Conservative party secured 49% and formed the new Government led by Stockton old-boy Harold MacMillan, with a one hundred seat majority, an increase of 46 over the Tory majority in the previous parliament[33].

As to music, the fourteen year-old leader of the Denvers was well capable of quickly mastering the latest Shadow's record, or the lead guitar riffs of Elvis Presley's principal sideman Scotty Moore. But his passion was country music, and his hero was Johnny Horton. Horton's song *The Battle of New Orleans* was a major crossover hit at that time as well as winning the 1960 Grammy Award for Best Country Western Recording. When visiting Roy's parents' house you could guarantee that the record either was not long off the turntable or would soon be put on. As with all heroes, the intensity of adulation was heightened by Horton's untimely death in November 1960, age 35, at the hands of a drunk driver in a head-on car crash.[34]

---

[33] Source: http://www.ukpolitical.info/Index.htm
[34] See *Wikipedia* http://en.wikipedia.org/wiki/Johnny_Horton for a brief biography and some interesting coincidences surrounding Horton's death.

When I joined the Denvers, it was natural that my relationship with him would develop. We were both grammar school boys, all be it from different schools that were fierce rivals. We were also quite a bit younger than the other band members. Roy was 15 and I was 14, with two of the other band members – the two Johnnies - at least four or five years older than Roy and Ron Telford much older than that. Roy had also taken a gamble on me, since I had no experience beyond Pedro's front room and at the point that John Hebb left and I joined, the group had clearly lost a better bass player. Roy was in a sense my patron and in those early days I looked up to him with much awe, even though physically Roy was shorter than me.

Two days after the encounter in my home street with Roy and Jack, I found myself on the stage with the Denvers at a Working Man's club in West Hartlepool. This really was a baptism of fire. We'd had no time to practise. I was hardly aware of the set-list, never mind practising and playing the numbers. A rudimentary knowledge of some scales and chord families helped me to busk a bass line for most of the numbers. And for those where I knew I was floundering I lowered the volume a bit and sought to act, if not play, the part! The other members of the band were encouraging and Jack and Roy were supportive, whatever they really thought. I'd effectively passed an audition and appeared to be accepted as a member of the band.

In early 1961, the band was just starting to play in some of the bigger commercial dance and club venues on Teesside such as the Maison de Danse, and Jubilee

CHAPTER 5

in Stockton, and the Astoria and Empire Continental in Middlesbrough. But their bookings were mainly in pubs, Working Men's clubs, and dances, whether in schools or community halls. The group had built up a solid reputation with these diverse audiences, and this was reflected in the considerable number of bookings the band had when I joined. With engagements at least three evenings a week, and sometimes four, or five or more, this was an exciting and intimidating world for a fourteen year-old schoolboy to enter.

While some of the bookings were in the Billingham and Stockton area many were further afield, for example, in Catterick, Northallerton, Spennymoor, Gateshead, Shildon and so on. Travel times of an hour or more were not unusual and given that band members had to be picked up and that it took time to set up our 'gear' we had to set out before 6pm for a gig that started at 7.30pm or 8pm. All of which didn't leave much time for tea and a schoolboy's homework. So, while my stock had begun to rise in the Saturday afternoon Burdon's music shop milieu it began to plummet in the classrooms of Stockton Grammar School.

To get to the gig we needed transport, hence the van that Roy and his dad were in when they came to offer me fame and fortune in the Denvers. Eric Clapton in his autobiography writes perceptively about travelling to gigs with *John Mayall's Bluesbreakers*:

> "We travelled in John's Ford Transit. Back in the sixties there was a lot of status attached to the kind of van a band had. A Bedford Dormobile, which was ugly and clunky and had sliding doors,

denoted lowly standing, but owning a Transit showed that you were top of the pile".[35]

Needless to say, the van that drove the Denvers to gigs in 1961 was, yes you guessed it, a Bedford Dormobile! Roy's father Jack, an ex merchant seaman and process chargehand at British Titanium Products Billingham, helped the band acquire the van and as well as manager was the band's principal driver. Both Roy and I were then too young to drive and as far as I remember none of the other group members possessed a driving licence. In 1961, young people in their late teens and early twenties were unlikely to possess a driving licence and were much less likely to own and drive a car than they are today. So, if Jack couldn't drive us because of work commitments, we had several reservists who would do the job for seven shillings and sixpence, or ten shillings! Clearly, the real value of ten shillings was significantly higher in 1961 than today and some indication of this is provided by the fact that the fee the band received at venues such as pubs could be no more than £5, was sometimes £4, and was rarely above £10. More context is provided when it is remembered that the average weekly wage in Britain in 1960 was £14/2 shillings, or £14.10 pence in decimal terms. Even in 1966, moderately successful local bands on Teesside, such as Micky Moody's Road Runners, began to get excited when their fees moved into double figures.[36] But a driver was essential and in Jack's absence

---

[35] Page 65, *Eric Clapton: The Autobiography*, Century, 2007
[36] Page 74 in Micky Moody (2006) *Playing with Trumpets: A Rock'n'Roll Apprenticeship*, SAF Publishing.

CHAPTER 5

it effectively meant that we had another band member to pay.

Trips to the Gateshead area to the north or Northallerton to the south could be quite exciting in a perverse sort of way. On cold evenings the van turned into a refrigerator, with the primitive heating system of the Dormobile only able to pump out tepid air in the front, to the benefit of Roy and Jack, while the two Johnnies, Ron and myself shivered in the back. The absence of side windows meant that the option of looking out of the window at the passing countryside was removed. We could only stare over Roy and Jack's shoulders at the oncoming traffic, wincing at the crazy overtaking manoeuvres of others – the van was quite slow – until sleep mercifully provided release. Relief would be provided when we had a different driver from Jack, who was a careful and responsible driver. I remember one occasion when returning from a booking in darkest Yorkshire, the van suddenly began to shake more than was usual. Startled out of my reclusive slumber I opened my eyes to see a rabbit being pursued by us as we careered along the grass verge, with the driver exclaiming that it wouldn't get away this time. But, thankfully, it did. Needless to say our rabbit hunter was not called upon to be our chauffeur much after that.

Our adventures in vans continued throughout the lifetime of the band. After our first vanless trip to France - nobody in the band could drive and Jack couldn't come with us for a six-month spell off work - we eventually acquired a Standard Atlas van. A Ford Transit it was not, but in terms of comfort and smoothness of ride it was in a different league from the Dormobile. The Atlas was roomier with more space for passengers in the back and for our expanding gear. I have always suffered from claustrophobia to some degree and so it was something of a relief to find that the roof of the Atlas was almost a foot above our heads. But safety provision was another matter. There were no seatbelts, and a lack of smooth surfaces with jagged metal protuberances waiting to entrap the unsuspecting passenger. This was brought home to us in a dramatic way on our second tour of US bases in France in the Autumn of 1963.

Roy having passed his driving test was able to drive the Atlas and so the group could travel to France under its own steam, commencing our second trip in late August 1963. Liberated to be travelling under our own steam we decided to take a few days vacation before we headed to our first meeting with our new agent in Paris (See Chapter 10) and then on to a monthly residency at the Enlisted Men's Club at a US base in Fontainebleau in France. So, our old 'Charlie' Atlas first took us to see the delights of the remnants of the 1958 World Fair just outside Brussels, with a visit to the Atomium, a structure shaped like an atomic molecule, being a particular highlight. Then after Paris and Fontainebleau we travelled for a month's residency to the United States Army General Depot base at Ingrandes just north east of Poitiers, to perform at the enlisted men's (EM) club for a month.

Having completed practice one afternoon early in April we got into the van to drive back to our hotel in Chatellerault before returning to the base for our show that evening. Sitting in the front passenger seat, I could see the base gates in the distance behind what appeared to be a parade ground area in front of the base headquarters' buildings. Being unfamiliar with the base Roy

CHAPTER 5

must have concluded that the best route to the gate was across the parade ground. Just as we moved to cut across the parade ground, the thought flashed through my mind that the "parade ground" looked as if it was covered in grass rather than asphalt, or concrete. Then everything went black.

I came to a few seconds after the impact, to find myself half in and half out of the van, the passenger door open and the windscreen shattered but lying on the grass in front of the van. Roy was conscious but severely dazed. Our two female singers, Jenny and Jackie could be heard moaning behind me. The van had driven off the base road directly into a shallow, grassy ditch. On impact it had managed to plough a furrow the width of the van and about three feet in length into the other side of the ditch. But amazingly, nobody was seriously hurt. My left foot had been pressed against the dashboard on impact and the force of the impact had led to the metal moulding itself around my foot. That is probably what helped keep me in the van following the crash after the door had flown open. No seatbelts were worn, nor was the van fitted with seatbelts as far as I can remember. So, again it is a wonder that we were not all seriously hurt. Nevertheless, both female singers had to go to hospital for treatment for comparatively minor injuries: cuts to their legs from the metal bulkhead that lay between the front and rear seats and burns from acid splashes due to a rupturing of the battery, which was positioned and visibly exposed between the driver and front passenger. We didn't make our show that evening but we were back in business the next night. The Atlas would I think probably have been written off back home since its frame was bent. However, an enterprising French garage in Chatellerault managed to patch her up and we used it until we returned home at the end of February 1964.

Worse was to come! With improvement in the band's finances, the Atlas was replaced by a new Commer van, a clear challenger to Transit supremacy. We returned to France at the end of March 1964 and a couple of months later we were working at the EM Club on the main US base in Orleans. Another English band, the Jaybeats from Cheshire and North Wales, was also working at one of the other US bases in Orleans. We had become friends with them and on this one particular evening they had turned up for the last part of our show. After which, we agreed to meet up for a drink near our hotel in the suburbs to the south of Orleans. Roy, Jackie, Jenny and Adrian Tillbrook – the band's drummer after our first tour to France – left in the Commer while I decided to travel with the Jaybeats in their mini-van. The attractions of being closeted in their cramped van with the Jaybeats' voluptuous female singer, Brenda Bardsley – not, I believe, her stage name! – my principal love interest at the time, far outweighed the benefits of the comparative roominess and luxury of the white Commer.

The N10 out of Orleans could be fairly busy even at midnight. As the principal route to Spain heavy trucks travelling in both directions were ever present. And with summer beckoning there were increasing numbers of tourists travelling in cars and buses even in those less-leisured days. On this evening, the traffic seemed heavier than usual. The Jaybeats' mini-van slowed first to a crawl and then to a stop, a traffic jam at midnight! But this was unusual and soon the sound of agitated French voices served to underline the point. Andy, the Jaybeats' lead

CHAPTER 5

guitarist, said he would get out and investigate and I offered to go with him. Proceeding up the line of stationary cars and trucks, passing gesticulating French and Spanish drivers the phrase "accident de la route" floated above the chatter. And even with my schoolboy French, I knew what that meant. I had a terrible sense of foreboding my heart began to pound. I shouted to Andy to speed up and we both began to jog trot up the line of vehicles. A queasy feeling gripped me, a feeling made worse by the pungent fusion of garlic, Gauloise and diesel fumes that enveloped us as the crowd of demonstrative drivers thickened. And then as we emerged from the crowd frightened anticipation became reality. There on its side like a beached whale lay the white Commer.

No police or ambulances were then at the scene, although I could hear the screechy sound of sirens in the distance. I tentatively approached the scene resisting a powerful urge to turn, run, and put as much distance as possible between the overturned van and myself. Then I saw Roy talking to Adrian, our drummer. Miraculously, all was well. Nobody had been killed or seriously injured. Jenny and Jackie were badly shaken and later went to hospital for checks but apart from bruises everyone appeared to be ok. Roy explained that he had been attempting to overtake a truck when a large black Peugeot 203 car suddenly pulled on to the road offering the prospect of a head-on collision[37]. Roy turned the steering wheel to avoid impact and caught the oncoming lorry a glancing blow. This was sufficient to flip the

---

[37] It was soon established that the driver was drunk and he was subsequently charged and convicted.

Commer over causing it to slide along the road on its passenger side for several yards. Jackie had been particularly lucky. Sitting in the front passenger seat as the van turned over she was pinned by the weight of Roy's body against the door her face against the window with the road rushing by only millimetres away. If the glass had broken ….. A day later one of the English tabloids – the Daily Mirror I believe – ran a short piece, tucked away in the middle of the paper under the headline: "Beat Group in Crash on Road to Spain." Fame, of sorts, at last!

Back in 1961, we would arrive at a gig in our Bedford Dormobile and proceed to get the gear out of the van and set up as quickly as possible. This would be rewound with even greater speed as soon as the gig finished, so we could all get home as quickly possible to get some sleep before school or work next day. The gig itself, our reason for being there, was never dull and offered a variety of experiences.

First, the audiences differed markedly depending on the venue and type of event. In pubs in places such as South Bank, Middlesbrough, Stockton, Thornaby and West Hartlepool, the audience was mainly working class men recovering after a day or shift in the steelworks, shipyards or chemical plant. Jobs were still largely plentiful and while there was clearly not a lot of money around there was enough to support several nights a week at the pub. Don't ask me what the consequences of that were for many household budgets. The north east of England, specifically Hartlepool, provided the inspiration for Andy Capp, a character I always thought was much overstated but who, nevertheless, does provide some insights into the north east working class men and women at that

CHAPTER 5

time. Florrie, Andy's wife was much more dominant in the family nexus than many have understood and the author, Hartlepool born cartoonist Reg Smythe, clearly intended us to appreciate that Andy might wish to portray himself as top dog but such status was largely on Florrie's sufferance. Indeed, I would assert after living for nearly 40 years in Scotland that the west of Scotland working class male was possibly less dependent on his wife and had a more clearly defined role than his north east England counterpart as mirrored in Andy Capp. To give one example, Andy Capp and my own father both cleared out of the house when there was decorating to be done and left it to the wife. My impression, clearly not based on any rigorous survey, is that such behaviour would not generally be observed in the west of Scotland. Decorating was/is seen to be the "man's job" in Glasgow but not so in Stockton. In Stockton and other parts of the north east if there was "man's work" around the home it would be the garden or allotment, an option that was probably unavailable to the average west of Scotland male housed in a tenement.

So, the audience at our pub gigs was largely male, certainly in mid-week, less so at weekends, with the few women who were there seated, almost without exception, with male partners. Solitary half pint glasses of shandy, or lemonade sat on the table in front of them, or maybe a Babycham at the weekend, while the beer in the pint glasses of their husbands or boyfriends diminished at an increasing rate as the evening wore on. As the drink and music intertwined and the haze from the many cigarettes smoked thickened, the evening began to build to a crescendo with strong vocal numbers such as Elvis Presley's *Frankfurt Special* from *GI Blues*, and

That's Alright Mama, belted out by our rhythm guitarist Johnny Maunder, particularly popular. Then the evening would be over, people would start to drift away, some would linger as we packed up our gear, a furtive smile might be exchanged with a girl friend or young wife as the couple departed and then the pub manager or owner would usually appear to thrust four or five one pound notes into Roy's hand. The lights would all come on, ashtrays would be emptied, tables would be cleared, and spilt beer would be mopped from the floors. Only the smell of stale cigarettes and beer remained.

The experience at working men's clubs (WMCs) was similar to pubs but there were interesting differences. Firstly, the WMCs were much more organised and less anarchic than pubs. There would be a Master of Ceremonies, usually the club secretary, who would introduce the band and provide the "intimations" of future entertainment, some of which was of the variety type: magicians – The Amazing Svengali – jugglers and, more frequently, comedians. At some clubs we were not the only act of the night and I remember one occasion when we were preceded by a middle-aged couple singing *The Indian Love Call*[38] with all the band members struggling to keep a straight face while almost wetting ourselves. For weeks afterwards, one of us would suddenly burst into song in a falsetto voice with the phrase *"when I'm calling you"* and the rest of us would dissolve into helpless laughter. And occasionally that would happen on stage to the bemusement of the audience.

---

[38] A duet made famous by Nelson Eddy and Jeanette MacDonald in the 1936 film version of Rose Marie.

CHAPTER 5

Now it was sometimes the case that the band had been booked by an Entertainments Secretary in the bigger clubs, so the announcer did not always know who we were and would have to scramble for a piece of paper to try and remember our name, especially when we were playing in the more remote Durham coalfield areas such as Spennymoor, Shildon, Tow Law, and Wingate, even though it was emblazoned right across the front of the bass drum. Or if he, and it was always a he, remembered our name he might have us coming from Sunderland – heaven forbid – rather than Stockton and greater Teesside. Secondly, being clubs there was a strong sense of community, further reinforced if the club was in a mining village as many WMCs were. The organisation and sense of community meant that women were more likely to be in the audience, but again only with male partners, and they would be more vocal. Everyone would be better dressed than in pubs, the visit to the WMC was more of a "night out". And, yes, there would be bingo! The parade of two fat ladies, Kelly's eye, Harold's den, took place in the interval between our sets, or between acts. We would participate too, munching crisps and cheese rolls that seemed to be freely available but maybe my memory plays tricks. The other food highlight of such occasions was the visit of the man selling small bags of seafood: whelks, prawns, mussels and shrimps, which we all loved, although the smell in the van going back home would often be of Billingsgate proportions.

The other main venue where we plied our trade was the dancehall. Playing at dances was in some ways more to our taste since the audience was much closer in age to us than the pub or WMC audiences. Of course people attending dances went there to dance not simply, or even, to watch and listen to the band, although many did and that, as we shall see soon, often caused us problems. Essentially, we were the background music so we had to be lively, varying the tempo occasionally to allow dancers to slow down a bit, and of course we had to be loud. We occasionally played the bigger dancehalls on Teesside such as the Maison and the Jubilee in Stockton or the Astoria in Middlesbrough, which were exciting events much anticipated by the band. But more frequently we played at smaller, and some not so small, dance halls in schools, colleges, tennis clubs, and private venues in Billingham, the suburbs of Middlesbrough, and Stockton.

Some of these venues could be very small, epitomised by Hartburn Tennis Club in the suburbs of Stockton. Being a tennis club meant that the dancers and audience were much more middle class than our usual dance venues and to my juvenile mind the young women seemed much more poised and desirable. At the start of the evening we would be placed behind a line of two benches that usually accompany trestle tables. There was no stage. The benches simply split the room between band and dancers and only slightly in favour of the dancers. By 10pm the place would be heaving with about 200 dancers packed together tightly, moving as one body to the music. There appeared to be little concern from the management about safety and as the numbers expanded heat levels rose and sweat dripped down from our faces onto our instruments as well as from the bodies of the dancers. Such occurrences prompted the joke that Hartburn planned to increase the capacity of the club to cater for another 50 dancers by moving the end wall of the 'hut' by half an inch. The

CHAPTER 5

heady mix of music, heat, alcohol and sexual excitement created tensions between dancers and also occasionally between the audience and the band. Occasionally, these tensions would explode into violence.

The risk of violence at one of our gigs was an ever-present if variable threat. It became an accepted part of what you had to put up with, at best to watch, at worst to endure, if you played in a rock band. The risk to the band also rose the more we, or one of our number, appealed to the female sex. And in Johnny Rocco – real name Ronald Porter – our occasional lead singer, we had someone who definitely stirred the hormones of the female of the species. Johnny was in one sense an Elvis clone. He sported thick, swept back, black hair; fleshy jowls, an intense stair and he sang Elvis songs, especially the ballads, beautifully. To use cliché, he had a heart of gold but was quick to rise and had fists of steel. He had no school qualifications that I remember and his normal work when he had a job was as a builders' labourer, hence the fists of steel. I remember every time the band drove in the van from Thornaby to Middlesbrough he would point out with great pride a concrete footbridge that *he* had built. He was a major asset to the band and indeed several bands because he had done the rounds with several of the main local groups including the Midnighters, but usually there would be a parting of the ways because Johnny, lovely guy that he was, could not be described as reliable.

So, one night as the Hartburn Tennis club throbbed to the sound of an Elvis Presley number and the dancers performed their sweaty gyrations, Johnny was to be seen dancing along the top of the bench that divided band from dancers. I am standing to the right of Johnny

Maunder who is directly behind Johnny R. and Roy is doing his Scotty Moore stuff at the left of the 'stage'. Keith Richards comment in his recent autobiography[39] that he seems to have spent a lifetime staring at Mick Jagger's arse reminded me of this moment as Johnny R's backside swayed to the left of me level with my face. Then suddenly he was gone. The singing had stopped while the music played on and there was Johnny fists flailing on top of one, or two, of the local youths. The dancers strained and a small circle appeared on the dance floor to accommodate the event, a not inconsiderable feat given the size of the Hartburn club – I'm trying hard to avoid the sardines and can simile! But the hero of the hour was not Johnny R. but Johnny M. who coolly stepped up to the second microphone stand and more or less took up where Johnny R. left off singing " ... that's alright mama, that's alright with you ...." The fight was soon broken up, the bleeding youths were helped away and Johnny R. clearly pleased with himself leapt back onto the bench to conclude the evening's performance with a rousing version of Johnny Kidd's *Shaking All Over*. And I can tell you he was not the only one who was shaking!

If actions have consequences then this truth was demonstrated two weeks later when we played at the Grangefield Grammar school annual dance. This was an important event for Roy, since he was still at school there and naturally we didn't want to let him down in front of schoolteachers and fellow pupils. The PT master, nicknamed "Rock", was there to use his

---

[39] Keith Richards "A Life" , 2010.

CHAPTER 5

formidable presence to keep order, chaperone the band and ensure the event passed off without incident. It was a good-natured affair located in the large school hall, which was big enough to accommodate the whole school at assembly and on speech days. The floor was full of dancers and so several hundred must have been present. Yet, the size of the place, with us perched high up on the stage well back from the dance floor and the fact that "Rock" had insisted that the lights could not be dimmed, meant that there was little atmosphere, unlike the Hartburn experience. Just another school dance, or so we thought, until Johnny R. left the stage after completing a set of five or six songs, saying that he was going to go outside for "a smoke". We launched into the Shadow's FBI, which had reached number 5 in the NME charts in February 1961. From our position high on the stage all that could be seen as we played the instrumental was a field of heads and shoulders moving to the music. Then almost magically a crop circle appeared as dancers rolled away and there was Johnny R. at the centre his mass of black hair held down tightly in one boy's hand while several other boys kicked his face and body viciously. Hearing and seeing the disturbance "Rock" hurried to make his way through the panicking dancers but too late. Johnny R. lay unconscious face down on the dance floor and badly beaten while his antagonists, savouring the taste of revenge[40] for Hartburn the previous week, had slipped out into the warm Stockton night.

---

[40] We learned later on the 'grapevine' how these youths plus mates had planned to get even with Johnny R. after their humiliation at Hartburn.

Johnny Rocco did recover from the ordeal but he never sang with us again. Soon after he would go to jail for some misdemeanour and I never saw him thereafter. Yet his talent was immense, he could sway an audience of any age by the beauty of his voice. Tears would be visible amongst the audience when he sang Presley's *"Can't help falling in love with you"*. In another time or place he might have been a big star but this wasn't always possible if you were born in Middlesbrough in the 1940s on the other side of the tracks.

Unfortunately, the fisticuffs didn't begin and end with Johnny Rocco. Fights were not infrequent at our pub venues but fairly rare in WMCs. Our main aim was to entertain the audience, not antagonise them and if there was a fight, keep out of the way. This we usually managed to do. However, occasionally this did not prove possible. So one evening we were playing in a pub just off Cannon Street[41] in Middlesbrough very shortly after I joined the band. We had just finished when an argument developed in front of us, a head butt went in and a dazed Middlesbrough drinker landed on top of Ron Telford's snare drum. This is not to single out Middlesbrough for special treatment because a similar event occurred at the Three Tuns pub in Northallerton a fairly quiet rural retreat. Here a local collapsed on top of the main cymbal after a blow from a fellow North Yorkshire farmer! But both our gear and us largely avoided direct action, at least until one night at a Thornaby community centre.

---

[41] Infamous for the race riot that occurred there in August 1961 precipitated by the stabbing and murder of a white boy by a young Asian man - http://journals.sagepub.com/doi/pdf/10.1177/0032258X6904201114

CHAPTER 5

The dance was for a youth club, which was run and organised by a kindly Irish Catholic priest. Our fee was probably £6. The evening appeared to be going well especially since a not inconsiderable number of apparently admiring young women had gathered at the foot of the stage. But I also noticed that there was a smaller number of less admiring young men who were trying hard to give us the "hard stare". The stage was not so high as to avoid contact, so at the end of one number when I came closer to the front of the stage for some reason a rather nasty and snearing young man said "who do you think you're looking at?" Rather stupidly I couldn't resist responding with "Nothing in particular!" Which as you might have guessed failed to pour oil on troubled waters. My antagonist's demeanour got steadily worse and buoyed up by several mates who had clustered behind him shouted: "You were looking at my bird weren't ye?" By then the seriousness of the situation had begun to dawn on me and the other band members: there was no escape, we had nowhere to run, our backs were literally to the wall. As soon as we had finished our final number to polite clapping and encouraging noises from the dwindling group of admiring girls, the boys stormed the stage. We had two advantages, height and our gear, particularly the screw in legs of the PA. Using the height advantage given to us by being up on the stage and the PA legs as clubs we managed to beat off the first wave of the attack before being rescued as the second wave began by the cavalry in the form of the kindly Irish Father and three bouncers. With the hall cleared and promises that the bouncers would stay with us until the van was loaded and we were on our way, the kindly priest turned to us and in an Irish accent that I can't mimic said "I can see that you boys have not had your troubles to seek tonight, so I think a little more consideration is required, here's £7/10 shillings. Goodnight and God bless!"

I wasn't completely oblivious to developments in the wider world during this period despite my obsession with rock and pop. My father kept reminding me to look out for the "commies" who were everywhere spreading their influence. " But dad it can't be all bad. They've just put a man in space." Major Yuri Gagarin had made the first manned space flight and orbit of the earth in April 1961. "Yes son but at what cost to the Russian people and the economy?" Good old Eisenhower had broken off diplomatic relations with Cuba in January 1961, in part in protest at the growing Soviet influence and military presence in that country. This was days before John F. Kennedy assumed office as President after his election victory over Richard Nixon in November 1960. Dad was not sure that Kennedy had the "balls" to stand up to the Russians. "Yes, dad but didn't the US bomb Cuban airfields in April and the invasion of Cuba by those anti-Castro exiles at the Bay of Pigs must have had the President's backing." "Maybe, son, but the invasion failed didn't it and the Russki's are now even more ensconced in Havana." Tensions over Berlin grew significantly over the summer as the flow of refugees to the West grew significantly and the Soviets and East German authorities began to build the Berlin Wall in August, ostensibly to keep western influence and people out but actually to keep East Berlin citizens in. All this seemed to prove my dad's point. Yet, to my Dad the US was still our only hope. Britain was "going to the dogs" aided by "fellow travellers" such as Canon John Collins, the new

CHAPTER 5

Chairman of the Campaign for Nuclear Disarmament (CND) and not one of my father's favourite organisations, to say the least. "Macmillan and the US killed us at Suez and now they want to sell us to Europe.[42]" Harold Macmillan, then UK Prime Minister had been Chancellor of the Exchequer at the time of Suez when the US threatened to withdraw financial support forcing Britain to stop its joint military intervention with the French in collusion with the Israelis. In July 1961, the UK had applied for membership of the European Economic Community (EEC), with tacit US support.[43]

Then in October 1961, to our horror, Tony Meehan suddenly left the Shadows, only weeks after *KonTiki* had reached number 1 in the charts. While Tony was not as important in our hearts as Hank, Bruce and Jet, this was still a bitter blow. For me the only comparable later experience was when Roy Jenkins and Shirley Williams left the Labour Party! Well perhaps not exactly

---

[42] On re-reading Christopher Booker's brilliant 1969 book "*The Neophiliacs: the revolution in English Life in the fifties and sixties*", I see that of the key social groupings that Booker identifies as playing a key part in the purported "revolution" he would have placed my father in *The old guard betrayed*: "Of course, 'Old Guard' political and social attitudes would by no means be limited to the upper and middle classes – as was to be seen all the way from Suez to the expressions of working-class support for Enoch Powell's racialist speeches in 1968-9." Page 101. Incidentally, I guess he would have placed me in *The young urban lower class* while placing himself, Shrewsbury and Cambridge educated, into *The Oxbridge 'intellectuals' and the upper-class young*. His fourth and final grouping was the *New generation in the unions*.

[43] Described by Booker *op cit* as "Macmillan('s) …. boldest gesture and his last throw" Page 164.

comparable. In retrospect, I felt Tony to be the greater loss. Would this be the end of our favourite band? Not so. Brian Bennett quickly replaced Tony and the Shadows soon went on to bigger and better things. The same could not be said of the Labour Party until many years after the Jenkins, Williams, Owen, Rogers[44] exit when another Tony emerged.

But there was also good news in October 1961. The Shadows were coming to Stockton to perform in the Christmas pantomime at the Globe Theatre. We had to go and see them. "Why don't we write to Hank Marvin and invite him to tea?" Roy said one Sunday afternoon as we messed about in his parent's living room after *The Battle of New Orleans* had stopped turning on the record player for the nth time. "What a smashing idea Roy" feeling slightly peeved that I hadn't thought of the idea! "Let's do it now. And Roy..." "Yes, Brian?" " ... don't mention *The Battle of New Orleans*." So the letter was duly written, past copies of the NME and Melody Maker searched for a suitable address to send it to, an envelope addressed, a stamp provided by Roy's mum and the letter put in the post for collection next morning. The days of October dragged slowly by and into November. There was schoolwork to be done, bass lines of songs to learn and gigs to perform. Routine was lightened by the news that Cliff and the Shadows were to release a new album in December containing the music for the film *The Young Ones,* which Cliff was starring in, to coincide with the Premiere of the film. Then one morning in early December Roy received a

---

[44] Labour MP for Stockton, interestingly.

CHAPTER 5

letter. "Dear Roy and Brian, Thank you for the kind invitation to Hank to have tea with you when the Shadows are performing in pantomime in Stockton later this month. Hank regrets that he will be unable to come to tea because of preparations for the show. However, if you report to the stage door on …(a certain date) …. and ask for Sam Curtis, he will introduce you to Hank who will be pleased to meet you. Best wishes ……" The letter seemed genuine enough: "WE ARE GOING TO MEET HANK MARVIN!"

So, on one cold December evening we presented ourselves at the stage door of the Globe. We showed the letter to the doorman asked for Sam Curtis and after a brief wait on a mezzanine floor on the stairs going down to the dressing rooms Sam appeared. "Hello boys" said this rotund and florid man sporting a substantial moustache that pressed down and around his upper lip. Then in a strong cockney accent "I'm Sam Curtis, the Shadows Road Manager, if you wait here I'll try and get Hank up to see you and I'll also see if I can round up any of the other boys." He disappeared. We shuffled in anticipation gazing at the duck egg blue walls. I felt that I was going to wet myself, an urge that fortunately I managed to stifle. Roy farted. We both giggled. And then there he was. Tall and thin, black horn-rimmed glasses set squarely on the bridge of his nose and a warm smile across his face. "Hi boys, how are you doing?" All the questions that we had earlier formed about guitars, chords, songs, shows, just drained from our minds as we shuffled our feet " … erm ok, fine." But it didn't continue like that. Hank put us at our ease and we talked about his Fender Stratocaster, first in UK - a present from Cliff, practising - a lot, but harder on the road, amplifiers – Vox, and so on. Roy, to this day, vividly remembers Hank responding to some comment about his red Stratocaster with "…. Yours is natural Blonde isn't it?" Roy was gobsmacked. How did he know?

Then Sam ushered Bruce Welch into the company quickly followed by Jet Harris. Jet was taciturn but not unfriendly. Bruce was more talkative and friendly but less clear in his answers to our questions than Hank and I couldn't stifle the thought that Bruce was "a bit dull" - grammar school boy arrogance perhaps. Soon Sam reappeared to take his charges back. They were to go on stage in the hour. As they turned, Hank paused, looked back at us and said that if we go to the box office there would be front row tickets for us for that evening's show, compliments of the Shadows. And before we could give due thanks to him he was gone. Less than two hours later the Shadows were playing their hits up on the Globe stage just a few feet away from us and as Hank played *Midnight* he gave us both a big wink.

As 1961 drew to a close severe snowstorms swept across the British Isles. March 1962 was the coldest month of the century so far[45]. Travelling to bookings became more of an ordeal and it was not unusual late on a Saturday evening to see the returning vans of the Bluecaps, the Johnny Taylor 5 and ourselves stopped on Stockton high street with band members warming their bodies holding and drinking steaming cups of tea purchased from the all-night stall located between the Shambles and the Town Hall. Amidst the steam and

---

[45] Booker *op cit* page 176.

CHAPTER 5

fluttering snow flakes the chat would turn to how the most recent gig had gone, what the bookings were like, what new venues were booking bands, or whether Ken Tyzak was still booking bands during the winter at the Rainbow Room, Seaton Carew, a small, shabby[46] seaside resort – "with a good beach" I hear my grandmother say – near Hartlepool just up from the north bank of the Tees. We all shivered.

Yet bookings were not going that well for us. In part, it was the cold winter with people less keen to go out and pubs and clubs therefore less ready to hire bands. It may also have been due to increased competition as the number of local bands rose. But our conversations around the late-night tea stall suggested it was more general than that. By the middle of 1961 the British economy was in trouble. The earlier boom of 1960/61 had generated a rising current account deficit, and a deteriorating balance of payments culminating in the heaviest run on the pound since 1949. On July 25th in response, the then Chancellor of the Exchequer, Selwyn Lloyd, raised Bank rate to 7% and introduced a 'Pay Pause'[47]. The effect of this was to lower real household disposable incomes, reducing household spending, leading to job losses and rising unemployment. By 1962, unemployment on Teesside had climbed from the lows of 1-2% in 1960 and 1961 to 5% and then rose further to 6% in 1963. Teesside was in recession.[48]

---

[46] As Mickey Moody *op cit* page 73, describes it.
[47] ".. the first recent peacetime attempt by a Government to impose an overall regulation of wage increases" Booker *op cit* page 163.
[48] H. Beynon, R. Hudson & D. Sadler (1994) *A Place Called Teesside*, Edinburgh University Press, page 69.

Average family incomes and spending were falling and venues were more reluctant to book bands. We needed money to pay the hire-purchase payments on our guitars, amplifiers, PA system and drums and after covering our transport costs we didn't have enough left to meet all the payments on our instruments. This was made worse by the fact that in early 1962 we had changed to an all Fender guitar line up. Both Roy and Johnny M. had blonde Fender Stratocasters and I had a blonde Fender Precision Bass. We had Vox AC 30 amplifiers and Louis Johnston, from Stockton, who had replaced Ron Telford as our drummer, had a large kit of Premier drums and cymbals. On top of this, Jet Harris had left the Shadows[49]. Damn! What to do?

"Why not hold a dance?" suggested my mother. "Hire the Billingham Tech College main hall, another couple of bands, make yourself the headliners, advertise it well in the college and you could make money." So, this is what we did, with my mother offering to cover the up-front costs of hiring Stockton Corporation buses to ferry people back to Stockton, Hartlepool and Middlesbrough after the dance ended. Roy thought it was a great idea and the rest of the band agreed. We all worked hard making the arrangements and the event went ahead on a Friday night in March just after my fifteenth birthday. We had sold quite a few tickets beforehand but we could not be certain that the event would be a financial success because on-the-door sales were crucial. Yet, the event was a success both

---

[49] Actually he was sacked just after the Shadows had recorded *Wonderful Land* largely because of his drinking which was beginning to interfere with Shadows' performances.

CHAPTER 5

financially and socially. The hall was almost full; there was no trouble – only one or two friends as bouncers – and even our parents enjoyed it! When all costs were paid off, including repayment to my mother, we had a sufficient surplus to reduce our debts considerably. Indeed, Roy and I could almost pay off the sums outstanding on our guitars.

But we still needed to fund the payments on the remaining guitar gear, amplifiers and PA equipment as well as Louis' drums. We had quite a few bookings lined up in the spring but would they be enough? In any event, Roy and I had begun to feel that the Tees, Ouse and Tyne should not set our horizons. There was a bigger world out there. Could we become part of it? We felt we were good enough for bigger and better things but in Britain at the time if you wanted to get on in the music business you had to go to London[50]. So we hatched a plan. In the school Whitsun holidays in May we would travel to London, stay with friends of my parents in Brixton and try and get bookings for the band during the summer holidays. Then who knows maybe fame and fortune would beckon.

As the train pulled into Kings Cross station at the beginning of the third week in May 1962 our excitement was palpable. We knew the stories about Hank and Bruce travelling from Newcastle to London and playing at the Two i's coffee bar in Soho, a path trodden by so many artists both before - Tommy Steele, Marty

---

[50] See Alan Clayson (1995) *"Beat Merchants"*, Blandford. If "Winchester's Arapahos …. hadn't a hope in hell of gaining a recording contract, living where they were" (page 51) how much harder was it for a band from Stockton?

Wilde, Terry Dene, Wee Willie Harris - and after – John Martyn, Bert Jansch. But were we living a small part of that collective fantasy that Christopher Booker contended characterised the social revolution in Britain in the Fifties and Sixties?[51] At our mundane individual level, we had high hopes for the future but it is probably fair to say that we were not grounded in reality. We had no idea how or where to look for bookings for the summer, nor had we gone into whether our band member colleagues with day jobs would be prepared to take time off work at risk of losing their precious jobs even if we did manage some bookings. With the whole of London and its anticipated opportunities and possibilities laid out before us such thoughts were far from our minds.

London in May 1962 had not yet become what *Time* magazine was later to describe as "the most swinging city in the world."[52] That would have to wait until the middle Sixties. The London that confronted us from the top of the red double-decker bus as we travelled across to Brixton was much the same as that greeting any visiting Teessider over the years: the sheer scale of the place, flows of traffic that never ceased, a kaleidoscope of faces from a range of ethnic backgrounds hardly ever seen in Stockton, the maze that was, and is, the underground, black taxi cabs, men in bowler hats, black coats and striped trousers sporting umbrellas, Lyons Corner House cafes, barges and river police, neon lighting and all the trappings of the Capital, the Houses of

---

[51] C. Booker *op cit*
[52] In the 13 April 1966 edition of *Time*, C. Booker *op cit* page's 8 and 294.

CHAPTER 5

Parliament, Buckingham Palace, statues of the great and the good, horses, soldiers, the changing of the guard, and a greater chance of seeing an E-Type Jaguar, a famous face, or a sexy woman!

Our bags had hardly touched the floor of Mr and Mrs Neave's pleasant terraced house in Branksome Road, Brixton before we were out again to explore London. "Where are you going?" Mr Neave asked. "Up to the west end and then perhaps to the pictures." Not a lie exactly, but still economical with the truth. We had only one destination in mind: Soho.

As we surface from the tube in Piccadilly Circus I can feel blood pumping round my body. The flashing Guinness Clock towers above us. We are enveloped in an embrace of neon. People are everywhere. I feel for my wallet. Then up Shaftesbury Avenue, left into Wardour Street and ... Soho! Dean Street, Greek Street, Frith Street, Berwick Street, these are names to conjure with. We gawp at everything: strippers walking from club to club dressed in tight leggings and mohair sweater with a tote bag containing their 'costume' thrown over a shoulder; Raymond's Revuebar, a very high-class strip-tease club - Raymond having being fined in 1961 the princely sum of £5,000 for keeping a disorderly house, yet the Revuebar did not close; "dirty" book shops, which I later learned to call 'pornographic' when they had lost their fascination; Greek, Italian, French, Chinese restaurants; then the Two i's with anticipation fractured on the 'Closed' sign that hangs behind the glass front door; 'clip' joints, where you pay 10 shillings to drink a heavily diluted glass of orange and talk to a seemingly lovely – the lights are dim – girl, who promises so much, after just another drink, then another and another, before disappearing into the beckoning anonymity of the Soho night. Sadly, thankfully, Stockton was never like this. Our senses sated we look for the late night bus back across the river, passing quizzical policemen who assessing our age are tempted to approach but think better of it. On, past drunks singing, couples arguing, newspaper sellers shouting, tea vans steaming, taxis queuing, buses coming, buses going then, yes, the bus to Brixton. I feel homesick. I miss my mam.

We started looking for work in the local pubs in Brixton. I remembered on an earlier visit to the Neave's with my parents that a pub in Branksome Road, or close by, had advertised Cliff Bennett and the Rebel Rousers as appearing at the venue. So next morning Roy and I knocked on the door and met the manager. Yes, we could come and play there, but there would be no fee. If the audience liked us the pub would re-book us at a fee. Much the same response was given to us at other venues that were suggested to us. We had tapes of the band but even if we had had them with us it wouldn't have been sufficient to win a booking. What appeared to be key was how the pub audience reacted to us. With hindsight we probably shouldn't have expected much more. In London and the rest of Britain there were literally thousands of beat groups like ourselves, there was an excess supply in relation to the demand from pubs, clubs and dances, hence the venues could pick and choose and pay low and even zero fees. This was going to be more difficult than we thought. Then Mr. Neave said "Boys, why not go up to the west end and visit some of the guitar shops and music stores in Denmark Street, Tottenham Court Road and Charing Cross Road. See who is hanging out there perhaps

CHAPTER 5

something will turn up." Good idea. Perhaps we could find a west end Burdons.

The music stores were like Aladdin's caves to us: guitars of every shape, size and description; solid electrics, acoustics, semi-acoustics, 6 string, 12 string guitars, 4 string, 5 string and 6 string basses! Fender Stratocasters, Telecasters, Jazzmasters, Precision Basses, Jazz Basses; Gibson Les Paul's, EBs, SGs, Southerner and Hummingbird acoustics, and ES-335 semi-acoustics; Gretsch Country Gentlemans, Tennesseans, Chet Atkins; and Martin and Guild acoustics. "Watch those guitars boys. Can you play?" sneered one assistant. "Cheeky cockney bugger!" Roy muttered as he tried to impress with part of the Shadows *Man of Mystery*. Even our hero Hank had been unable to record this cleanly and Norrie Paramor their producer at EMI's Columbia had, inexplicably, allowed a blemished version to go to final pressing and general release.[53] But not all music stores were unwelcoming. At Ivor Mairants, the great guitarist himself took down a Guild semi-acoustic from the wall and proceeded to demonstrate the guitar to us with a series of jazz riffs that made our jaws drop. "Yes dad that Django Reinhardt guy must be something else!"

Situated on Charing Cross Road was Jennings music store. The unprepossessing name of the company that manufactured Vox amplifiers and guitars, the British answer to Fender. In fact Vox amplifiers, if not their guitars, were world class. The AC30 twin amp, which we had at the time became a legend in the music business and behind many fine rock guitarists you would

---

[53] Alan Clayson *op cit* page 50.

often find, if not a great woman, certainly an AC30! We walked through door of the glass-fronted shop past the banks of Vox amplifiers displayed down the side of the store and approached a glass counter behind which stood two sales assistants. "Hello, can I help you?" "Erm, yes, we have Vox amplifiers." Both assistants give us a blank stare. "That's nice, did you want to buy anything? I'm afraid we don't sell parts here, although we might be able to order ...." "Well ... the truth is," Roy interrupted, "we run a band up north in Stockton and we are down in London to try and get some bookings for the summer. So far, we haven't had much success." I butted in. "We just want names of venues, or even a manager or agent, who might help us get work." "Joe!" His colleague Joe had just gone to the back of the shop. "Wasn't Sam Curtis in here the other week looking for bands to take to France to play for the yanks?" Joe comes back in. "Yeah, Sam split from the Shadows when Jet Harris left. His son Paul is running a band called the Londonaires and Sam wants to book his son's band and maybe one or two others over in France. He sees himself as an artist's manager now and not simply a road manager." "We know Sam", Roy interjected, "we met him last year in Stockton when he was with the Shadows." "I'm sure he'll remember us. Would you pass on to him our names and perhaps give him our 'phone number. Brian, what's your mam's number?" "Stockton 54270." I shot back. "No problem, best of luck with the bookings lads." We gave our thanks and left.

"Do you think anything will come of it, Roy?" I mused as the train pulled away from Kings Cross station, flecks of soot and the smell of steam drifting in

CHAPTER 5

through the open carriage window. "Wasn't that Mallard[54] just there?" "I don't know, what was its number?" "6 00 something." "All streaks are 6 00 something. Mallard's number is 60022." "No, I think it was 60024." "That would be Kingfisher. But Roy what do you think?" "I think we need to get our feet back on the ground. I've got my O-level exams in a few weeks time. You've got end-of-year exams. I take it Stockton Grammar still do exams? Maybe when we're older." "But Roy, what about London?" Silence. "Never did like bloody cockneys anyway!"

The next day, Friday, the last day of the Whitsun holiday and school on the Monday. I wander bleary eyed into the kitchen and make a cup of coffee. Images are running through my head from the last couple of days. It's nearly 11am mam and dad are at work. I slump down in a chair in the living room. The sun's rays are streaming through the windows past the curtains throwing abstract shadows on the living room floor. I light a cigarette, "shouldn't smoke in the house, mam doesn't like it", reach for the NME and the 'phone rings. Drag myself from the chair through the alcove into the dining room, place cigarette in mouth and pick up the phone. "Is that Roy?" "No, it's Brian." "Bet you don't know who this is?" "Sam Curtis?" I venture. "Clever boy, Brian. Clever boy. How would you like to go to France?"

---

[54] The Gresley A4 Pacific steam engine that held the world's speed record for a steam engine, set in the 1938.

Mum & Dad's wedding, March 1940

BKA with mum & dad, 1947

CHAPTER 5

BKA and dad, 1948

BKA and parents at seaside, 1947

BKA (top 3rd from right) Wolviston Primary School, circa 1954

BKA Wolviston Primary School, 1955

CHAPTER 5

BKA with mum and his Hercules Jeep

BKA First day at Stockton Grammar School, September 1958

BKA (bottom 2nd left) - Stockton Grammar School Choir - circa 1960

The Denvers at The Astoria, Middlesbrough, early 1962

CHAPTER 5

The Denvers off to London & France, May 1962

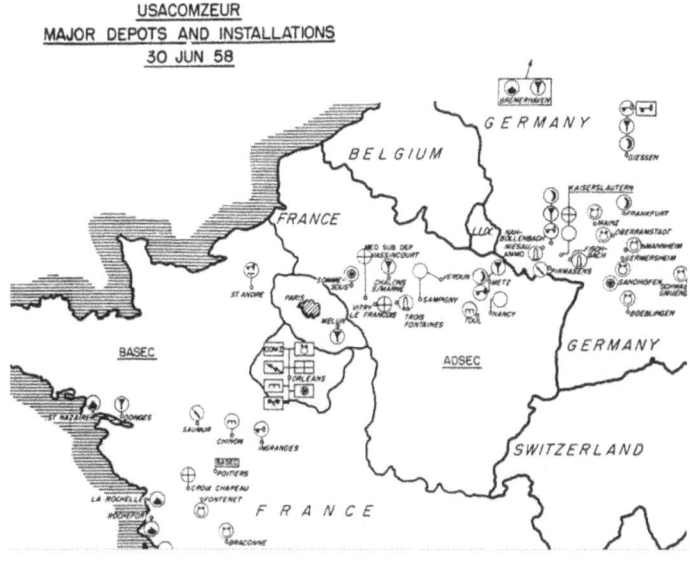

US Army COMZ Europe Bases, 1958

The Denvers, US Army Medical Depot, Vassincourt, August 1962

Clowning around at the Hotel de Metz, Bar-le-duc, July 1962

CHAPTER 5

The Denvers, US Army Garrison,
Fontainebleau, September 1963

The Denvers, US Army Garrison, Fontainebleau,
September 1963

With the Everlys, Fontainebleau, September 1963

CHAPTER 6

SAM CURTIS AND THE FRENCH CONNECTION

The Commer van draws up outside Starlite Artistes' plush offices in busy Albemarle Street London on a chilly May morning. Large pictures of the Brooks Brothers[55], and Brian Poole and the Tremeloes adorn the front windows. Roy is sat up front with Jack his father and the driver of the hired van. I'm sat behind with Louis and Johnny M, while our gear is stacked behind us. Today is Tuesday, 29 May 1962. It is only 4 days since Sam's 'phone call. We are professional musicians, off to play in France. Roy (16 years old) and I (15) have both left school, Roy days before his O-levels! Louis and Johnny M., both painters and decorators, have packed in their jobs. Howard Flatley, the band's singer, has stayed behind, perhaps wisely, not wishing to give up an apprenticeship at ICI Billingham.

What were we thinking about? What, more to the point, were our parents doing letting us go so readily? I can only imagine the stick that my mother must have

---

[55] Then heralded as "Britain's answer to the Everly's."

CHAPTER 6

got from my paternal and maternal grandparents. Yet, my parents had not objected. "Is this what you really want to do? Are you aware of the implications of giving up Grammar school? No qualifications, no apprenticeship and if all this fails maybe a labouring job is all you'll be able to do." " But mam I can get qualifications later. This is a chance of a lifetime." At that they gave me their blessing and never raised the issue again. They clearly, I think correctly, reasoned that if they had stopped me, I would likely have rebelled, let my schoolwork drift and all our lives would have been made miserable for no real benefit. At least, this way, I had to stand on my own two feet, take responsibility for my actions and I couldn't blame them. It was a heroic decision on their part. I loved them for it and I still do to this day.

"Wotcha boys!" says Sam as he peers into the back of the van. "This is my dad, Jack," says Roy squirming a little. "Bet you're glad to get rid of this lot then, Jack?" is Sam's breezy reply. We all climb out on to the busy pavement. "What's going to happen when we go back to Stockton in the van?" Jack asks. "Don't worry mate I'll take 'em to France, so there's no problem." But Roy said you were taking another band as well, the Londonaires or something." "Yes, that's right Jack and a good band they are especially when Paul is kicking up a storm. Don't worry, Lenny's promised to help me out." "Whose Lenny?" "Lenny? Lenny's me brother. Owns an upmarket photographic emporium just off Piccadilly. Photographs the stars; maybe the Denvers one day. I've got a vehicle and Lenny's got a vehicle." "But you said that the group would play for a month at one base then travel to another base for a month. How are they going to move around Sam?" "No problem, Jack. I'll be there." "You'll go over at the end of each month to pick them up?" "Yes, love France I do. I'll move the Londonaires as well. Got to do something for my money, know what I mean?" "But what happens at the end of the six month tour?" "Now there you got me Jack. Maybe if the boys saved a bit by then you could have a van and you could pick them up, London or Dover maybe?" "Oh, and one thing Sam." "Yes, Jack." "Who's in charge? Who runs the show?" "That's easy Jack. I'm their manager, them over there, Starlite Artistes, is their London agent and a German geezer Herr Carl Friedrich from Chateauroux France is their French agent." "Seems like there'll be a lot of deductions from the band's fees." "That's show business Jack!"

Lenny Gurvitz[56] arrives within the hour. Sam disappears to round up his "boys", meaning the Londonaires, and we begin to unload the van and load Lenny's car. Yes, car! A large maroon Wolseley with a roof rack on top, which is where most of the gear is precariously stacked. Jack says goodbye and our past life recedes into the London haze back to Stockton. Several honks on a car horn announce the return of Sam in his pale blue Commer caravette, or what the American's call a Winnebago. Out jumps three male Londonaires and a female. Paul Curtis/Gurvitch sporting a goatee beard, is taller than his father, slightly aloof but friendly enough. We learn he is a hairdresser in an upmarket London salon. Mark is an altogether more flashy character, bass

---

[56] Sam's real name was Samuel Gurvitz a second-generation immigrant with a Russian-Jewish background.

CHAPTER 6

player, full of (to us) cockney arrogance, while Steve, the drummer, is a moon faced, gentle guy who is incredulous - "really?" - at every statement or fact offered about our lives. Sandy, the female vocalist is pleasant, yet reserved and is clearly not going to get too familiar with these lads from up north. Could you blame her?

"Let's go." Shouts Sam. "We've got the early evening ferry from Dover to Calais to catch. Wagons roll!"

Unfortunately, we didn't make the early evening boat. As the Kent fields rolled by Sam's vehicle began to slow down on the outskirts of Charing a small village in Kent, then pulled over to the side of the road. "Think I've blown a gasket" he shouts through the car window to Lenny." You go into Charing and see if you can find a garage. In fact, I'll squeeze in with you." In Charing a garage is found. Sam explains the urgency. No problem. The van will be picked up and the gasket replaced in a couple of hours. "No point hanging about," says Sam, "let's give the locals a show." Off to the church. Sam locates the local vicar and offers to put on a show in one hour in the church hall, "2s/6d entry, all proceeds to the church." The vicar has just had an offer he couldn't refuse. Sam instructs us to begin setting up the gear, the Londonaires on first us on last. Then Sam is off through the streets of Charing like a Town Crier of old, " Special concert 6 o'clock this evening, church hall, two top professional pop bands – 2s/6d, almost free!"

At 6pm about 25 young people, mainly girls, are gathered outside the church hall. The Londonaires start their set and they are first-rate, the bass player especially. His arrogance is not simply bravado; he can really play, better than me – bollocks! More people arrive, so that by the time we start our set there must be about 60 people in the hall. The Londonaires had clearly gone down well and I can see Mark surrounded by several admiring girls. I begin to understand the meaning of the term "metropolitan sophistication". We go down pretty well and are not displeased, when, just as we are about to start our penultimate number Sam bursts in, "right boys and girls, show's over, got to get these performers on the road to fame and fortune. Remember you saw them first here. Something to tell your grandchildren!" At that, the audience began to drift away. We started to pack up our gear and began carrying it to Lenny's car. On my third trip through the churchyard I noticed Mark's white backside rhythmically appearing then disappearing from behind a tree. What was it about bass players? No let me rephrase that. What was it about bass players other than me?

By the time we reached Dover, we had missed the last ferry. But no worry Sam had a solution: we could sleep in the van and car! So we all snuggled down. Louis, Johnny M. and myself in the back of Lenny's car and Roy and Lenny in the front with poor Sandy sandwiched between. So all on our best behaviour, that is no farting from the lads from up north, less sure about Roy and Lenny though, sleep overtakes us, when what seems like minutes later Sam is banging on the top of the car: "ferry leaves in twenty minutes." We board the boat and within the hour we are disembarking. France. My first time on foreign soil.

At a Les Routier café, I sample my first glass of red wine and a jambon. I am not impressed. Well the ham was ok, but I wasn't so sure about the hard bread, and the wine, couldn't think what people saw in it; give me Coca-Cola any day. "Ok, guys this is the programme. We stay in Paris tonight and tomorrow we travel together to

CHAPTER 6

the northeast near the German border. The Denvers will then peel off with Lenny and go to Toul while the Londonaires will go on with me for a few miles further up the road to Nancy. Tonight we shall eat a nice French meal, then have a little tour of gay Paree. Tomorrow you will be paid and then you are on your own. Any questions?" "Why pay us tomorrow Sam, why not now?" "You a barrack-room lawyer sonny boy? Let's just say, I am looking after your welfare and thinking about your mums and dads. You'll soon understand."

Paris, like much of the rest of France, had still not shed the physical scars of the Second World War. The war had been over for almost 17 years but there were still many vacant lots and few new buildings visible. Paris had not, of course, suffered the bombing of the London blitz, so there were not the massive boarded up bombsites that were still visible in London in the late fifties and early sixties. But if you were to look carefully you could see the impact marks of bullets on some walls around the city. We would see much more evidence of the detritus of the war when we got to Toul. The city bustled though. Cars honked their horns much more than in England, even London. Taxis seemed to be driven by homicidal maniacs. Sophisticated looking women, with dark hair, golden skins, carrying tanned handbags, and wearing smart skirts and tops of muted colours adorned with scarves and gold jewellery, seemed to be everywhere. Our spirits rose further as we confronted the usual sights: the Eiffel Tower, the Champs Elysee, the racetrack that was the Etoile and the Arc de Triomphe besieged in the middle. Café's perfumed by garlic and French cigarettes reinforced the perception of a new and different world. And, as if to underline the point, to the delight of our still juvenile minds, the pissoirs! Behind curved sheets of metal about 4 feet deep we could see mens' heads, shoulders, legs and feet but not their torsos. "What's going on there Lenny?" I asked, tongue in cheek. "It's a French custom, the parade of the todgers. Better than doing it on the road as you'll see when we drive out of Paris." Then as we turned the corner: "What lesson does that teach you boys?" "Dunno, Lenny." "Never shake hands with a Frenchman!"

After steak and chips and a few coca-colas, we all, except Sandie, scramble into Sam's caravette. Paris is even more beautiful after dark: lights dancing on the Seine, the shiny white dominating presence of the Sacre Coeur, rivers of light flowing down the Champs Elysee into and around the Place de Concorde, the grandeur of Paris Opera and then, for us, the main course after the hors d'oeuvre, Montmartre and Pigalle. "Tonight you will see sights you've never seen before," announced Sam like a Ringmaster fronting a circus. "On our left is the Moulin Rouge, even better than Raymond's Revuebar! In this café," we are now in Place Pigalle, "the band is led by Benny Waters, Muddy Waters' brother." Could that be true? "Over there, that's the café where Sartre used to write and meet with de Beauvoir, Camus and all his existentialist pals. What was his book? *Coming and Going?*" "No I think it's *Being and Nothingness* Sam, Roy pipes up from the back. "Same thing! And there, that's the old *Hot Club de France* where Django Rheinhardt used to play. What might he have done with four fingers?" Thoughts of my father flood into my mind. I start to feel homesick. But not for long. "Now for the floor show," Sam announces.

CHAPTER 6

The van is turned into narrower side streets. Streets that seem to be lined with young and some older women, almost shoulder to shoulder. Our faces press hard against the windows. The women are invariably slim, quite heavily made-up but attractive enough for me to begin to experience a stirring between my legs. Men, usually suited, walk down the street looking at, and inspecting the girls. Some are engaged in earnest conversation with the object of their desire. Bargains struck, others disappear with their quarry into the shuttered windowed properties behind, while new men emerge, adjust their clothing, and look furtively up and down the street before drifting off into the night. A young woman looks up and winks at me. I blush but my loins stir further. The parade seemed to go on for street after street. I had never seen anything like it, either before or since. The gendarmerie didn't seem to bother. Indeed, I noticed several, resplendent in uniform, guns in white holsters, in casual conversation with some of the women. If only I could describe to my classmates back at Stockton Grammar School, the sights that lay before me, one could imagine the effect on the back row of Mr Murray's Latin class.

"And in the next streets we have the high-class hookers," Sam promised. Sure enough, women of even greater beauty and alluring adornment lined the streets. The spectacle was altogether subtler: young women in long clinging shift dresses revealing a mouth-watering curve of hip and breast; others in long flowing skirts, reminiscent of the fifties, topped by tight sweaters highlighting well-shaped breasts; and some in fur coats suggesting a hidden promise of bliss. "Better get you boys back to the hotel. Don't want you expiring." As the van pulls up at the front of the hotel, "Now, you see why payday is not until tomorrow! We must meet after breakfast in the hotel lobby at 9am sharp; we have a long drive ahead of us. Sleep well boys. And your doors will be locked!"

The heat of the Paris night was intense. Images of the evening flowed through my mind. I couldn't sleep. I was thirsty but we had been told not to drink the tap water in Paris. I threw open the shutters of the already open windows. Sounds drifted up from the street below. Roy snored in the next bed. An Algerian pedlar continued to sell carpets and God knows what else even at midnight. I thrust my mouth under the running tap and take great gulps. Would I catch the dreaded lurgy? At least I wouldn't be thirsty. Oh those girls ......

There is a hammering at the door. It is Sam. "Get up. Hands off cocks and feet in socks! It's past 9am. You've got twenty minutes to get dressed and grab a coffee and some bread before we leave. We're rolling."

We would not return to Paris for another year at least.

The endless, straight, tree-lined roads are what I remember most of that trip from Paris to Toul. Memories of the night before and the bustle of the great city began to be replaced with the anticipation of what Toul would be like and what experiences lay ahead. Of course, we had already exhausted the obvious jokes about Toul that you can imagine most male teenagers would come up with. What would the American soldiers be like? My main knowledge, such as it was, was from the movies: John Wayne, Charlton Heston, James Dean, Elvis Presley, Jimmy Stewart, Gene Autry, Roy Rogers and Trigger. But as to your average American I knew little.

Sam's van slows and pulls into a lay-by. Lenny follows. He winds the window down, while Sam comes

CHAPTER 6

over and crouches at the side of the car. "The turn-off to the hospital is just up the road. Lenny will book you in at a small hotel just outside Toul, drop your bags off and then take you up to the base. The hotel is cheap but ok and will meet your needs. Don't expect the Ritz! I'll see you at the end of the month. Best of luck boys." And with that he was off, his pale blue caravette bobbing away into the distance.

Lenny follows his instructions to the letter. The hotel is fairly isolated, set back off the road slightly between the town of Toul and the Toul Jeanne d'Arc, US military hospital that was to be our place of work for the next month. The bigger Toul Engineering base, the other US military facility in the immediate area, lies at the other side of town. The woman who runs the hotel is friendly, almost motherly, and we – at least Roy and I - get to practise our schoolboy French. Roy and I are to share a room near the top of the building with creaking floorboards, two single beds, a small mahogany wardrobe and a washstand with a jug of water covered with a cloth. The loo, lies along the corridor, and we find to our shock, horror, that it is a simple ceramic hole in the ground. Lenny comments that this is in the French tradition.

Bags unloaded we set off for the base; up a winding hill until a guard post comes into view. One guard sporting a white helmet, well-pressed khaki fatigues and a large black armband with the letters MP in white written across it approaches the car. "I'm bringing the new band in," Lenny explains. A quick look at the three of us sat in the back of the car and the guard signals for the barrier to be raised. "Hope you do better than the last lot! Welcome to Toul Jeanne d'Arc, US military hospital."

"What do you think the guard meant when he said 'hope you do better than the last lot'?" Roy inquires of Lenny when the last of our gear has been stacked at the back of the stage of the Enlisted Men's or EM Club. Lenny looks a little sheepish. "Well you know soldiers, they want to hear music but they also like to see, as they would put it, 'a piece of arse' up on the stage. That's why all bands have a girl singer. The last band's girl singer got homesick early on in the month and returned home. The band were fired the following week." "So does that mean they haven't had a band for nearly three weeks now? Roy exclaims. "And we don't have a girl singer," chimes in Johnny M. "Yes, I know. Sam is going to bring one out for you at the end of the month when he comes to move you. Didn't he tell you?" Roy looks first at me, rolls his eyes, and then looks at Johnny M. and Louis.

"What are we going to do Lenny," Louis pleads. "I think you might have to learn to wiggle your arse. See you back in blighty."

CHAPTER 7

GUESTS OF UNCLE SAM

At the end of the Second World War, U.S. troop deployment in Europe began to fall. By 1950, there were just over 120,000 troops based in Europe, about 23 percent of the number based outside the United States and about 8 percent of the total US armed forces.[57] There were still almost 100,000 U.S. troops in Germany but less than 1,000 in France. From 1950, relations between the West and the Soviet Union started to deteriorate. The Cold War had begun. U.S. troop numbers in Europe rose again, and quickly, with Germany seen as the potential frontline and primary battleground for World War III.[58] By 1962, U.S. forces in Germany had peaked at above 274,000 and were to remain at around a quarter of a million until the end of the 1980s. In France, U.S. troop numbers also began to rise. The main reason for this was the realisation by the US and NATO High Command

---

[57] All data on US troop deployment are from the US Department of Defense.
[58] Source: Tim Kane (2004) **Global U.S. Troop Deployment, 1950-2003,** Center for Data Analysis, Report No 04-11, Heritage Foundation.

that their supply-line through the north German port of Bremerhaven was vulnerable to seizure by Soviet forces in the event of hostilities. Bremerhaven was quite close to the East German border. A new safer supply route was desired and so the port of La Pallice, the industrial harbour of La Rochelle in western France, was chosen as the entry point for supplies into the European theatre[59]. France thus became a critical link in the logistical support[60], or supply line, to the potential frontline in Germany. Troop numbers grew quickly peaking at just over 71,000 in 1957 and by 1962 there were 53,000 U.S. troops serving in France. Numbers then started to fall as relations between France and NATO soured and by 1968, after France under De Gaulle withdrew from the integrated command structure of NATO, but not NATO itself, there were less than 100 U.S. troops in the country.

Of the 53,000 U.S. service personnel in France in 1962, 37,000 were in the army and 16,000 in the air force, housed in around 40 army bases and 11 major air bases. Most of the army bases were situated in a 'dog-leg' from Bordeaux, La Pallice and Braconne in the mid-west, through depots at Ingrandes, just north of Chatellerault, Chinon, Orleans, a cluster around Paris such as Camp des Loges and then east through Verdun, Vitry, Bar-le-Duc, and Toul to Nancy close to the German border. The air

---

[59] La Pallice with its deep water harbour became a German U-Boat base in World War II and one of the last to fall to the allies in May 1945 with one boat U766 found intact in one of the pens. This boat was subsequently commissioned into the French navy. La Pallice was used as the base for U-96 in the well known film Das Boot - see http://www.uboat.net/flotillas/bases/la_rochelle.htm.

[60] The organization of U.S. military supply bases in France was officially known as Communications Z, or COM Z.

CHAPTER 7

bases were more dispersed but still on a south-west, north east axis, at places such as Bordeaux-Mérignac, Chambley-Bussières, Châteauroux-Déols, Chaumont-Semoutiers, Dreux-Louvilliers, Étain-Rouvres, Évreux-Fauville, Laon-Couvron, Paris-Orly, Phalsbourg-Bourscheid, and Toul-Rosières. The United States Air Force in Europe wanted all its tactical air units to be located west of the River Rhine because of the vulnerability to Soviet attack if based in Germany.

Little, if any, of these strategic military and political issues entered our young minds as we walked from the hotel to the base, which being van-less we did on most days. But there were times during the next two years, as we shall see, when geo-political events broke through our teenage solipsism. As we walked we would buy a large 'Pain' and share it between us, scooping handfuls of the soft, fluffy, bread from the inside of the loaf. The slowest to scoop got the crust! To say this was our 'breakfast' does an injustice to the term because often by the time we had dragged ourselves out of our beds it would be mid-afternoon. But some days we felt the warm June morning sun on our faces as we went in 'early' to practise, trying to spot cars with an 'English'[61] number plate from the limited traffic on the road and then cheering with thumbs-up signs when, on a rare occasion, we did see one.

The Jeanne d'Arc hospital[62] was situated on top of a small plateau, in a quiet location close to a forest. From

---

[61] I never fully appreciated the significance of our conflation of 'English' with 'British' until I moved to Scotland in the mid-1970s!
[62] The French for Joan of Arc was the name chosen by the US military authorities not the French. It was built on land adjacent

the base, the 13th century Cathedral of Saint-Étienne, and the wine hills to the north of Toul were visible.[63] After our trudge up the hill, we entered the base and found our way to the hangar-like Enlisted Men's (EM)[64] club, where we would manage to get cokes and then start practising. After practise we would go and get something to eat. We had access to the snack bar on base, if accompanied by a GI, but not the Post Exchange or PX - the on-base department store that sold US branded goods and services to the GIs, and to be distinguished from the Commissary, which sold groceries to the GIs and their families[65]. Occasionally, we would eat at the EM club itself if its kitchen opened early enough before we were scheduled to play. The snack bar was cheaper than the food sold at the EM club, although the EM club in offering largely burgers, steaks and French fries appealed more to our teenage taste buds.

Our concern about prices reflected the limited size of our income. The result, in part, of the various managers

---

to an old French cavalry barracks where US Army and US Medical Corps personnel had been based in World War I. Source: http://translate.google.co.uk/translate?hl=en&sl=fr&tl=en&u=http%3A%2F%2Fwww.professeurs-medecine-nancy.fr%2FHopital_J_dArc.htm

[63] Source: http://translate.google.co.uk/translate?hl=en&sl=fr&tl=en&u=http%3A%2F%2Fwww.professeurs-medecine-nancy.fr%2FHopital_J_dArc.htm

[64] To be distinguished from the Non-Commissioned Officers (NCO) and Officers who both had their own separate clubs.

[65] Most married officers and many married NCOs had their families with them and lived in US army built accommodation off base. School age dependants went to the US schools, which served the families of several of the US bases that were located relatively close to each other.

CHAPTER 7

and agents percentages that were applied to the fees paid by the USO for the band's services. We were paid £15 per week each. Not that much. In fact, a little less than the average weekly wage in the UK in 1962 of £15.17s.3d.[66] But we didn't get £15 in our hands, we got half of it! The other half was sent home to our parents - in fact to Roy's dad as home manager of the band - to save. That meant we had £7 10s 0d to cover our hotel, food, drink and everything else, including cigarettes. At the exchange rates of the time that roughly translated into 20 US dollars, or 100 new French Francs and we usually had to carry a mix of both dollars and francs in our pocket. A cheese burger, French fries and salad would cost about 75 cents at the EM club and a steak would be $1 25c, or more depending on the quality of the steak. So if we ate at the EM club most nights it would devour a good portion of our income. Cigarettes, if memory serves me correct, were about 25c for a pack of twenty Lucky Strikes or Camel at the club while a carton of 200 from the PX, which a GI had to use his allowance to get for you, would be around $2. A can of coke would be 20c and a bottle of beer: a Schlitz, Budweiser, Miller or Heineken was, I think, 25c. And, there were other temptations inducing us to part with our money.

The most visible of these were the slot machines that were usually found in a side room just inside the entrance to the club. The machines took either nickels

---

[66] Average regular weekly pay excluding bonuses in July 2011 was £434, equivalent to an annual salary of around £22,500. Source: http://www.ons.gov.uk/ons/rel/lms/labour-market-statistics/september-2011/statistical-bulletin.html#tab-Earnings

(5c), dimes (10c) or quarters (25c) and many GIs were clearly addicted to them because often the same GIs could be seen pulling the handles of the machines as soon as the EM club opened. Of course to a fifteen-year old these machines at first held a terrible fascination: the prospect of a $10 dollar or $20 jackpot for an outlay of a dime. I soon started to play the machines watching with anticipation as the counters spun down in front of my eyes and then first one line stopped, then the second and finally the third. Two cherry bunches in line paid 5 nickels or dimes, depending on the machine - the 25c machines I tried to avoid - a line of three cherries paid 20 coins out. A jackpot was achieved if you managed 3 watermelons in a line. Needless to say the thrill and risk of the gamble, the fascination of the spinning counters and the delicious anticipation began to overtake my sense of what I could reasonably afford. I began to realise that I'd lost just over $10 and there were still 6 days to go until the next payday. I had to cover all my needs for nearly a week with less than $10. That gave me a salutary wake-up call. I hardly ever played the machines after that. A lesson learned that was to last me a lifetime: I never gambled with money again apart from an occasional bet on the Grand National, or the purchase of a Tony Parsons novel!

The fear of being sacked was real. We had to play 6 nights in a week with Monday night off, a convention that applied to all the EM clubs we played at in France. We knew quite a number of popular songs and instrumentals but filling 6 times 3 to 4 hours per week requires an extensive repertoire. On top of that, was the stuff that wowed them at the Hartburn Tennis club going to impress Uncle Sam's finest? And the killer concern: no

CHAPTER 7

girl singer![67] We decided that we would put a lot of emphasis on the songs of Elvis Presley, Chuck Berry, Bo Diddley, Buddy Holly, Jerry Lee Lewis, with some Hank Williams and Johnny Horton numbers thrown in. Our hope was that Country and Western, essentially American roots music, would go down as well in Toul as in Stockton, and perhaps better. It would also please Roy! But this was going to be tough.

Yet it wasn't as bad as we feared. Johnny Maunder had a great voice and could sing Elvis songs with a lot of panache and the young medics, Specialists[68], dump truck drivers[69] and motor pool guys seemed to like us. As the beers were downed, the audience livened up, requests for songs would come up and we would manage to do many of them. For those songs that we didn't know, we promised to learn them within the week, which in turn enthused our practise in the next few days. But I guess we showed willing and the young GIs seemed to appreciate it. They even seemed to like Cliff Richard songs and Shadows' instrumentals, which was a relief since we could play a lot of their numbers

---

[67] The use of the term 'girl singer' seems sexist and chauvinistic these days but that is the term we used and so I shall stick with it!

[68] In the US army Specialist Grades existed with the purpose of rewarding enlisted men with higher degrees of experience and technical knowledge, or particular military occupational skills such as mechanic or bandsman.

[69] An engineer company was also stationed on the base - 525 Engineer Company (Dump Truck) - a company of 48 dump trucks that worked on military building projects in both France and Germany. There was also a transportation company operating tractor trailers. See comments by an ex GI who was based at Toul in 1961: http://www.topix.com/forum/city/long-beach-ca/TEO8RKFCNSLACF9PG/p45

but it was surprising to us since neither had 'made it' in the US.

One night after finishing a poor rendition of the Everly Brothers recent 1961 hit *Walk Right Back* we stepped off the stage for a 15-minute break when a GI came up to us and said, "You just missed him". "Who?" "Curtis". "You mean Sam Curtis? Has he been here tonight?" "No, never heard of that guy.... Sonny Curtis of the Crickets who wrote that Everly Brothers song you've just played." It turned out that Sonny Curtis had been stationed in Toul Jeanne d'Arc for eighteen months and a week or two earlier had finished his national service and gone back home to the States. He had written *Walk Right Back* while doing his basic training at Fort Ord, California and had offered it to the Everlys on a 3-day pass trip to Los Angeles where they had been attending an acting class! Only the first verse had been written but since they seemed to like it Sonny promised to go back to his new base, Fort Gordon in Georgia, and write a second verse. But a little later, indeed on the first day of his tour of duty in France, Sonny heard the Everlys had released the song with the first verse sung twice! At that moment we did not know that the Everlys would also be in our future in France. Our main thought was what bad luck we had missed a musical legend, a great guitarist and a great song-writer whose brain we would have ruthlessly picked for musical tips and gossip if we had overlapped.[70]

---

[70] 'Sonny Curtis a native Texan, played lead guitar on Buddy Holly's first Decca sessions. His fluid guitar playing style was a major influence on Waylon Jennings. In addition to his work with the Crickets, Sonny has enjoyed enormous success as a solo

CHAPTER 7

As in all club entertainment, the highlight of the week was invariably the weekend and Saturday night in particular. This was the night when 'floor-shows' often visited the clubs. These were organised by the USO[71] and could range from Turkish belly dancers - much appreciated by the hormone-ravaged young GIs - to top US entertainment stars such as the Everly Brothers. The atmosphere of the club on these Saturday evenings was electric, and we often had to go on both before and *after* the belly dancers, with, yes you've got it, no girl singer. But we got by, courtesy of good old rock n' roll, amplification and our wits! Indeed, as the booze flowed, the GI's excitement increased and our music became at first an unwitting vehicle for modulating their emotions. So, if we played an up-beat rock number at high volume

---

recording artist and as one of Nashville's most respected songwriters. His songs have been recorded by artists from Bing Crosby to the Bear on the Andy Williams Show. Among his hit song credits: "Love Is All Around" (the Mary Tyler Moore Television Show Theme song which Sonny also sang on every opening segment of the show), "I Fought The Law," "Walk Right Back" which was a big hit for the Everly Brothers, "I'm No Stranger To The Rain," recorded by Keith Whitley, and many others – including his own Elektra Records hits "The Real Buddy Holly Story," "Good Old Girls" and "Cowboy Singer."' Source: http://www.thecrickets.com/bios.html

[71] "United Service Organizations Inc. (USO) is a private, nonprofit organization that provides morale and recreational services to members of the U.S. military, with programs in 140 centers worldwide. Since 1941, it has worked in partnership with the Department of Defense (DOD), and has provided support and entertainment to U.S. armed forces, relying heavily on private contributions and on funds, goods, and services from DOD. Although congressionally chartered, it is not a government agency." From Wikipedia.

such as *Johnny Be Good* they would tend to become more assertive in their demands of us and each other. A quiet ballad such as Elvis Presley's *Can't Help Falling In Love With You*, from his 1961 movie *Blue Hawaii*, would calm them down as they perhaps thought of their girlfriends and mom's back home. Recognising this we began to use the music to adjust the emotional temperature of the club. This insight would be unexceptional to most musicians and even club managers but to us it came as a mini-revelation. You might ask, after the events with Johnny Rocco at Hartburn Tennis club why were we surprised? But we were and to a certain extent we revelled in this mini god-like power to boost our popularity with the GIs and to ingratiate ourselves with the management, who were pleased when we quickly switched to a slow ballad or instrumental if a fracas arose or a fight started. Yet, our naivety sometimes betrayed us.

One Saturday, late in the evening we were asked to play *Theme from Dixie*. This we were happy to do because it was something of a speciality and before we came to France we'd had a tape of the instrumental played on Radio Luxembourg. What we didn't at first twig was that the request came from GI's whose home was in the southern United States, where *Dixie* was still something of a national anthem. As several of the GIs began to breast-beat about the nirvana that was the 'South', other GIs clearly from the 'North' demanded that we play *Yankee Doodle Dandy*. It is a fairly simple tune to play, so it wasn't long before we were belting it out. But while appeasing the disgruntled 'northerners' it made matters worse with the 'southerners' until blows were being exchanged by first two, then four, then six

CHAPTER 7

GIs until the Civil War was being played out before us. Several bouncers struggled to prevent Gettysburg or Fredericksburg from being enacted on the floor of the EM Club until the Military Police arrived swinging their 'nightsticks' and restored order. The best that could be said was that the battered and bruised would get treated quickly; the base was, after all, a hospital!

This was a salutary lesson to us and we resolved to be more careful in the future. Moreover, some of the trust that we had started to build with the EM club management as a reliable, popular band had clearly been eroded. Our fears at lacking a girl singer began to resurface. And there was still more than 2 weeks to go before June ended and we were to move on. No contact from Sam. Had he found us a girl singer? We decided to try and meet up with the Londonaires on Monday, our day off, and ask Paul if he had heard from his father. Despite playing at the US General Depot in Nancy, we found out that the band was staying at a hotel near the centre of Toul, so after a telephone call to the hotel we arranged to meet them there late in the afternoon.

Mondays were a sort of oasis in our busy week of practise, playing, eating and sleeping. When we eventually secured a van for our second stint in France in 1963 we would drive out to the nearby sights and places of interest on our days off. But in 1962, we either used much of the day to catch up on sleep, or went up to the base to get food and then chat with the GIs over a drink or two. However, when we stayed in the centre of town as we did in Bar le Duc - our next location after Toul - there were more options available. We could go for a late lunch in a local cafe and often play the fool as bands tended to do. Bar le Duc was a case in point. Not far from the Hotel de Metz where we stayed was a small cafe/bar that offered cheap but tasty lunches. To enter the cafe you went down a side street, turned right, entered the cafe/bar and then were shown to a table in the back dining room of the cafe. But the dining room had a window at ground level that looked on to the side street. Often the window would be ajar. We would open it quietly, look in and if the room was empty we would all climb through the window, closing it behind us and then take seats at a table. When the waitress came into the dining room for something she would get quite a shock seeing us sat there while we innocently inquired why she hadn't seen us come in. She would then start to doubt her own sanity and we would chuckle to ourselves. But she got her own back. The next time we did it, after we had finished the meal and paid, she barred the door from the dining room to the front of the cafe and pointed to the window insisting that we leave the way we had come in. And we did!

Our meeting with the Londonaires gave us no new information on Sam's whereabouts, or whether he had secured a girl singer for us. Paul simply hadn't heard from his father. Of course, that wasn't unusual. Obviously, there were no mobile 'phones and land-line telephone calls were expensive. Communication back home was mainly by letter. My mother wrote to me a couple of times a week and I replied with letters and postcards. About once a fortnight, my mother would in addition mail me a 'food parcel', or more accurately a 'chocolate parcel'. She would include in the parcel a clutch of my favourite chocolate bars such as Cadbury's

CHAPTER 7

Dairy Milk, Mars Bar, Fry's 5 Boys,[72] Lucky Numbers[73], and a Kit Kat. There would also be a letter inside and some cuttings from the local newspaper the *Billingham Express* or the *Evening Gazette*, on some local news that she thought I might have an interest. The care she took in putting together these parcels fills me today with love and admiration for her. I just wish I had shown a little more gratitude at the time! Upon discovering a parcel from home downstairs in the hall or small lobby of our hotel, I would race upstairs, tear the parcel open and with a lot of assistance from Roy consume a good proportion of the parcel's contents there and then. Occasionally, I would also share the contents with Louis and Johnny M. but sometimes our greed prevented that. At other times I would try and ration my/our consumption of the parcel's goodies in an attempt to spread the benefit until the arrival of the next one.

---

[72] The Cadbury website describes this bar as follows: "Launched in 1902 it was once the most famous chocolate bar in the world, with its five pictures of a five-year-old lad called Lindsay Poulton showing emotions from Desperation (no chocolate), to Realisation (finding out he's got Fry's Chocolate). Apparently at the photo session, Lindsay wasn't looking miserable enough for the first photo, so his father (the photographer) tied a cloth soaked in nasty smelling ammonia round his neck to achieve the 'Desperation' face! The bar was retired in 1976" http://www.cadbury.co.uk/ourproducts/yesterday/Pages/Yesterday.aspx

[73] This was an assortment of chewy sweets, some covered in chocolate and some not. These Lucky Numbers each had an individual number on the wrapper, hence the name. The brand was launched by Cadbury in 1958 and retired in 1968. Source: http://www.cadbury.co.uk/ourproducts/yesterday/Pages/Yesterday.aspx

But this intention was, as with Hamlet, more honoured in the breach than in the observance.

We finished our game of cards with the Londonaires, bid them goodbye and set off on the 2 to 3 mile walk back to our own hotel. It was late on the Monday evening. The streets of Toul were dark and dimly lit. As we walked I noticed what appeared to be holes or marks in the stonewalls of the ramparts that looked as if they were caused by bullets or shrapnel. Whether these were recent, or dated back to the Second, First World Wars, or the Franco Prussian War in 1870[74], I could not say nor would I have known. But just as these thoughts were drifting across my mind and as we were crossing a bridge over the Moselle, or the Marne-Rhine Canal, we came face to face with a French soldier in a heavy military great coat, carrying a rifle and wearing what appeared to us to be a First World War style steel helmet, or "tin hat". This wasn't something you normally came across on the streets of Stockton and Middlesbrough apart from the occasional Mackem[75] supporter trying to sneak unnoticed into Ayresome Park! As they say in comics and cheap novels "our blood froze". Perversely, the title of the Ventures 1960 hit *Walk Don't Run* suddenly jumped into my mind and I decided that that was

---

[74] "During the siege of 1870 during the Franco-Prussian War, the last time that Toul's defenses were used as a classic fortress, 64 guns opened fire at 6am on 23 September, and the fortress surrendered at 3pm after 2,433 shells had been fired." From Wikipedia.

[75] A term used to describe people of the Wearside and Sunderland area but more specifically the supporters of Sunderland football club.

CHAPTER 7

good advice to follow. Whether the others had had a similar epiphany I do not know but we ceased our chatter and tentatively approached this arm of the French state. But, the soldier just shuffled past us without giving us a second glance. We concluded that he was probably guarding the bridge and eventually we understood that this must be connected to the French-Algerian War, which had been going on since 1954, the consequences of which were now coming to a head.

The Algerian pro-independence group FLN, led by Ben Bella, had been waging an increasingly violent guerrilla war against French colonists for seven years, and this had caused a political crisis in France. Indeed, the then President of France, Charles de Gaulle, had come to power as Prime Minister in 1958 and as President of the new Fifth Republic in January 1959 with a mandate to retain Algeria as part of France and to prevent the war spilling over on to French streets. But upon gaining office he soon reversed this policy and sought to allow Algerian independence. In January 1961, the French and Algerian people voted in a referendum by large majorities in favour of Algerian independence, even though the FLN urged Algerians to boycott the vote, which many did. On the other hand, with more than a million settlers of French descent living in Algeria, the opposition to Algerian independence was severe both in Algeria and France. This led to the formation of the Organisation de l'Armée Secrète (OAS), an extremist organisation of French settlers determined to fight the independence movement and led by the former French military commander in Algeria, General Raoul Salan.

So, with the extremist OAS prepared to violently resist independence and the FLN prepared to use violence to secure independence on its terms, the French people could be said to be caught in the middle.[76] Ben Bella began to negotiate with the French authorities and in March 1962, following talks that had begun in May 1961 after a 30-day ceasefire, an agreement was signed in Evian ending the war and granting Algeria independence. On the 5th July 1962, a couple of weeks after our encounter with the French soldier on the bridge, Algeria was to become formally independent. At that time it was therefore the potential actions of the OAS that were the perceived threat in France, even though parts of the FLN continued to commit atrocities. An extreme example was the Oran massacre on the day of independence where estimates of the deaths of French civilian settlers and Algerians ranged from 95 through 1,500, to 3,500. After the agreements signed in Evian, the OAS attempted to prevent the move to Algerian independence by a campaign of assassinations and bombings in Algeria but also in France. This campaign culminated in Jean-Marie Bastien-Thiry's assassination attempt against President de Gaulle in the Paris suburb of Le Petit-Clamart on 22 August 1962[77]. But the

---

[76] These comments should not be seen as whitewashing the French state, which through its colonial and internal security policies had precipitated many of the problems it sought to avoid. The Muslim population in Algeria had been given little political or economic power, and few legal rights, and by January 1961 discontent was now at such a level that half a million French troops were stationed in the country. Source: http://news.bbc.co.uk/onthisday/hi/dates/stories/january/8/newsid_4464000/4464264.stm

[77] The assassination attempt was given fictionalized prominence in Frederick Forsyth's book *The Day of the Jackal*, and in the 1973 film of the same name.

CHAPTER 7

capture of Salan in April 1962, the execution of key OAS leaders by firing squad in June 1962, and finally Bastien-Thiry's execution by firing squad in March 1963 effectively spelt the end of the OAS.

At the time we were oblivious to almost all of this. Apart from our 'confrontation' with the soldier, I remember seeing the letters "OAS" scrawled on walls in and around Toul and some of the other towns we visited during the second half of 1962. Equally, most of the GIs we came across had little to say about the political developments in France and Algeria. If anything political was discussed it would be the position of Cuba and how developments there threatened the spread of Soviet influence into the United States back yard[78]. Yet, if the GIs seemed indifferent to current French politics they were aware of some of the consequences. Several regaled us with stories about atrocities allegedly committed by the French police or the military on Algerians in France: young men rounded up, taken away, then shot and their bodies left in some remote spot; beatings, and even stories of rape. How true any of this was we never found out. Some events are well known such as the so-called Paris Massacre in 1961[79]. But in this

---

[78] The Cuban Revolution led by the Fidel Castro swept the corrupt and unjust Batista regime from power in January 1959 after a long struggle. While the US government had become frustrated with the corruption and injustice of the Batista regime, sufficient to impose an arms embargo on the Batista government on 14 March 1958, it nevertheless felt threatened by the Marxist and apparent pro-communist sympathies of the revolutionary leaders and their favourable posture towards the Soviet Union.

[79] From Wikipedia: "On 17 October 1961 ... under orders from the head of the Parisian police, Maurice Papon, the French police

conflict, which had aspects of a civil war as well as a colonial war, one cannot escape the conclusion that atrocities were committed by people on all sides: the French state, the OAS, the FLN and rival Algerian groups.[80]

With the extreme political turmoil in France at this time the presence of more than 50,000 US troops added an extra edge. If for some the French state was threatened by the possible and eventual secession of Algeria, it was also threatened, or perceived to be threatened, by the ostensibly friendly military force that was camped within its boundaries. The presence of US forces was a key ingredient in NATO's military stance towards the perceived invasion threat of the Soviet Pact forces and therefore it could be argued crucial to the defence of France. In addition, the US bases provided much needed jobs and income for many peripheral areas of France. First, there were the one-off benefits to local suppliers and labour from the construction of the bases. Then there was the impact of the recurrent expenditures of the bases. Jobs were provided for those providing services on base, such as ourselves, although our salary remittance home diminished the local spending impact

---

attacked an illegal but peaceful [citation needed] demonstration of some 30,000 pro-FLN Algerians. ... After 37 years of denial, the French government acknowledged 40 deaths in 1998, although there are estimates of over 200."

[80] There is evidence that torture was used by the French and the FLN (http://en.wikipedia.org/wiki/Torture_during_the_Algerian_War and http://www.hartford-hwp.com/archives/61/118.html) and there were many documented atrocities (Jim House and Neil MacMaster (2002) "*The Paris Massacre of 1961 and Memory*" Ch 13 in Kenneth Mouré, Martin S. Alexander (Eds) **Crisis and Renewal in France: 1918-1962**, Berghahn books)

as we knew only too well! But the indirect effects of the spending of the incomes of the French employees, and most importantly the GIs themselves, in local stores, cafes, restaurants and especially bars, provided a major boost to income in many local economies.[81]

Yet, the relationship was bittersweet. The young French loved the American culture that came with the GIs, the large motor cars, jazz, rock, and blues music, the comics, the books, the movies, even the fast food. The French were also envious of the domestic appliances that the US households living off base possessed: large refrigerators, fancy cookers, automatic washing machines and dishwashers. But admiration and envy was also tinged with hostility. Hostility, towards the evident wealth of the GIs, towards the perceived arrogance and felt superiority of many of the US personnel, towards the sexual permissiveness of the GIs and their evident attraction to young French women, and to the threat to French culture of US cultural imperialism. The French are rightly proud of their culture and are extremely protective of it. Yet, the evidence suggests that the cultural influence of the US bases on French life was highly localised, although it is accepted that the US presence had a modernisation effect accelerating changes in French society that had already begun to happen[82]. Indeed, it might be argued that the US bases

---

[81] See Axelle Bergeret-Cassagne (2008) **Les Bases Americaines en France: Impacts Materiels et Culturels 1950-1967**, L'Harmattan, Paris.

[82] Hilary Footitt (2011) "American forces in France: Communist representations of US deployment" pp. 85-98 **Cold War History** Vol 11, No. 1 and Axelle Bergeret-Cassagne (2008) *op cit* p.242

in France and Europe were the vanguard of the modernising influence of the US on Europe through the flow of US multinationals that was beginning to strengthen at that time. The recognition of the significance of this development was to be the subject of the seminal book published in 1967 by Jean-Jacques Servan-Schreiber, *Le Défi Américain* or *The American Challenge*. The book saw Europe and the US engaged in a tacit economic struggle, which Europe was losing on all fronts: in management techniques, in technological tools, and in research capacity. This international best seller had much influence and was instrumental in creating a resurgence of French nationalism, drawing attention to the importance of transnational cooperation in Europe and the pressing need for modernisation, in contrast to the conservative instincts of de Gaulle and his followers[83].

Nevertheless, in 1958 De Gaulle had swept to power on a wave of nationalism and was committed to the protection of French interests. The loss of Algeria was a blow to French imperialist pretensions, while the presence of US troops on its soil was a clear reminder, if any were needed, that the days were long gone when France could defend itself on its own. De Gaulle was always uneasy about the American forces in France and it could be argued that he adopted a negative stance towards the US presence because it boosted his nationalist credentials with the French people but also because it conflicted with a sense of his own destiny as a world historical individual who would lead the French people to greatness. His decision to withdraw from NATO's

---

[83] See http://en.wikipedia.org/wiki/Jean-Jacques_Servan-Schreiber

integrated military command structure in 1966 and his request that all non-French NATO military personnel should leave France may have been a blow in favour of French cultural, military and political independence but it was damaging to NATO, to the French economy[84] and ultimately to France.

As we stood each evening on the stage of the Toul Jeanne d'Arc EM club to play American rock n' roll and British versions of it we felt more culturally attuned to the Americans than the French. We spoke more or less the same language as the GIs, we were similar in age to many of them and there was the shared music. We played largely US music with some British music, mainly The Shadows and Cliff Richard, thrown in. But we were often embarrassed when GIs posed the question, what good music is coming out of Britain? America seemed to rule the popular music waves. Little did we know that in that very month, June 1962, the Beatles were being successfully auditioned by George Martin for a recording contract with EMI. So, with our immersion in American culture we adopted some of the contempt for the French that many, but not all, GIs exhibited. As a result we tended to hang about the base more than was necessary and I viewed myself as an honorary American. But I think we deluded ourselves. In their hearts I fear that the GIs were no more willing to see us as one of them than they would a French band. As largely disciplined soldiers they were invariably polite and kind but there was a deeper cultural divide between us that I consciously failed to appreciate at the time.

---

[84] Axelle Bergeret-Cassagne (2008) *op cit* pp 233-239.

The GIs were in France to protect Europe but the sub-text was that Europe was unable to defend itself. Hence the graffiti "US go home" which had spread through France in the early 1950s at the instigation of the French Communist Party (PCF)[85] and could still be seen on the walls of some French towns, rankled with most GIs. Moreover, the US had supported Europe through Marshall Aid to help reconstruction after the Second World War, but Europe and France, in particular, was felt not to be grateful and had squandered the "gift". I heard it said by GIs on a few occasions that France had spent the aid on planting trees along the sides of its very straight roads, with little thought for the dangers the trees posed to motorists and presumably to US military trucks plying the logistical supply route to Germany! French literature was a closed book to most GIs with the possible exception of some officers, NCOs and the odd enlisted man. Jean Paul Sartre would have been a "commie mother f****r". Jean-Luc Godard was no Alfred Hitchcock and another "commie mother f****r"[86]. The wine was undrinkable. Pernod was a no-go area, and while some GIs expressed a preference for cognac I saw little evidence of much consumption of it when GIs went off-base[87]. Much the same would be

---

[85] Hilary Footitt (2011) *op cit* p. 96
[86] Forgetting of course that Hitchcock was actually English!
[87] In *Cold War Heroes*, a novel by Tom Johnson set in and around the small Caserne-Aboville US base in Poitiers during the early 1960s, the 'heroes' were US military police (MPs) who delighted in the consumption of cognac. The novel, which I found interesting and which stimulated some of my own memories of the US military, is based on Johnson's experience in the US military in Poitiers.

CHAPTER 7

said about French food, with its focus on fussy sauces and consumption of unspeakable creatures such as snails and frogs legs. Even French women were condemned because it was believed that they refused to shave their armpits![88]

Of course, these opinions may have been those of young enlisted men with limited education. A group of British squaddies might have been little different. But I do believe it was more than age and education. At best, there was a lack of a willingness to appreciate other cultures and, at worst, a contempt for most things French and indeed European. But clearly, as with all generalisations, there were exceptions.

One exception appeared to be black US servicemen. Again it is risky to generalise, but as a rule black GIs seemed more willing to go out 'on the economy'[89], were more willing to learn the language and more willing to absorb French culture. There were several reasons for this. African Americans were a large minority in the US forces, and while all races were now integrated in the US forces[90], there were continuing racial antagonisms.

---

[88] A flavour of GI attitudes at the time is given in this quote on a vets website from a member (David A. Gillespie) of the 202nd Deuce O' Deuce Military Police stationed at Ingrandes and writing in 2005: "La Slavia, or Panther Pssst beer, that smelled like a skunk, no money, no Frauleins, Gitane cigarettes, unwashed men in blue jackets, pants and red rubber boots reeking of garlic and women with hairy armpits, what the hell are we doing here?" http://www.pbase.com/202mpco/image/39926081

[89] The term used for going out into, and buying goods and/or services in, the French economy for which the GIs would have to change dollars into French francs before they went off base.

[90] Segregation in the United States Armed Forces did not formally end until 1948 when it was abolished by Executive Order of

The extent to which black soldiers mixed with white soldiers varied from base to base. In some EM clubs, such as the main base in Orleans, where we played in 1963, the black GIs sat down the short side of the L - shaped club while the whites sat on the long side! On other bases, such as Vassincourt, in August 1962, we heard whispers of an active chapter of the *Ku Klux Klan* and a black counter group known as the *Trench Foot Squad*. So, for many black GIs there was probably less of an incentive to stay on base than was the case for white GIs. In addition, black culture was clearly not the same as white culture. African American soldiers tended to be more interested in jazz and the blues and had greater kinship in this respect with many French people, young and old, than with their fellow white GIs. One got the sense that they were more willing to blend in despite, or maybe because of, the clear difference signalled by their black skin. The French in return clearly appreciated this and so were more welcoming to them than perhaps they were to white GIs.

Another exception would be those GIs who formed a life-long attachment to popular French singers such as Edith Piaf and Charles Aznavour.[91] Indeed, it should also be said in defence of the GIs, white or black, that the French sense of the importance of their own culture and the place of France in the world made it just as likely that some French people would look down with

---

President Harry S Truman. But segregation continued in practice until the disbandment of the all-black 24th Infantry Regiment in October 1951.

[91] Source: http://groups.yahoo.com/group/caserne_aboville/message/2394

CHAPTER 7

some hauteur on US culture and its representatives in France: the US military. Fast food, pop art, rock n' roll and country-blues would be viewed as culturally inferior to haute cuisine, impressionist painting, jazz and the conservatoire. How much more difficult to take when the cultural upstart had saved you from Nazi occupation and was there to protect you from the threat of Soviet invasion, which a large part of the leftist intelligentsia in the 1950s and early 1960s refused to acknowledge or contemplate[92] - *plus ca change*!

Of course, the US bases were not wholly enclaves. GI's occasionally brought French girls onto the base for an evening at the EM, NCO or Officers' Club, or a movie at the camp Theater[93]. Many hundreds of French citizens came to work at the bases in support roles each day. There were community links, some formal and some informal such as the parties given at Christmas for the children of French employees, or at Easter for French orphans,[94] and participation in automobile

---

[92] Several historians and commentators have noted " ...the remarkably long-lasting blindness of French intellectuals to the repressiveness of communist regimes and the shortcomings of revolutionary politics ...(and that) Intellectuals would only be awakened from the long slumber of their critical faculties by the publication of ... Solzhenhitsyn's *Gulag Archipelago* in 1974 ... the failure of post-1968 revolutionary politics and the collapse of third-world revolutionary utopias ...." This view is discussed and assessed in Michael Scott Christofferson *French Intellectuals Against the Left: The Anti-Totalitarian Movement of the 1970s* (2004) Berghahn Books, from which this quote is taken, pp 1-2.

[93] Of course, the girls couldn't just walk into the base willy-nilly, they had to be signed in by the duty desk sergeant; see Tom Johnson *op cit*.

[94] See photograph on this veterans website: http://groups.yahoo.com/group/caserne_aboville/photos/album/987469651/pic/

rallies. And finally, an international flavour was added by the presence of large numbers of Polish guards.

The presence of women at the EM club, by and large, tended to have a civilising influence usually bringing out the better angels in the GIs and the band as well. I say "usually" because on some occasions it had the opposite effect. As Tom Johnson notes[95] soldiers who had previously dated a French girl might get annoyed when another GI brought the girl into the club. As more alcohol was consumed this annoyance could fuel arguments and occasionally fights. From our experience, the potential explosiveness of such situations was heightened if the present and previous suitors were of a different race. For these reasons, many GIs preferred to meet their dates off-base away from the prying eyes of their comrades.

The presence of Polish guards, or "Polaks" to the GIs, known officially as the Polish Labor Service (PLS) constituted an interesting political anomaly from World War II that had serious human consequences. The history of the PLS is something of a mystery and I have failed to find any authenticated source records. Some records are alleged to exist in the US National Archives but there is nothing accessible on the web[96]. It is contended on some US veterans websites that the PLS was composed of Free Poles that fought against the Germans in WWII, mainly in units equipped by the

---

1300764002/view?picmode=&mode=tn&order=ordinal&start=1&count=20&dir=asc
[95] *Cold War Heroes* op cit
[96] See communication here http://dir.groups.yahoo.com/group/caserne_aboville/

CHAPTER 7

British Military. After World War II they could not go back to Poland because their liberty would be threatened under the Soviets. It is not clear why their lives would have been threatened by the post-war Soviet domination of Poland, unless the Soviets viewed them as collaborators with the Nazis, or feared their links with the west. One veteran also claims that documents on the creation of the PLS in France in 1950 held in the US National Archives, reveal that the French gave permission to the US military authorities for 700 Poles to be recruited from "displaced person" camps in Germany for service at US bases in France.[97] Whatever their provenance, the PLS were a separate unit in the US military and had their own distinctive uniform and insignia.[98] They were effectively stateless, unable to go back to Poland and unable to go to the US because they were not citizens. The guards were usually quite a bit older than the average GI, often in their thirties and some much older. They could be very well educated and several had been doctors or other professionals back in Poland. But in the PLS their role was basic guard duty, and they were considered to be a valuable support to the US military in France. It is a tribute to the humanity and compassion of the US authorities that the PLS were

---

[97] Source: http://dir.groups.yahoo.com/group/caserne_aboville/message/2335

[98] One vet describes their uniform as being "a light tan and they had their rank insignias on shoulder boards. All wore a patch with polish colors and I think it included an eagle. They were armed with M-1s (rifles) and patrolled the fence as well as manned the gates." Source: *People in military bases in France in the sixties* at http://www.topix.com/forum/city/long-beach-ca/TEO8RKFCNSLACF9PG

treated so well in their work for the US forces. But there was a downside. This was the suspicion that some of the PLS were spying for the Soviets even though all had been vetted and scrutinized very closely before being allowed to serve in the PLS. Some of these suspicions were probably not unfounded as the Warsaw pact forces were clearly keen to know what the NATO, and particularly the US, forces were up to. Spy mania was always present and not just focused on the Poles, with 'commie' hating and suspicion of the Russians increasing with the intensification of the Cold War during 1962.

We met many Polish guards while working on the military bases in France and became friends with some. Most were separated from their families and we would soon be shown photos of wives, daughters and sons 'back home' once we got into conversation with them. This separation and statelessness meant that many were very maudlin, quite reasonably, leading to much consumption of alcohol when off duty. And could they drink! At Toul Jeanne d'Arc they had their own 'Polish Club' which served Polish food and beer. It was popular with the regular GIs because the club offered interesting food alternatives to the meat loaf, hamburgers and hot dogs served at the PX Snack Bar and the EM club. The Polish sausage was especially tasty and very valuable to us because it was cheap and wholesome.

Often we would sit in the EM club with our tummies rumbling but wary of buying more food because we were short of money and there were still two or three days to go before we could pick up the money order from La Poste in Toul. The maddening thing was that the GIs kept offering to buy us drinks, anything we wanted, when what we really needed was food. But it

CHAPTER 7

seemed impolite and even mercenary to ask for a hamburger instead of a coke, or a beer - don't tell my mother! Yet, accepting offers of drinks seemed to be culturally ok but it wasn't ok to ask instead for probably cheaper food, since requesting the substitution brought us closer to begging. Somehow additional hamburgers, cheeseburgers and fries found their way to us but we did have pause for chauvinistic thought that maybe having a girl singer would make it easier in the free food and drinks department!

Then our prayers were answered. One evening, two days before we were due to finish our month at Toul Jeanne d'Arc, Sam Curtis walked into the EM club while we were in the middle of our set. Accompanying him was a tall brunette. All eyes in the club shifted from the band to follow this young woman as she moved to a table close to the stage, smiling at us as she sat down. It was Thursday and the club was half empty, so we played one more number and then announced that we would take a break.

"Wotcha boys! This is Jenny from Ealing. That's in west London for the information of you northern yugger duggers." Jenny smiled again. We responded with nervous nods and hellos, slightly intimidated by the apparent sophistication of the young woman. But as we began to shuffle in our seats an overweight GI clumsily brushed past our table knocking Jenny forward as he progressed. "Fack me!" Jenny exclaimed in a strong cockney accent. At that moment our inhibitions fell away and we knew instinctively that Jenny would fit in with the band. Jenny Paul (real name Hutchins) was, as Sam said, from Ealing. She was on the books of Starlite Artistes, nominally, our London agents who had mentioned to her that there was a band in France that had to have a female singer and was she interested. A positive reply led to a 'phone call from Sam a few days later and a few days after that they travelled to France together. For Sam any female was a challenge, and so, once we got to know Jenny better, she told us that during the journey out from London Sam had "tried it on, of course." The fact that his behaviour was expected says a lot about the music business and the role of managers and agents in the 1960s who had a lot of power over artistes and frequently would seek sexual favours[99]. I doubt whether it has changed all that much today, although following the film industry allegations of sexual misconduct against Harvey Weinstein and the growth in late 2017 of the #MeToo international movement against sexual harassment it is to be hoped that the music industry has not escaped its effects.

The next night, our last at Toul Jeanne d'Arc, was fun. It was the end of the month. The weekend was beginning. The GIs had received their pay cheques and were keen to party. We played a great set. Sam sat beaming in the audience. The GIs were responsive, especially after Jenny got up to sing a couple of songs that we had rehearsed in the afternoon. Next day we were to move to Bar-le Duc. We had survived.

---

[99] I base this judgement not simply on this one comment but from what we heard from other female singers that we talked to during that period.

CHAPTER 8

FROM TFAD TO DEFCON-2

"You're sitting on a powder keg son!" announced a friendly GI as he joined our table while we munched our cheeseburgers before our first gig at TFAD Bar-le-Duc. "Yes, Trois Fontaines Ammunition Depot, there's enough explosive here to blow up the whole of North East France. So, when the balloon goes up and those Ruskies go on the march, you'd better watch out!" And the GI was correct. TFAD, like its counterpart in Nancy, stored the full range of conventional explosives used by the army, especially tank shells, grenades and bullets. The proximity of the base to the German border meant that supplies could be shipped out and delivered fairly rapidly to front-line forces if the cold war turned hot.

The presence of such a large quantity of ordinance meant that security on the base was much tighter than at Toul Jeanne d'Arc. We couldn't just amble into the base like we did at Toul. We had to show the passes that had been issued to us every time we entered. The MPs on the main gate took their role seriously and always looked at our passes, giving us the once-over before they let us in. My admiration for the efficiency and dedication to duty of the camp-gate MPs was dimmed somewhat when I realised, as we arrived one day in a local taxi, that the scrutiny was more about getting a good look at Jenny's legs than any concern that we might be the advance guard of the Red Army.

The rules were that the MPs on the gate had to have their pistols loaded with an ammunition clip in when a senior officer pulled up in his staff car to the gate. He would then have his ID checked, the barrier would be raised and the MP would stand to attention and salute. All so very military. But of course pulling guard duty can be quite boring, even on the main gate of a busy US army base, especially in the evenings when the work traffic had subsided. So the MP guards would try and find things to do to amuse themselves. And being young men they often chose pastimes that might be considered 'juvenile'. One of these was to emulate Tom Mix and see who was quickest on the draw.

The reader will, of course, see where I am going here. So one evening when 'Gunfight at the OK Corral' was reaching its peak, an army staff car turns into the short track up to the main gate of the base. The two MPs quickly rush to put their caps on and ammunition clip in. ID checked, barrier raised, officer saluted, staff car disappearing, an MP turns, draws and BANG! The other MP, his right hand clasped round a pistol only half withdrawn from its holster, slumps backwards and turns his head slowly to the left where a few inches away a sizeable bullet hole can be seen in the wall of the gatehouse. Fortunately, Tom Mix had not been knocked from his perch but needless to say the gunslingers in the future kept their guns in their holsters and the would-be Tom Mix lost a stripe. The bullet hole remained unrepaired, however, visible to us every evening when we left the base, perhaps as a reminder to would-be cowboys

CHAPTER 8

that such activities are best left to Hollywood and the silver screen.

After our arrival in Bar-Le-Duc and TFAD, Sam Curtis stayed for a couple of days and then left for London. But not before he had indicated to Roy that the band should replace me and get a more experienced bass player. Fortunately, I fared better than Pete Best the drummer of the Beatles who had been rejected by George Martin after they had test recorded "Besame Mucho" for him and Parlophone at EMI studios a few weeks earlier in June. Ringo Starr replaced Best in the August while we were playing at Vassincourt, another base near Bar-Le-Duc. We knew nothing of the Beatles then but that was soon to change. Roy said to Sam we were one band, had come a long way together, and stood or fell together. "Fire Brian and you fire the band." I don't think I deserved such loyalty from Roy or loyalty displayed with such courage. But his support helped salve a bruised ego and I resolved to work hard at becoming a better bass player and repay his faith in me.

Safe behind the cloak of security provided by the MPs we played the EM Club at TFAD six nights a week as in Toul. Our daily routine of sleep, eat, practise, eat and play was similar to Toul except with Jenny now in the band we had a new repertoire to learn. Peggy Lee, Brenda Lee, Ella Fitzgerald and Skeeta Davis were added to Elvis Presley, the Everlys, Buddy Holly, Cliff Richard and the Shadows. Learning new songs was much harder then than it is today, where the Internet gives you access to the chords, tabs and standard music notation of almost everything. Access to mp3 files for playback on ipods, iphones, or other players, is cheap and ubiquitous. Back then we relied principally on our ears! Jenny did bring some sheet music with her, which was like gold dust but we were largely on our own trying to work out key, chords, guitar riffs and, in my case, the bass line.

Back in England we had learnt songs by repeated playing of 45rpm singles, the arm of the multi-disc holder pushed out so that the record played over and over again, much to parental disquiet. If you wanted to learn a particular riff and avoid playing the whole song through each time you could work out where the section roughly was then drop and raise the arm of the record player at the riff. Needless to say this was not very accurate and also risked damaging the records due to the repeated impact of the needle on the shellac surface of the disc. It also meant a lot of fumbling from guitar to record player arm back to guitar and so on, which was not conducive to the best learning experience! In France in 1962, we had no record player and it wasn't until 1963 that we acquired a small tape machine that allowed us to play and record ourselves but more importantly to record, listen to, learn and rehearse the latest hits or other songs that took our fancy. The EM Club jukebox, along with jukeboxes in the occasional French café or bar, became a key source of information and we would often sit listening and even take written notes as the GIs put nickel after nickel into the machine. In the afternoon we would try and get the club management to play records on the jukebox for free so we could listen and try to work out the root notes and chords as we sat with our guitars. So, through this rough and ready process we augmented our repertoire.

Jenny fitted in well with the band, both musically and personally and the GIs at TFAD loved her and liked us. The index of approval was measured by the amount

CHAPTER 8

of drinks we, and of course she, were offered. The desire for food rather than drinks was a constant issue and I know that Jenny feels sickened to this day at the felt humiliations she endured in asking for food instead of drinks for us as well as her. By this time our sense of Sam as the "cheeky Cockney Jewish chappy" had begun to change to Sam the "fat Cockney bastard!" Now that the thrill and self-importance of being a professional musician had started to pale a little, the reality of our situation began to sink in. The amount we were being paid, at least the £7,10s in our hand, was way too little to live on. Sam probably spent more on one lunch back in London we mused.

Added to this we had no transport. The base was a couple of miles outside Bar-Le-Duc. The distance between the Hotel de Metz where we stayed to the base was too far to walk every day and so we occasionally had to use local taxis, which although cheap still ate into our limited funds. On other days we might be able to catch a US army bus that took GIs to and from Bar-Le-Duc, and this became a little easier once we began to be known at the base. At night, after our playing session had finished, no bus or taxi was available, so we had to rely on the charity of one of the GIs, the club manager, or one of his staff, to run us back to the hotel.

Sam had also told us that we had to move ourselves in future when we changed base and that added to our anger and feelings of betrayal. What to tell our parents? If we were too honest with them about our situation we feared they would drag us home. Even an admission to them that things weren't working out exactly as promised and expected was hard to make. Roy and I had both given up a grammar school education and Louis and John their jobs as painters and decorators. We had not attained the musical Promised Land that we thought Sam had offered us. Older and wiser heads would probably have seen through Sam's blandishments but we were growing up fast and were determined that we would not be beaten by Sam's exploitation. But for the moment we had to put up with our lot, serve out our contract, then go home and look for a better deal.

After little more than six weeks away from home, the pressures of being frequently hungry, feeling homesick and worrying about our future were starting to get to us. We were arguing more and one of us, Louis, was drinking more. Louis was tall, his face was thin and more often than not he would have a cigarette in his mouth or hand depending on what stage he was at in the smoking process. He had light, but not blond, hair and this was swept up and back in what some might then have called a Tony Curtis quiff but for other observers the first impression was probably "Teddy Boy". He smiled a lot, appeared to be an extrovert and was very likable, yet he seemed always to be in need of reassurance. Some would say he was a typical drummer! When his drum solos were in full flow he would be flying, in his element and it was sometimes difficult to bring him down to earth to end the number. He needed a good supply of drumsticks because often in a solo one, sometimes two, would break or shatter and slivers of wood would fly past the ears of Roy, Johnny or myself. As the paradiddles and rolls swept around his gold Premier drum kit he would smile at one or more of the band, clearly enjoying himself but inviting our approval. Back home in Stockton Hilda was the love of his life and his rock. Without her Louis was rudderless and he missed her terribly. So as the weeks

CHAPTER 8

dragged by he was drinking more even while we were playing and this made him touchier. Then one Monday, our day off, it all came to a head.

The Hotel de Metz was located on the main street in Bar-Le-Duc. It was rather grand but had an air of faded gentility. The hotel had clearly seen better days. But it was no dump and on any calculation was well above our pay grade. We stayed at the hotel for two months because in August we moved from TFAD to Vassincourt a much smaller base but still in the Bar-Le-Duc area. On this Monday in particular we got up fairly early by our standards and John and Louis decided that they would buy a crate of wine from the local alimentation just along the street from the hotel. The vin ordinaire came in clear, reusable bottles with ceramic tops and a rubber seal that was connected to the bottle by metal wire that lifted and closed on a lever principle so allowing reuse. I remember my parents in the 1950s taking a regular delivery of lemonade, which had similar reusable bottles and good money would be paid on their return. The same principle applied here. The crate of 10 or 12 bottles was incredibly cheap, how much I can't remember, but given our impecunious state it had to be cheap. By midday Louis and John were well into the bottles. Roy and I had a few sips as they say but we decided to leave them to it and go and get something to eat. This was where the qualities of the Hotel de Metz began to be demonstrated. The restaurant was of a high standard, certainly by English standards, and the food was excellent and not that expensive. But the deciding factor influencing our choice was that we could charge the cost of the meal to our hotel bill and so could eat when we had run out of, or had little, cash.

The manageress of the hotel a tall, ample, severe woman, who we use to mimic endlessly, took great pride in her restaurant and frequently took the orders for meals from the guests. On this occasion Madame approached our table. "Messieurs, what like you to eat?" She said in broken but better English than our French. We ordered roast potatoes, roast beef and petit pois. This was probably our first 'proper' meal in terms of meat and two veg. since leaving home. The smell of the food, the silver serving platter, the taste of the petit pois still linger in my mind today. Then profiteroles for desert followed by coffee. All too good for a fifteen year old! By then Jenny had arrived at our table and said that she had seen Johnny leave the hotel and when she came down past their room she could hear cursing sounds coming from it. I said that since I had finished my meal and felt in need of some limited exercise I would go and check the room to see if Louis was ok.

Part of the inside of the Hotel de Metz was built like a large atrium, open to the ceiling with each of the five or six floors opening out on to a balcony. Much of the structure was composed of filigree metal work, with fairly low, open metal railings, and greenery such as vines and ferns intertwined with the metal work. We four boys had a sort of super room on the second floor, with Louis and John staying at one level on the second floor and mine and Roy's room on the third floor but accessed via John and Louis' room on the second. I walked through the hotel, up the stairs, along the balcony of the second floor and tried the handle of the room door. The door was obviously locked. So, as you would do in such a situation, I shouted through the door "Louis are you ok?" Silence. Again, "Louis, are you alright?" A pause, then

CHAPTER 8

"Fuck off, Ashy." "Open the door Louis, we can chat about what's upsetting you." Another pause and then the door is unlocked. I tentatively open the door and move slowly into the room. Louis is sitting facing me on the bed. "Are you ok, Louis? Your hands are bleeding."

"You poncy grammar school boys you don't know what a real job is. If you're so smart why don't we have any money? Roy should stop licking Sam's arse, get on the 'phone and get us more cash, or get his dad to send us the rest of our wages; bloody £7,10s a week. I wish Hilda were here. Fucking Yanks. Fucking French. Have you got a fag? Fucking room!"

I raise my eyes from Louis and begin to look around the room. The place looked as if a herd of elephants had run through it. Only the bed was standing. Everything else: table, chest of drawers, the far bedside table, chairs, even the wardrobe, seemed to be smashed to greater or lesser degree. "I think I might have a couple upstairs. I'll go and see." I start to rummage through a jacket looking for the cigarettes, when I hear the sound of wood cracking downstairs. "Louis, what are you doing?" I race downstairs to see Louis demolishing the near bedside table. "Stop it Louis. We'll get thrown out of the hotel." I attempt to pull the little table, or what was left of it, away from him. "Piss off, Ashy." He then grabs me and starts to push me towards the still-open door. Before I have chance to think we are on the landing/balcony. Louis has dropped the table and he keeps pushing. It then dawns on me that in his alcoholic lunacy he is trying to push me over the balcony. I turn and look down to see several waiters, residents and other hotel staff gazing up at us open-mouthed some twenty feet below. My head and upper body are being bent further backwards over the low balcony rail. I look back up to be confronted by Louis' snarling face, empty of reason and in another place. Instinctively, I use all my fast diminishing strength to throw myself to the side, which is sufficient to release me from the weight of Louis' body and propel me towards the balcony floor. Of course, that movement while saving me leaves Louis pushing at air and he starts to go over the balcony. By chance I manage to grab the top of his trousers and the momentum of my dive to the floor pulls Louis down on top of me. We land in a proverbial heap. Silence. Louis then begins to cry, whimpering "Hilda, Hilda." I respond "You crazy bastard" trying to shift Louis' weight off me. In so doing I turn my head to where a foot or so away from us I can see a pair of heavy black brogues, above which like a pair of cooling towers, extends two thick, grey, stockinged legs, then a skirt, and a blouse encasing an ample bosom, topped by a stern face. "Messieurs, les residents.. !"

That incident was a turning point in the life of the band. We all instinctively knew that Louis couldn't stay with the band in France. But Roy and I were not sure what to do about it. Roy dealt brilliantly with Madame from the hotel, related an unrepeatable sob story about Louis' family circumstances, offered to pay for the damage in the room while suggesting maybe an insurance claim was a better route and kept us from being thrown out of the hotel. So, on the face of it things continued as before. But in the background Roy and I decided that he should write to his father and ask him to look out for a good drummer who would be willing to travel to France at short notice. I had a telephone conversation with my mother who revealed that

CHAPTER 8

she would like to come and see us in August next month and that she hoped Hilda would come with her. Hilda had received letters from Louis revealing his unhappiness. I made no mention to my mother of Louis' madness but confirmed that he was unhappy and missing Hilda.

The month of July soon passed and we received confirmation from our agent Karl Friedrich in Chateauroux that we were to move to Vassincourt a few miles away from TFAD on the first of August. The transfer itself was easier than anticipated. Willing GIs offered transport and assistance with the move, which reinforced our contempt for Sam at leaving us in the lurch. So on August first we left the comparative opulence of TFAD and arrived at the EM Club in Vassincourt.

Vassincourt was less an army base like TFAD or Toul and more an outpost. The buildings appeared flimsy, less permanent and were connected by dirt roads. The place would not have looked out of place if Custer's cavalry had ridden in, tied up their horses and drifted across to the saloon. The EM club itself was largely a single room about two cricket pitches in length contained within a Nissan hut type structure. Fittings were basic and our 'stage' was a dais raised about 9 inches at the end of the room. The dais was not sufficiently large to accommodate the entire band so Louis was forced to set his drum kit up at the side of the dais near a window. Jenny had to sit at a table in front and to the right of the stage while we were playing instrumentals or doing our own vocals before stepping up to join us to perform her songs. This meant that she could be vulnerable to a degree of harassment from less than sober GIs, so we had to ask the management to designate the table as the band table, which was out of bounds. We were prepared to mix and solicit French fries, hamburgers and steaks but we would go to them. At the other end of the club was the bar that ran for about ten feet on the right as you walked into the club after the toilets. On the left was a small room containing about ten slot machines. Next to the toilets was the manager's office.

The manager, whose name sadly escapes me now but let's call him Ricky, was a staff sergeant in his day job, he was short, of stocky build, displayed a large beer belly, and had a rotund, florid face, on which were set a pair of spectacles, all capped by swept back hair. Ricky spoke in a strong southern drawl, was outwardly friendly but you knew instantly that this wasn't a guy you should cross. He had an aphoristic way of speaking and so would come out with statements such as "Let the big wheels roll!" This phrase would be used as a form of abuse, the big wheels being those people who were getting above themselves and failing to do what he wanted, and so should roll away. Alternatively, he would use the epithet as a galvanising statement, meaning, "Let the wagons roll" or more prosaically "Let's get on our way." You had to watch for the context!

Ricky was also slightly crazy. After we had finished our set and the club had closed he would keep the bar open and serve free drinks to the band and club staff that he trusted. There was a clear risk in this because if the MPs found out and raided the club Ricky would be likely to loose his lucrative job as EM Club manager and probably a stripe as well. This was the first time that I really consumed much alcohol. The club was strong on cocktails so there were sloe gins, Tom Collins, margaritas, whiskey sours, and mint juleps to name but a few. These drinks were usually fairly sweet tasting and to a fifteen year old

CHAPTER 8

were close to lemonade, a hint of today's alcopops. Ricky encouraged the drinking and I did wonder whether this was all a grand plan to get inside Jenny's knickers. But knowing Jenny as we soon did the prospect of this was highly unlikely whether she was drunk or sober. There was always something to celebrate or mourn and an excuse for a party. On August 6th we heard that Marilyn Monroe had been found dead. Many strong men on the base wept. But Ricky decided to mark her passing in his own way by a marathon drinking session in which Jenny was invited to sing songs from "Some Like it Hot" while we nodded into our Tom Collins. Later that night I would wake up on the floor of the club toilet, feeling sick and vowing never to drink alcohol again. Some hope!

Some of the club and bar staff were Polish Guards and a couple of them befriended the band. They gave us lifts into Bar-Le-Duc and generally looked out for us in the club environment. On some nights Ricky would announce at about 1am in the morning "Hey, let's go to St. Dizier." St. Dizier was only 17 miles away from Vassincourt and had some clubs that welcomed GIs. So off we would go, some of the band driving with Ricky in his '59 Chevy Impala and the rest of us with one of the Polish Guards in their Citroën or Peugeot. There would be more drinking at the French club and occasionally live music. So, while Ricky and his pals were doing the serious drinking of cognac and local beer we, at least Roy and I, would go and inspect the band and their instruments. Of course this would be a French band playing jazz tinged music with accordion, violin, snare drum, double bass, and the occasional acoustic, or semi-acoustic jazz, guitar. Nevertheless, they were a pleasurable alternative to the boorish excesses of Ricky.

At about 5am Ricky would announce, "Hey, let's go get breakfast." Off we would go charging through the countryside until we found a French café that was open at 6am. There we would drink fantastic coffee and eat oeufs en plat dipping chunks of fresh French bread into the runny yoke of the eggs. That for me would be the highlight of the 'evening'. At around 7am to 8am we would be dropped off at the Hotel de Metz, where we would try and creep past the concierge and up the stairs into our beds before the censorious eyes of Madame settled upon us.

It was into this milieu that my mother and Hilda descended around the start of the third week of August. Louis and I, all spruced up, met them off the train from Paris at Bar-Le-Duc station. My mother's first, and oft repeated[100], comment was "You look so thin." Now wasn't the time to tell her that if it wasn't for the charity of the GIs and her own food parcels to me I wouldn't be here. So, I mumbled something about getting lots of exercise without a van to transport us around. But she gave me a funny look, which I now know is the look of a parent who knows when her offspring is being economical with the truth. We had reserved separate rooms for them at the Hotel de Metz. Upon our arrival, Madame greeted us warmly with no hint of the devastation and mayhem that Louis and I had caused a few weeks earlier.

The visit was a success and all my anxieties about how my mother would respond to the environment we were living in proved groundless. The rest of the band

---

[100] See Chapter 14.

CHAPTER 8

were pleased to see her. Louis and Hilda largely went there separate ways. Presents were distributed and in addition Roy was given a sealed letter from his father. In it Jack said that he had found a very good drummer, who had a reputation as "a bit of a rum character" but he was available and could come over to France at short notice. Max Temple was his name.

My mother spent some time with me alone and asked probing questions about the band's situation. I gave her some of the truth about Sam and mentioned Louis' problems but I put a gloss on them. She was well received by Ricky, our Polish friends and the other GIs. Everyone was polite and formally correct and nobody tried to bed her as far as I was aware. Two days before they were due to leave was the 21st of August, my mother's birthday. She would be 45. On the day itself, we sang and played happy birthday to her from the stage at the club. She was flattered by the reception she received from the GIs and the club staff. But my heart sank when, after the club had closed, Ricky came up to her and us and said, "Let's party." My mother's tipple was a Babycham, or a lemonade shandy. Now she was faced with offers of exotic drinks she had never even heard of before never mind drunk. But she rose to the challenge and I had to admit I had a sneaking admiration for her chutzpah as she seemed to take all this in her stride. But then my heart sank further when Ricky shouted, "Let's go to St. Dizier." I asked my mother "Would you like to go back to the hotel?" She said that she wasn't tired and what was this St. Dizier place anyway? I replied it was just a boring club, with a crappy French band and a few drunken GIs. But she was not to be deterred and, as if to put me in my place, she mused that it sounded interesting and that she would love to go. My mother as guest of honour was invited into Ricky's Chevy and I accompanied her along with Jenny who was brave enough to sit up front with Ricky. Sitting in the back seat she marvelled at the sumptuous red leather upholstery with me jealously responding *soto voce* that it was almost certainly plastic. And off we went.

As it happened we were the last to leave and so we were at the end of a convoy of about four cars. This didn't suit Ricky's leadership pretensions, so after a failed attempt to get close to them on the road he made a decision to turn off, first onto a farm track and then across a field. I almost had my head in my hands, glancing up and rolling my eyes at Jenny who kept looking back anxiously at my mother and I. But she did not seem to be fazed and looked to be enjoying the experience. Fortunately for me if not for my mother, Ricky did not drag out the experience and after about an hour at the club he asked my mother and me if we would like to be taken back to the hotel. I looked across at my mother, who said that she'd had a wonderful birthday and that Ricky had made it really special. Ricky beamed, puffed out his chest and said "My pleasure ma'am." Back at the hotel, I walked her back to her room and she thanked me for giving her a great birthday: "Such nice people, but tell Jenny to watch out for that Ricky." With that, she kissed me goodnight and closed her door, leaving me to try and make sense of the night's events as I walked back to my room.

"Wake up Ashy, wake up!" Roy's insistent voice finally begins to force me into consciousness. "What's up? What time is it?" "It's 12.30pm and Louis has just told me he is leaving the band and going home with

CHAPTER 8

Hilda tomorrow." All I could think to say was "What about his drum kit?" "Silly bugger, there's more things to worry about than his drum kit." "No, Roy this is serious. He can't take his kit with him, so we should hang on to it and get your dad to ask Max to come over straight away and use Louis' drums. I can't see Louis wanting to do much during the next three months because he has to sort himself out and he'll want to spend time with Hilda. We can drop them off in December when we come home in the van that your dad is going to buy." "Hm, maybe you're right and maybe we can find a GI to play Louis's drums until Max arrives." And that is what happened.

I then hear a soft knocking on the room door downstairs. I pull on my jeans and go downstairs, the room is empty, Louis is with Hilda and I'm not sure where Johnny is. I open the door and there is my mother. "I've just been to the café over the road for a coffee and a read of the paper I got at the station earlier this morning. The whole place is in uproar. Police are everywhere. As far as I can tell, someone has tried to kill de Gaulle in Paris." I finished dressing and went with Roy and my mother down into the lobby area of the hotel. People were huddled in groups, many were gesticulating and Roy thought he'd heard mention of the OAS. Finally, we tracked down a waiter whose English had been buttressed by a stint at an English hotel on the south coast. He told us that shots had been fired at President de Gaulle's motorcade as it travelled through the Paris suburb of Le Petit-Clamart. The radio was saying that de Gaulle was uninjured but people didn't know what to believe. Some were saying this was the start of a coup by the OAS who hoped to reverse France's withdrawal from Algeria and Algerian independence, which had been officially proclaimed the previous month. Others said it was likely to be the FLN who despite Algerian independence were angry at the slow progress towards independence under de Gaulle and the atrocities visited on Algerians by the OAS and the French state[101].

Our response to the mayhem was, of course, to ask how this affected us. Nobody had mentioned the Americans, so presumably the post assassination recriminations would not affect the presence of US troops in France. The only problem it seemed to me was whether my mother would be able to get the train to Paris the next day and then home. A bizarre thought passed through my mind that this might be a way to keep Louis but it dissolved as soon as it emerged. The next day my mother, Hilda and Louis departed, with much hugs and great sadness that a key figure in our band for the past eighteen months was leaving. We had been through much together in a short space of time and the bonds created between us had seemed strong. The train left on time and apart from the heightened security they were little detained in Paris and were back home on Teesside the next day. The Denvers minus one continued in Bar-Le-Duc.

We now had to make preparations to move back to Toul but this time it was going to be the Toul Engineering Base and not the Jeanne d'Arc hospital. The greater distance meant that we thought we couldn't rely on the casual help of friendly GIs. We had to try and get hold of a van. But none of us were qualified to drive. Roy and I were too young, and Johnny and Jenny had never

---

[101] Of course, as detailed in Chapter 7, it was the OAS that attempted the assassination.

CHAPTER 8

felt the need to learn. We asked around the EM Club at Vassincourt and to our surprise Ricky offered to take us in his Chevy with some of our gear in his capacious boot and the rest would be taken by one of the Polish guards, Teddy, who generously offered to assist. "Hell, I ain't seen Toul in a while. Good to see them big dicks roll!" Ricky enthused. We graciously accepted his offer, although not without tacit reservation. The thought of the damage that might be inflicted on our expensive Fender guitars and Vox amps if Ricky decided to go off-road didn't bear thinking about. The move was set for 1st September and we had one week to play out at Vassincourt. One of the GIs stood in on the drums for us and while he was no rock drummer and was more used to marking time on military marches, his contribution was incredibly valuable. Our fear was that Ricky would lose it with us after Louis had gone and take his exit as a personal insult, but he didn't and there were no complaints. The fact that we had a GI substituting on the drums probably helped pacify Ricky and the club audience and, apart from the drum solos, little would appear amiss to most non-musicians.

Little had been heard from Stockton after Louis' departure. My mother sent me a letter thanking me for looking after her in which she noted, amidst exhortations that I should eat more, that she thought Jenny was "such a lovely girl." Nothing further had been heard from Roy's dad and so again we began to worry what would happen when we got to Toul. The GI substitute could not go with us because he had a day job and while the lack of a drummer might on the face of it be less of a problem than the absence of a girl singer it seemed unlikely that a rock band could survive without one.

But our worries proved groundless, for three days before we were due to leave for Toul there was a knock on our bedroom door – it was mid-afternoon and we were preparing to go to the base. We opened the door and confronting us was a stocky, yet slim, shortish man, with a round beaming face and short hair, wearing a crew neck jumper, a silk scarf tied round his neck just visible above the sweater, a pair of jeans, heavy boots and an army style overcoat. Under his arm was a snare drum. "I'm Maxy Temple and this is my girlfriend Linda." Linda smiled but said nothing. "They say you need a drummer. Well here I am. Aren't you going to invite us in?"

Max was from Darlington, had hawker connections and had not long left the army after staying on for three years following his National Service. He was a lot older than us, around 30, and the phrase that comes to mind when thinking about him is "hard as nails." He wore a permanent, but cynical, smile and said very little. But you knew if you crossed him he would probably give you a good kicking. His musical tastes were different from ours and, perhaps reflecting his age, leaned towards jazz and standards. Yet, there was no doubting his talent as a drummer. Much less flamboyant than Louis he nonetheless kept time better and probably could be described as a proper musician. He fitted into the band extremely quickly. His talent and experience meant that one or two run-throughs of the numbers we played were sufficient for him to get what was needed and to deliver it thereafter. For a bass player he was a godsend because he knew how to keep the beat, which helped me to do so and what he taught me about timing and rhythm revealed how little I knew before.

CHAPTER 8

We were a band again. Two new members in two months but in the remaining performances at Vassincourt it felt musically that we were a tight unit and could go on to do bigger and better things. But on another level the loss of Louis was a metaphor for a loss of innocence. Roy and I and Johnny and Louis tended to pal up together but we were a bit like four musketeers, "all for one, one for all etc" and that disappeared when Max came on the scene. Clearly age, and the presence of Linda, was a factor but I think there was also something about Max's personality that led to a desire to keep himself to himself. Nothing unusual about that you might say. Band members often go their separate ways when off-stage. Indeed, it might be argued that such behaviour is better for the welfare of a band because, as with an intense marriage, 24-hour contact can be its downfall. But there was something shifty about Max, which made one feel that you couldn't completely trust him, and if that is not good in a marriage it certainly is not good in a band. Jenny was the first to notice and sound the alarm to the rest of us.

She had heard noises from their room at night that seemed to go beyond what one might expect to overhear in a normal relationship. Max could be heard shouting, Linda could be heard crying and then there were the crashes and bangs. Jenny noticed that Linda carried bruises on her legs but all attempts by Jenny to get close to her and ascertain whether she needed help were rebuffed. The rest of the band often discussed the situation and we concluded that there was nothing to be done about it unless Linda complained and perhaps, rather glibly, the behaviour was consensual! It is also worth saying in support of that view that Linda was no mouse. She might have been quiet at the beginning but once we got to know her better she would be forthright in argument and often acted as Max's minder by seeking to protect his interests, or give his point of view. While Max was taciturn and covert in speech and behaviour, Linda was loquacious and expansive. She also had a tendency to act first and think later.

A classic example of this is given by our experience on the last day in France of that tour, while waiting in Boulogne for the channel ferry our gear piled up on the harbour waiting to be carried on in individual pieces before the hoped-for meeting with Roy's dad and the new van in Dover. We were sat in a café prior to eating biftek au cheveaux et frites when Max and Linda came into the café. There were four glasses full of beer sitting on the table untouched as we waited for the meal to arrive. Linda strode over picked up one of the glasses and turned it completely over. Naturally beer spilt everywhere over the table and over our clothes. I thought Jenny was about to hit Linda but we just sat open mouthed. Then Linda said "Sorry, I thought the glasses were empty and upside down!" None of this, of course, justifies Max beating her, if indeed that was what was happening.

Max was clearly not happy with the wages we were getting, even though he was paid the full £15, largely the consequence of Linda's representations to Roy and his dad. However, while we tended to economise and rely on the charity of the GIs, Max, aided and abetted by Linda, took more direct action. They would go into cafés and restaurants, sit near the door and after they had eaten their meal they would do a runner. They would look out for each other in markets, while one stole food or goods the other provided a distraction or served as a lookout. This behaviour scared the life out

CHAPTER 8

of the rest of us because we felt sure that the police would track them and us down leading to us all being sent home, or worse, being incarcerated in some mediaeval French jail.

So, when we moved to Toul and then onto Nancy General Depot in October there was much about the band to occupy our minds. But this didn't last because the consequences of events thousands of miles away began to creep into our lives.

In January 1959 The Cuban Revolution led by Fidel Castro swept the corrupt and unjust Batista regime from power after a long struggle. While the US government had become frustrated with the corruption and injustice of the Batista regime, sufficient to impose an arms embargo on the Batista government on 14 March 1958, it nevertheless felt threatened by the Marxist and apparent pro-communist sympathies of the revolutionary leaders and their favourable posture towards the Soviet Union. Tensions began to build and in April 1961 the United States backed CIA-trained forces of Cuban exiles to overthrow the Cuban government. This became known as the Bay of Pigs invasion and it ended in humiliating failure for the US, with many of the invaders captured. The failure of the Bay of Pigs invasion also served to embolden the Soviet Union, who believed that the new US President Kennedy, who had assumed office in January 1961, was inexperienced and weak. Hence, he would be less likely to stand up to the Soviet Union than his predecessor President Eisenhower, who had been a 5-star general and led the allied forces in the D-Day invasion of Europe in 1944.

Throughout 1962 US relations deteriorated both with Cuba and the Soviet Union. On January 9th Cuba and the Soviet Union signed a trade pact. This prompted the Organization of American States, following US pressure, to suspend Cuba's membership on January 22nd. On February 3rd the US announced a trade embargo against Cuba. This was followed on February 7th by bans on all US - related Cuban imports and exports. Relations deteriorated further when on April 14th a Cuban military tribunal convicted 1,179 of the Bay of Pigs attackers.

As we went about our daily business at Toul and then Nancy the word Cuba increasingly entered into conversations either directly or overheard. But it appeared at first to be nothing more than GI ranting at the communist pre-disposition of Castro and his loyal lieutenant Che Guevara. Given our tender age our knowledge of politics was very limited but we were sufficiently aware to be sceptical of the GI's foreboding. After all, communist parties and communist sympathies were much more prevalent in Europe and therefore more familiar and perhaps less threatening to us than to US citizens, where even post-McCarthy to be a 'communist' was often viewed as being synonymous with the 'devil'. Moreover, the US military were our hosts and we didn't want to rock the boat by challenging some of the presuppositions of the GIs. In any event, if the truth be told, we were more interested in news about the latest Cliff and the Shadows record than international politics. But that quickly began to change.

In late September some of the GIs at Toul pointed to the fighting that had erupted between China and India over a border dispute as an indication that "the commies were on the march." By October 10th when we were playing at the Nancy General Depot, the news that the border dispute had developed into a full-scale war

CHAPTER 8

between China and India, the two largest countries in the world, gave further pause for thought. Then a few days later matters took a significant turn for the worse. On October 14th a US reconnaissance U-2 flight over Cuba took photos of Soviet inter-mediate nuclear missiles being installed. The Cuban Missile Crisis had begun.

On October 21st further U-2 flights revealed additional missile bases in Northern Cuba and that the numbers of Soviet bombers and Mig fighters were increasing. Of course the world including us knew none of that until the evening of Monday October 22nd, when President Kennedy addressed the US nation in a televised speech, announcing the presence of offensive missile sites in Cuba. But even before Kennedy's address we knew that something was going on. The whole rhythm of the base changed. There seemed a purpose in everyone's actions. Gone was the laid-back style of most GIs. Everyone seemed to sense that this was something serious and their training was beginning to kick in. There was a sharper edge in the EM club. GIs were drinking less and talking more. Patriotic songs were more in demand. Even the criticisms of President Kennedy disappeared. Kennedy wasn't that popular amongst the military personnel we met, principally because of the Bay of Pigs fiasco and his weak showing at the June 1961 Vienna summit meeting with Khrushchev. Some hated him simply because he was a rich, Catholic, Democrat. And even more bizarrely some suggested he had played a part in the 'suicide' of Marilyn Monroe back in August.

Our response to the crisis was first to stop listening to Radio Luxembourg and switch to listening to the American Forces Network (AFN) on the couple of portable transistor radios we had with us. Secondly, we talked to the GIs more and tried to get more information. In this connection we became friendly with a US military plain-clothes policeman, a CID officer. Such officers frequently worked undercover on straight criminal work, such as seeking out and arresting black marketers, but they also had a security role to uncover and prevent spying in and around the bases. Dave was altogether more serious than your average GI. He was older and very thoughtful. He said that most of the GIs didn't appreciate how serious the situation was. This worried and scared us because we had been sceptical and less serious about the situation than most GIs we met. But our scepticism evaporated when on October 22nd the troops moved to a higher state of alert. This was DEFCON 3.

Monday was our day off and so when we arrived at the base on Tuesday the 23rd it was another world from Sunday. Getting into the base was much more difficult as security was considerably tighter. All personnel were in their battle fatigues, more weapons were on display, and vehicular activity had clearly increased. Once inside the base, we could see tanks being loaded onto transporters, and artillery pieces were being brought out of storage, checked and hitched to trucks as the flow of trucks and other military vehicles entering and leaving the base increased dramatically.

At this point I made a rare 'phone call to my mother and asked how my dad and her were. Was she worried? Surprisingly, she said that she was concerned but not terrified. She took the view that the Americans were sabre rattling over a few Russians on Cuba when there were US missiles in Italy and in Turkey right next to Russia. She thought it would pass. I said I wasn't so sure

CHAPTER 8

and it was certainly being treated very seriously here. I said I would ring her back later in the week.

We know now that President Kennedy and his advisers had chosen the option of a blockade of shipments of offensive weapons to Cuba. This was considered to be a sufficiently robust response that stopped short of direct military action. And, while it was a violation of international law it differed from the Soviets' blockade of Berlin in 1948, which had sought to prevent all materiel, civilian as well as military, from entering the city. So, on the Tuesday October 23rd U.S. ships took up position 500 miles offshore to blockade Cuba. On the Wednesday all talk was of the Russian ships approaching the US blockade. Was this the flashpoint that would cause a nuclear war?

We went through the motions that night as we played our set. Hearts had lifted when we heard that the Soviet ships approaching the blockade had slowed down and some had turned around. When we stepped down from the stage, Dave who had come in late to the club told us that he had heard that one ship had refused to stop. "Let me run you home and we can listen to AFN in the car." Jenny, Roy and myself said we would go with him. Max, Linda and Johnny said they would stay and see if they could get another drink and get a lift back to the hotel later.

We got into the car. Dave started the engine and then switched on the radio. The tone of the commentary on AFN was not calm. A lot of the talk was about when the war would start and how it would start. It was speculated that the US would make a direct attack on Cuba. Others said that if the US did that the Soviets would attack and overrun Berlin. Others again worried about a

US nuclear first strike on Russia, or an attempted Russian first strike on both the US and the NATO forces in Europe. This didn't sound good, to say the least. The commentators were talking like you might discuss the tactics of a forthcoming football match, or the possible moves in a chess game. I wanted to shout at the radio, "this is not a game, the future of humanity is at stake!" After half an hour we hadn't moved. We were all absorbed by the radio. Dave switched the heater up in the car, pulled out a couple of cans of beer from the glove compartment and said "We may as well make ourselves comfortable. This could be a long night!"

After a while, tiredness crept over me and I began to doze off in the back of the car. I wondered whether I would see my mam and dad again. Were they safer in Stockton than I was on this US military base in Nancy close to the German border? I forced myself back into consciousness: "Dave, if it all starts what do you think will happen to the base here? Will we be attacked by nuclear missiles?" "No, I don't think the Russians have enough strategic missiles to attack an army base like this. They will be targeted on the main population centres in the US mainly but also Europe as well. The limited tactical nuclear weapons are likely to be used on the battlefield in Germany in response to our first use of them on the battlefield. No, what we can expect here is attacks by Russian bombers. That's why we have been putting a lot of effort into ensuring the anti-aircraft missiles and gun batteries on the perimeter of the base are fully operational and have the ordinance to deal with a sustained attack." Roy and I both said that we hadn't noticed. "No, you were not meant to." Dave smiled.

CHAPTER 8

I then asked the question that had been troubling me for some time, "Nancy is a major general depot and seems to store all levels of military equipment, are nuclear weapons stored here as well?" Dave turned his head towards me and gave me a fixed stare. "Am I going to have arrest you as a Russian spy? And, you know if the balloon goes up we'll probably shoot you!" I shifted uncomfortably in my seat. "Dave, I'm not a bloody spy. I'm just interested. My dad was in the RAF." As if that was a clinching defence. "If the Soviets thought we had nuclear weapons here then we might be hit by a nuclear strike. So if the Ruskies are your friends don't go telling them that or you might get a thermonuclear device on your head." Dave brushes away my attempted protestations. "But think about it logically, strategic nuclear weapons are delivered either by missiles, or bombers. Missiles are kept in silos and most of these are in the US given our inter-continental ability. Some intermediate range missiles are in Europe. So, that leaves us with nuclear bombs. Let us just say that since a war might blow up quickly, you need your bombs close to the delivery system. Hence, they will be kept on an air force base. And you wouldn't want such prize assets to be close to Russian attack, so between you and me if they are here it will be a US airbase in the mid west, or south of France." "You mean like Chateauroux airbase near where our agent stays?" I interjected. "Perhaps." At this point, Jenny who had seemed to be sleeping, stirred and said "Yes, Dave that's all very well about those big bombs but what about those nuclear bombs that they use close up?" "Tactical battlefield nuclear weapons" Roy suggested. "Yes, thanks Roy. Do they store any of those here Dave?" Dave looked out through the car windscreen across the EM Club car park to the club and surrounding buildings, lights were being turned off in the club. "I don't think we should go there Jenny. No ma'am. I'd better get you all home." And at that he pushed the transmission stick into Drive, put his foot on the gas and drove slowly out of the base.

During the next two days, Thursday 25th and Friday 26th of October, the crisis continued. Dave said that if the balloon went up he would try and get us out. But realistically, nowhere was safe and given the scale of the US air force based in the UK and the UK's leading role in NATO, it was no safe haven even if we could reach it.

On the 25th AFN reported on Adlai Stevenson's, US ambassador to the UN, presentation to an emergency session of the Security Council, of reconnaissance photographs of the Russian missiles *in situ* in Cuba. The Russian ambassador would neither confirm nor deny the existence of the missiles. The two super powers seemed to be hurtling towards war.

We learn later that in response to intelligence about the move to operational readiness of the Cuban missiles President Kennedy issued Security Action Memorandum 199. The order authorised the loading of nuclear weapons onto aircraft under the command of SACEUR, which had the duty of carrying out first air strikes on the Soviet Union. That's Strategic Air Command Europe and would include US air force bases in the UK, France and Italy. This made sense of a comment overheard on the Nancy base the next day, in an echo of Ricky at Vassincourt, "I hear the big one's are rolling."

But it was not all bad news. We hear, again via AFN, during the day, that the Soviets have responded to the blockade and quarantine by turning back 14 ships

CHAPTER 8

presumably because they were carrying offensive weapons. Our emotions are on a roller coaster and we find it hard to sing what seem now to be trivial songs while the world teeters on the edge of oblivion. Yet, our Friday night performance is lifted by changing the emphasis and words of certain songs to bring in aspects of the crisis. So in the Johnny Kidd number *Shaking all over* we slightly change the words from Jenny singing "When you move in right up close to me, that's when I get the shakes all over me. You give me shivers down my backbone. Shaking all over." to "When we move in right up close to you, that's when you Ruskies get the shakes all over you. You get shivers down your backbone. You'll be shaking all over." And so on. Naturally, this was a big success with the GIs and I guess we did out bit for morale. We felt useful.

On Saturday lunchtime, the 27th, we hear in our hotel room from AFN that they are getting reports that a US U2 reconnaissance or spy plane has been shot down over Cuba. Was this the first act of war? We get a taxi into the base. At first we can't get in. "But you've seen us playing on the stage at the EM Club." Roy pleads with the MP guard on the gate. "This ain't no place for civilians." The guard replies. "Look call the EM Club. We are here to work. We have a contract to fulfil. Let us in to do that" Roy adds. The call is made. Words are exchanged. The guard looks at us while on the 'phone, nods at us and then raises the barrier. The EM Club is deserted. No staff making preparations for the opening in the evening, no bottles being stacked, no food being brought in, nothing. Finally, we find the managers office and there is a light on, so we knock and go in. The manager looks up from his desk. "Sorry guys, no show tonight, or tomorrow … We've gone to the highest alert. We are at DEFCON 2"

"What the fuck's that?" said Max in one of his rare sallies into politics and military affairs. "It means war, son; a nuclear war. You all better go over to the snack bar, get yourself something to eat and then go back to your hotel and wait for us to contact you. That is if we are still here!"

Wikipedia writes that on October 26th, at 10:00 pm EDT, the US raised the readiness level of Strategic Air Command forces to DEFCON 2. "For the only confirmed time in US history, the B-52 bombers were dispersed to various locations and made ready to take off, fully equipped, on 15 minutes notice. One-eighth of SAC's 1,436 bombers were on airborne alert, some 145 intercontinental ballistic missiles stood on ready alert, while Air Defense Command (ADC) redeployed 161 nuclear-armed interceptors to 16 dispersal fields within nine hours with one-third maintaining 15-minute alert status."

We had been cast adrift. There was no Dave. Everyone was going about their serious business and, quite reasonably, had little time for us. But the gloom was lifted slightly by Johnny, "I bet Sam and his fat arse are already deep down in a bunker in Mayfair." We sniggered half-heartedly. "Perhaps Karl Friedrich in Chateauroux can help us. Maybe we can go there?" said Jenny. "Not if that is where the big bombs are." Roy mused, less than reassuringly. "Let's go into town and get pissed," said Max. And for once we all agreed.

The weekend seemed to go on for ages. Sunday the 28th saw us fighting off hangovers and return to listening to AFN in our hotel rooms even though the batteries in our radios were beginning to run down through constant use. We learn that there is still a standoff of US and Soviet

CHAPTER 8

ships, including submarines, at the quarantine line off Cuba. Rumours of US-Soviet proposals and counterproposals are aired. Then late in the day we hear that Soviet Premier Nikita Khrushchev has announced over Radio Moscow that he has agreed to remove the missiles from Cuba. In return the US has agreed not to invade Cuba. It comes out later that in a secret deal between Kennedy and Khrushchev, Kennedy had agreed to the withdrawal of U.S. missiles from Turkey. But the fact that this deal is not made public makes it look like the Soviets have backed down.

Tuesday morning, the 29th, there is call for us downstairs in the hotel. It is the club manager, "We won, let's party! See you on the stage of the EM Club tonight."

Two more days at Nancy, then we were to move to a small base at Brienne le Chateau, closer to Paris. How would we get there? It had completely slipped our minds. But the US cavalry again came to the rescue in the form of Dave, a friend and a US army truck. Don't ask me how he wangled it. On the afternoon of Friday, 1st November we rolled into the new base, unloaded our gear and bid Dave and his friend goodbye. Our battered radios reported that aerial reconnaissance showed that the Soviets had begun to dismantle their missiles in Cuba. The crisis seemed to be over.

Everything immediately after that was an anti-climax and the month at Brienne passed without incident. News that the Cuban missile crisis had definitely ended came on November 20th when following confirmation that the missiles had been removed from Cuba the US ended its blockade.

Roy hired a French driver and van to take us to Boulogne and the ferry to England on the morning of

December 1st. We were all keen to get home. On arrival in Boulogne, the white cliffs of Dover were faintly visible, or so it appeared. As I looked out of the van window towards England I felt a wave of patriotism and love for my country that I had never experienced before, or since. Those cliffs seemed to symbolise a haven, a place of safety, a bosom in which to bury my head and escape the threats of violence and war. At that moment I never wanted to leave England again.

Then in the café after Linda and the beer incident I discovered my passport was missing. I thought I definitely had it with me. Max and Roy said I would probably have to stay in France until the embassy had provided me with a new passport. But don't worry they would tell my parents I was ok. I broke down in tears. After the events of the past few weeks, emotions were running high. And now, to be on the threshold of returning home and to be prevented from doing so because of the loss of a passport seemed so unjust. Had I done something to displease the gods? I couldn't help myself I just kept sobbing. Until Max reaching into his greatcoat pocket said, "Ok Ashy, we found it for you!"
"Bastards!" I cried.

But I couldn't have been happier.

CHAPTER 9

OUT OF THE SHADOWS

We shivered in the back of our Standard Atlas van as Roy's father, Jack, drove us to gigs from North Yorkshire to Tyneside in the early months of 1963. Drifts of hard packed, grey snow pushed back by snow ploughs on each side of narrow lanes often towered over the van as we drove into places such as Spennymoor, Northallerton and Catterick to play the local working men's club, pub or NAAFI[102]. The winter of 1963 was colder than the winter of 1947, when I came into this world, and in fact the coldest winter in England since 1740[103]. At times temperatures dropped below -20 degrees centigrade. Like the children we still were, we delighted in the first snows

---

[102] From Wikipedia "The **Navy, Army and Air Force Institutes** (**NAAFI**) is an organisation created by the British government in 1921 to run recreational establishments needed by the British Armed Forces, and to sell goods to servicemen and their families. It runs clubs, bars, shops, supermarkets, launderettes, restaurants, cafés and other facilities on most British military bases..." http://en.wikipedia.org/wiki/Navy,_Army_and_Air_Force_Institutes

[103] See http://www.metoffice.gov.uk/education/teens/case-studies/severe-winters

as the blizzards swept in from the north at Christmas. Little did we know that in large parts of the northeast the snows would remain until March. The cold weather accentuated the difference between our band life on the US bases in France and life at my parents' home in Billingham. All the rooms in the buildings on the bases were super-heated. But at 17 Matlock Gardens, the only heating was the coal fire in the living room. On nights when the band wasn't playing my mother and I huddled close to the coal fire, curtains drawn, eating our supper and watching *Thank Your Lucky Stars*, *Z-Cars* and the *Avengers*, my favourites, or *Songs of Praise*, *Emergency -Ward 10* and *Coronation Street*, my mother's, on the flickering TV set, while my dad, as ever, enjoyed the warmth of the Kings Arms.

My mother remained a staunch fan of the band as we soon found out when we arrived back in Billingham. We were met off the Boulogne channel ferry at Dover by Jack, keen to show us our new - to us - van: the Standard Atlas. With the gear hand-carried off the boat and stowed in the van, we all squeezed in the back with Roy and Jenny up front. Off we drove to drop Jenny off in London and then up the A1 to Darlington, dropping off Max and his girlfriend, then to Stockton and home.

After a warm greeting from my parents and real feelings of relief on my part that I was home at last, my mother broke the news. She had organised a "Welcome Home Party", with properly printed invitations for the coming Thursday evening the 6th December. More than 150 invitations had been sent out and she had received nearly 100 acceptances, so she hoped that we would be able to play at the event, which was four days hence! Needless to say after gratitude came consternation: Jenny

CHAPTER 9

was in London, Max in Darlington and I had no idea what plans Roy and Johnny had. A panic 'phone call to Roy soon followed who was more sanguine since my mother had kept his parents informed about what she was doing and they had already briefed him.

So, four days later the band, minus Jenny, turned up at Wolviston church hall to be greeted by an assorted mixture of relatives and friends, including my old guitar tutor Mr Evamy and his wife. The band played a set of about 10 to 15 numbers, with Johnny taking the singing burden, offering a good leavening of Elvis numbers, which seemed to please Maureen from Burdon's music shop and the many young women from my mother's work whom she had encouraged to attend. My mother's *piece de resistance* was to contact the local press about the event, with the *Billingham Express*, and the Middlesbrough *Evening Gazette* sending reporters and photographers.

The *Billingham Express* had faithfully followed our adventures in France and would continue to do so. On November 22nd they had published an article with the headline "'Rock' Group Will Be Home For Christmas" and gave details of the forthcoming welcome home party and concluded the short article with the words " ...it will be interesting to see what six months' professional experience has done for the youthful rock n' rollers." In the event they confined their reportage to a photo with a small caption in the following week's edition of the paper.

The *Evening Gazette* on the face of it did us proud, with a photograph and an accompanying article under the headline "Home from successful venture" which charted the recent history of the band - 'group' in their, and our, terminology of the time. The sub-editor had clearly felt justified in adopting his/her headline because in the caption under the photograph we are described as "The Ventures" rhythm group! Perhaps revealing that we were not as well known on Teesside as we had either thought or hoped.

On December 27th the *Billingham Express* ran an article under the headline "Rhythm group now seeking fame at home" in which it reported that we had been offered another six-month contract to return to France starting on the first of January 1963. The reason given for turning the contract down was that our parents had advised against it and so we planned to stay in England. The *Express* then reported me as saying that we had also been offered engagements in London for two months, so we were going to take that option instead. At a distance of more than 50 years I cannot be certain that we hadn't had such an offer to play in London, the offer to go back to France was real enough, but I fear the London offer may have been a product of my 15 year-old fancy, not wanting to admit that we were a lot further away from the "big time" in England than we were prepared to admit.

Moreover, the influence of our parents was real enough. Both Roy's family and mine were concerned that we had sacrificed a good grammar school education, the fruits of passing the eleven-plus, for the extremely uncertain prospect of finding success as a rhythm group, or rock band, one of the many thousands of bands seeking fame and success at that time. The reader might reasonably object why our parents hadn't stopped us going to France in the first place, rather than seek to exercise parental control over us on our return. I think the answer, as noted in Chapter 6, was that our parents feared

CHAPTER 9

rebellion and withdrawal from school if we hadn't been allowed to go. They gave us the opportunity to get it out of our system but now after our return was the time to think again about careers for the long term. The settlement agreed with our parents was that Roy and I would seek to complete our GCE O' levels by registering for full-time classes at Stockton and Billingham Technical College, while continuing to promote the Denvers and seek engagements in the evening. We were back to being a semi-pro outfit.

There were also other practical problems. While Roy and I were still more or less of school age, the others in the band were definitely not. Would they want to go and get day-jobs? And if they wanted to remain full-time musicians could we generate enough income from evening engagements in northeast England to keep them in the band? Bookings further afield would not be feasible if we had to be back in college next day. Was this actually the end of the Denvers, despite what our parents said? Or at least was it the end of the band that had wowed the GIs, almost wrecked the Hotel de Metz in Bar le Duc, bombarded French soldiers with rotten eggs in Toul, and survived the Cuban Missile Crisis? Amazingly, no! Max said he would continue as the group's drummer and see what he earned with us. Johnny said that he didn't want to go abroad again. Dorothy and he were thinking of settling down and getting married; Johnny was looking for a painter and decorator's job but was happy to continue playing in the group as long as we stayed on Teesside. And Jenny? Well her home was in Ealing and Stockton seemed a much less attractive proposition than London for bookings amongst other things. But she agreed to come and stay in Stockton if we could get a reasonable run of work for the group. Which is what she did, lodging for a while with my maternal grandmother in Stockton, sampling her exquisite Yorkshire puddings, home baked pies and fantastic dessert puddings: steamed egg, spotted dick, rice and semolina, then staying with the families of some of the other group members. Yet, Roy and I knew that we were likely to lose Max soon. If we wanted to move the band back up to another level we would lose Johnny and if we didn't try to do that we would lose Jenny. It was with such uncertainties and fears that we entered 1963.

Making the Denvers a success was the main motivating force in both my life and Roy's life at that time. I was fifteen going on sixteen and Roy was already seventeen. We were both intelligent and knew that what our parents were saying about getting some qualifications and building a career while continue to play in the band as a hobby was probably the sensible thing to do. Yet every time I got out of bed in the morning - if I could get up in the morning! - it was the Denvers and how we might go on to bigger and better things that was usually at the forefront of my mind as I tucked into the, by now cold, bacon sandwich that my mother had left me before she went off to work. I am sure Roy was little different from me. With the advent of the Beatles, pop music was becoming central to popular culture in Britain. Moreover, popular culture was, for better or worse, beginning to influence, even break down, traditional British authority structures in politics and religion as well as in music and the performing arts. As Christopher Booker notes in his seminal book about the 1960s *The Neophiliacs*:

CHAPTER 9

"It was about this time that, as their second record *Please Please Me* reached the top of the hit parade, the world outside Liverpool was becoming dimly aware that the Beatles were no ordinary pop group - and indeed that pop music itself was beginning to exert some peculiar fascination, expressing the spirit of the times."[104]

Furthermore, he contends that

"It is impossible to question that the events and character of 1963 stand out as more remarkable than those of any other year in Britain since the war - or that they represented the central hinge between one kind of Britain and another."[105]

We were probably little aware at the time of the momentous change that was occurring but we felt that pop music was the key to an exciting and rewarding future. A 9am to 5pm existence, commuting between Billingham and Stockton, or Middlesbrough or West Hartlepool, to some anonymous desk job, lacked the glamour of performing centre stage belting out a rock number breathing in the, hoped for, adulation of teenage girls. Neither Roy nor I had much of a sense of politics at that stage in our lives. It would be another ten years before I read Hegel and Marx at university. We were not "angry young men". Young, yes, but certainly not angry. We certainly had an, all be it hazy, dream of what we

---

[104] Christopher Booker *The Neophiliacs: The revolution in English Life in the fifties and sixties* (1992) Pimlico Edition. Page 192
[105] Booker *op cit* page 190.

wanted to achieve, and this dream may have been part of what Booker describes as the "collective fantasy"[106] of the sixties. But fantasy or not, if you had asked us then, we certainly would have wanted to be part of it. Nevertheless, back in reality, as I scraped the crumbs of my breakfast bacon sandwich from the plate, there loomed the question of how to attain the glamour and avoid the desk job.

We needed to get bookings immediately. We had to change the music and style of the band to adapt to the changes largely emanating out of Liverpool and led by the Beatles that had occurred while we were away in France. Then if we were to be free to travel we needed to change the personnel in the band: a new drummer, a new rhythm guitarist, or keyboard player, or an additional (female) singer. The latter would be exceptionally valuable if we were to return to France and the US bases.

Getting local bookings didn't prove too difficult. Despite being misnamed by the Evening Gazette, we were reasonably well known on Teesside and so bookings at the smaller venues such as pubs, working men's clubs and dance halls were relatively easy to obtain. Roy's dad had plenty of contacts from our pre-France time, while Roy and I separately wrote to some of the bigger venues on Tyneside, Wearside and Teesside as well as to booking agents, since the bigger venues preferred to use such agents[107] rather than deal directly

---

[106] Booker *ibid* page 9.
[107] Keith Roberts ex lead guitarist of the Crestas writes on the Picture Stockton website "I introduced Roy Smith of The Denvers and his father Jack, their manager at that time, to Joe Postgate in the early sixties and as a result got them their first

CHAPTER 9

with the bands and artistes[108]. Within weeks of the start of the year we were playing at three, four and more venues a week. Hence the shivering in the van as the cold winter held the north east in its icy grip, followed in the morning by a bleary-eyed walk for Roy and I from our respective homes across Billingham to the Technical College; a trip I often missed as a lie-in proved more attractive than seeking solutions to quadratic equations or explaining why Brutus betrayed Caesar!

Several venues stand out. At one extreme were pubs such as the Cleveland Hotel, South Bank. We had always enjoyed playing there before we went to France and so it was something of a homecoming to play there again in early 1963, although I am not sure we did that much better for a fee than the £4 we received - for the group not each of us! - back in 1961/62. If my memory serves me correct we used our success to bargain an increase to £7-10s. At the other extreme, again in South Bank, was the Sporting Club, which had been transformed from the Hippodrome cinema into a cabaret club that booked a range of top variety artistes as well as bands[109]. The headliners were often some of the top names in the entertainment business and were booked

---

booking with Southern Border Dances." The Crestas drummer Louis Johnson joined the Denvers in 1961 not long after I joined. http://picturestocktonarchive.wordpress.com/2006/03/08/the-crestas-60s-group/

[108] I still have a letter from the McKiernan Agency, of Stockport Cheshire written on 18 July 1963 offering us a choice from 5 dates in August at The Swan Hotel, Redcar, and from two dates in September at The Billingham Arms.

[109] See http://search.catflaporama.com/post/search?query=%22 Sporting+Club%22+South+Bank&board=2

there for the week! So, you could find yourself, as we did, following a snake charmer act onto the stage, having had the privilege of being allowed to handle the snakes - my one and only time - in the shared dressing room before the act went on stage; an experience worth the snakes since the 'charmers' were two beautiful young women, which made the shared dressing room more bearable!

The club was similar in concept to the Empire Continental, which was located next door to Middlesbrough Town Hall and which some argue was Middlesbrough's first night club[110]. We had played there in 1961 with Johnny Rocco, our lead singer capturing a lot of mature female hearts with his renditions of Elvis ballads. But by 1963 I believe it had closed down as a cabaret venue, with bingo no doubt proving more profitable. By 1991 the building was derelict when it was purchased by Barry Faulkner and turned into a successful nightclub/music venue and is still operating to this day.[111] Sadly, the future treated the Sporting Club less kindly than the Empire: it burnt down one Christmas Eve (in the 1970s, I think).

---

[110] See the quote from Eric Whitehouse of Bluecaps fame on the Picture Stockton website" The first night club on Teesside was, I think, the Empire Continental next door to the Town Hall. Variety and cabaret artistes and the odd "beat group" were booked for 7 day stints around '61/'62ish ish. The Contessa and the Bongo followed and then the Marimba. The South Bank Sporting Club was another popular live cabaret venue. Mick Kemp's Blue Caps supported a young Gerry Dorsey complete with Jerry Lewis impressions back in early '65" http://picturestocktonarchive.wordpress.com/2006/04/07/flyers-from-the-fiesta/

[111] http://www.themiddlesbroughempire.co.uk/about.html

CHAPTER 9

There were many other venues that were memorable. The working men's - or 'social' - clubs in north Durham and south Tyneside, such as those in Shildon, Consett, the Team Valley, Tow law - a town later to enter musical legend in Mark Knopfler's magnificent Hill Farmer's Blues - Horden, Shotton, Blackhall and Easington among many others, offered regular bookings in a world that to us, even then, seemed strangely archaic. I discussed some of our earlier experiences playing these clubs in 1961 in Chapter 5. Roger Smith of the Kylastrons and the Six Leaves writes evocatively of his experience of them in 1965:

"Most villages and districts in the North East had at least one Working Men's Club and most of them provided entertainment including local bands (or beat groups as they were called back in 1965). Bands were booked by the club's concert secretary who would address you as 'bonny lad' and refer to your band as 'the torn' (turn in English). It was the concert secretary's job to regularly tell you to turn down the volume. He had the power to pay off the band or give you more bookings depending on how you went down. Audiences were mainly seated but in some clubs towards the end of the night people would get up to dance. The upside of playing at these clubs was that the beer was incredibly cheap and it didn't cost much to get rat arsed and look as if you were enjoying being there. A pint of Federation beer could cost as little as eleven pence (less than 5p in new money). As a comparison, a pint bottle of Newcastle brown ale at that time cost around two shillings and six pence (twelve and a half pence in new money)."[112]

What Roger doesn't stress is that these clubs were male bastions, where miners and colliery workers, or steel workers in places like Consett, were able to drink and chat to their mates of an evening in privileged exclusion from the female of the species, usually their wives. But things changed at the weekend. Wives and girlfriends were encouraged to attend, for drinks, entertainment, bingo and often pie and pea suppers. The men, at least early on in the evening before the cheap Federation beer started to work its way through their bloodstreams, were better behaved and keen to ensure that their partners were content: another shandy, or a Babycham pet? So any band or group that thought they could get away with smutty asides, or a volume of music that might bring the house down had another think coming. As Roger says, the rule of the concert or entertainment's secretary was supreme: transgress and you would be off the stage, your set cut short never to play that club again.

It was while we were playing one of these clubs in the North Durham coalfield that a rather natty bespectacled man approached us in one of our breaks and asked if he could chat with us. He said his name was Tony Kish and he was a producer and director at BBC Newcastle. Our ears pricked up: could a TV or radio performance be in prospect? But no, Tony said he was involved in news and current affairs; although I believe he is the same Tony Kish that went on to direct Byker Grove in the early 2000's. He was a live music fan and would travel locally

---

[112] http://www.readysteadygone.co.uk/category/my-bands/

CHAPTER 9

to see and hear bands that he liked. He had heard about us, hence the reason why he had come to the club and he wanted us to know that we were probably the best local band he had heard .... . Our heads began to swell until he added .... south of the Tyne.

"So who's better than us north of the Tyne?" Roy asked.

Tony clearly sensing that he might have offended us, or damned us with faint praise, was quick to reassure that no they weren't better but just different. The name of the band was the Alan Price Rhythm and Blues Combo, who nine months later in January 1964 would change their name to the Animals.

"What's so special about them?" I queried.

"Well, they have a fantastic earthy blues sound that is unique, featuring a gutsy blues singer and great musicianship, although there are some groups coming out of Liverpool that do American blues in a similar style." Tony replied.

Next day as Roy and I sat droopy-eyed drinking coca-colas in the Billingham Tech canteen Roy said

"I think we have to change."

"Do you mean the music we play, or the members of the group?"

"Both", he replied. "You heard what Tony, whatever his name, said last night. The music that is starting to become popular is Beatles-type music. I know that Cliff and the Shadows have just had *Summer Holiday* reach No. 1 and the Shadows have had *Dance on* and *Foot Tapper*. But it's songs like the Beatles' *Please Please Me* that we need to start playing. The Beatles' sound is very different from the Shadows it is more earthy and less 'nice'. Look that George Harrison doesn't use an echo chamber for his lead solos in the way that Hank does. He also plays a Gretsch semi acoustic and not a Strat."

"And, they don't seem to do any instrumentals like the Shadows." I interjected.

"Yes, it is American rhythm and blues and soul type music that seems to be the key influence. We need to start going back to the Chuck Berry, Carl Perkins and Elvis's Sun recordings that we used to do. We need to get out of the Shadows."

"But", I cautioned, "we are going to lose Johnny Maunder and he's the only one of us that can do songs like *That's Al'right Mama* and *Blue Suede Shoes*."

"Yes, that's true. But Jenny is pretty good at belting out rock songs like *Shakin' All Over*. And groups of girl singers such as the Shirelles and the Marvelettes are becoming popular in the States."

"So, when Johnny leaves maybe we should replace him with another girl singer!" I exclaimed.

"That's just what I was thinking. In fact, I have someone in mind."

"Who?"

"She's called Pauline Riley and lives in Norton. My Dad heard her sing at the Buffs club on Norton Road. He thought she was great and by chance found that he was talking to Pauline's mam."

"Old Mother Riley?"

"Now, now Ashy, get serious. Her mam said that she was keen to work with a group and thought the Denvers would be great."

"But we can't have a singer called Pauline Riley. How naff is that?" I complained.

CHAPTER 9

"No, like Jenny she doesn't use her real name on stage. She sings under the name of Jackie Peters."

Within the month Johnny had left the band and Pauline/Jackie had joined the group and started rehearsing with Jenny, Roy and I. Max was increasingly reluctant to come over to Billingham or Stockton for rehearsals, and we'd heard that he'd been playing some bookings with a trio in Darlington. We knew Max had to go. As I noted in Chapter 8, he was a good drummer: no frills, and kept perfect time. But quite frankly, he scared us. His age, and tough disposition meant that you always feared that if you had a disagreement with him about, say, how he was playing a particular song, he was just as likely to leap off his drum stool and fill you in rather than discuss it with you. Then we had a stroke of luck. One of the group's contacts suggested that we should audition a young guy from West Hartlepool. He was only 15 years of age but he had built a reputation playing in various Hartlepool bands and doing charity shows in working men's clubs. His name was Adrian Tilbrook. We auditioned him at some rehearsal rooms in Stockton and were very impressed, so Roy offered him the job on the spot. Adrian - or "Tilly" as we always called him - immediately accepted. We had a new band.

With two new members it became easier to change the style of the band. We practised hard encouraging Jenny and Pauline to sing together and develop harmonies as well as singing their own songs. The need to have them both sing well together was important because having lost Johnny's rhythm guitar playing a line-up of lead guitar, bass guitar and drums sounded a bit thin. On the positive side, having Pauline in the group as well as Jenny meant that we could do justice to many Shirelles, Marvelettes, Ronettes - a little later - and Crystals' numbers. In 1964, we would add the Supremes to that list. The response to the new line-up and material at some initial bookings appeared to be favourable. Two 'girl' singers made us different from most other groups and the response to the band from the paying customers at the clubs and dances seemed to be favourable. Moreover, the sound of the band began to evolve in other ways.

Roy and I decided that we should say goodbye to our trusty Fenders and replace them with guitars that we believed might better help us attain a country/blues sound. So, using the good offices of Mr Camplin at Burdons we traded in our guitars.[113] Roy purchased a Gretsch double cutaway Chet Atkins and I bought a

---

[113] Many musicians at the time subsequently regretted selling their instruments. Most of us could hardly afford to upgrade our guitars never mind buy additional ones, like many of today's bands with their array of guitars present on stage. I guess a blonde 1961 Fender Stratocaster or Precision bass would be worth quite a bit today. But for every action there is a, sometimes favorable, consequence. Mike Gutteridge writes on the Picture Stockton website: "One afternoon, I was in .... Burdons on Yarm lane, Stockton, and Mr. Camplin the manager showed me a second hand blonde Stratocaster. It had belonged to Roy Smith of the Denvers and it was for sale at £99.00. A new one at the time was £190.00. Most of our fathers would not have been earning £20.00 a week so it really was a fortune. I don't think I went to bed that night. I just played and played. I later traded it in for what I believe was the first Gibson 345 in the area. A price tag of £320.00 which could have almost bought you a house in Tarring Street. How, I wish I'd kept them both...." http://picturestocktonarchive.wordpress.com/2005/01/06/local-60s-group-from-stockton/

CHAPTER 9

Gibson EB-3 bass. I loved my Fender Precision but the Gibson suited me better: it was a smaller scale with frets a little closer together, which was more tolerant of my stubby fingers as they moved up and down the fret board. I had decided to develop bass rhythms that embraced eighth and sixteenth notes in 4/4 time as a way of filling in for the lack of a rhythm guitar. This did not meet with Adrian's approval since he preferred a solid bass beat behind the melody line and not cascades of bass notes scattered all over the neck. The risk of me doing this was that it was harder to keep time, running the risk of each number becoming a race to the finish, something that was anathema to any decent drummer.

But were these changes in personnel, instruments and musical style sufficient to create a sound that would stand comparison with the increasingly popular R&B bands emerging out of Liverpool, Manchester, Sheffield and London? We were soon to find out!

Teesside might have been slow overall to embrace the 'Swinging Sixties' in terms of tastes in clothes, music and other aspects of style. But there were some oases. In early 1963 one of these was the Outlook, Middlesbrough. The Outlook was a small purpose-built department store on Corporation Road. Chris Bailey[114] writes:

---

[114] A graphic-designer, who designed all the publicity for the Teespop'68 Festival and who was involved personally and professionally in many of the popular cultural developments in the 1960s writing eloquently about the period, particularly on the Picture Stockton Archive website.

"It had been purpose-built as a mini-department store, as an investment development by Sinclairs. It contained very high quality ladies and men's fashion departments, a record store, and a hairdressing salon. ...... After shopping during the day you could go downstairs into the "club" (or basement) and enjoy a Hamburger for 1/6d (8p) or a Cheeseburger for 2/- (10p) whilst listening to "popular music"..... The Outlook "cellar" coffee bar was essentially the "Club" each evening. This retail "concept" was 40yrs before the much vaunted Psyche in present day M"bro, and in general far ahead of anything else for years."[115]

The 'Club' downstairs was called the Alcove, reflecting probably the seating and table areas which as Bailey notes were arranged in slightly raised alcoves around the walls, but neither bands nor paying customers new it as such. It was always the Outlook. And a key feature of the Club, which would be anathema to present day clubbers, is that it was alcohol free. Chris Bailey eloquently explains:

"Most people left school and were quickly wage-earning by age 15-16, i.e. two years under the legal drinking age. Many young apprentices were earning almost as much as their own "unskilled" dads. So, the emergence of unlicensed clubs was a viable option. Whilst the "licensed" Astoria

---

[115] http://picturestocktonarchive.wordpress.com/2006/04/04/outlook-club-advertisement/

CHAPTER 9

ballroom in Wilson St had opened (on the site of the Hippodrome Cinema) in 1961, it catered mainly for the "Brylcreem 'n Winklepicker" brigade and their gals, who were by default, post 1950's rooted. The Outlook (unlicensed) therefore provided an alternative for the new breed of young people who were rapidly becoming more interested in both "style" and music, and had a fair amount of disposable income."[116]

The Club was the brainchild of John Benedict McCoy, an amazing blues musician and entrepreneur, who probably did more for the popular music scene on Teesside than anyone else in the 1960s, although the Lipthorpe Brothers,[117] Brian Tennet[118], and Bari Chohan[119] deserve honorable mention. McCoy, thin, bespectacled and always coolly dressed, had an incredible antenna for the future trends in popular music, culture and style. He was well connected to the London scene through friends such as Long John Baldry and was aware before most people of the unique musical sounds coming out of Liverpool, Manchester, and Sheffield as well as London. So, McCoy

---

[116] http://picturestocktonarchive.wordpress.com/2006/04/04/outlook-club-advertisement/

[117] Founders of the famed Fiesta Club in Norton and other venues in Sheffield and elsewhere.

[118] Founder of the KD Club in Billingham and elder son of building contractor Charles Tennet, Tennet Contsruction and then Task Construction, my mum's and my boss, for a while, before I went to University in 1970.

[119] Local impresario, from aged 18, and agent of several local bands, involved with John McCoy in setting up the later Teespop'68 Rock Festival.

managed to book rising bands into the Outlook from Liverpool and elsewhere some time before they became nationally and internationally known. Tony Hargan writes:

> "What I remember most about the Outlook was the number of Liverpool bands booked including The Searchers, The Undertakers, Rory Storm & The Hurricanes, Earl Preston & The TTs etc. I remember seeing Cyril Davies and for me one of the great live club bands at the time – Cliff Bennett & The Rebel Rousers."[120]

And in 1963 we can add the Mersey Beats, the Big Three, and Dave Berry and the Cruisers, from Sheffield, with the *piece de resistance* being the Hollies and the Rolling Stones, who appeared on the same bill at the Club on 12 July 1963. This was the first booking the Rolling Stones had done outside London: for a fee of £65 of which £60 was paid in cash and the remainder paid as a sub to Brian Jones of three packs of Players cigarettes.[121]

So one day after our new line-up had been together for about a month, Roy got a call from John McCoy asking if the Denvers would like to play at the Outlook. Roy agreed a fee, I think of £15, and McCoy said that we would be the local support for a visiting band from

---

[120] http://picturestocktonarchive.wordpress.com/2006/04/04/outlook-club-advertisement/
[121] http://picturestocktonarchive.wordpress.com/2006/04/04/outlook-club-advertisement/

CHAPTER 9

Liverpool. This would be the first of several bookings for us at the Outlook. I can't remember the sequence but we supported the Searchers, the Mersey Beats, the Big Three, Dave Berry and the Cruisers, Cyril Davies Rhythm and Blues All Stars, with Long John Baldry, and jazz legend Johnny Dankworth. Typically when we played at the Outlook I remember that we would get changed upstairs in a room in the store then go downstairs through the store into the club. There was a small changing room at the end of the club to the left of the stage as you looked at it, which was for the use of the 'star' visiting bands and we could use the room when the other band was on stage. But usually after we had played our set we would go out to watch the band as they performed on the low stage. Through observation and from chatting with the members of these groups before and after the gig we picked up a host of tips. In this way the Denvers embraced and adapted the Liverpool Sound: Roy's guitar echo chamber - a Binson Echorec - was finally ditched, although we still retained reverb on the Reslo mikes for vocals, Shadows' instrumentals were off the set list while the blue mohair suits and black under-the-collar ties remained in the wardrobe.

By this time my short career attending classes at Billingham Tech was in ruins and Roy's was only a little better, bolstered by the extra year he'd completed at Grangefield Grammar on his O' Level courses. There seemed little point in concentrating on our studies when most of our daily thoughts were focused on how we could take the Denvers onto another level. It was on one such day in 1963 that Roy and I walked in bright sunshine across to the new Billingham Town Centre during our lunch break at the Tech. I was secretly proud of our new town centre. Largely funded by the substantial rates income that came from the ICI, and in part a product of the energy and enthusiasm of Fred M Dawson, the Town Clerk, the Centre was probably unique in the north of England at that time. Although not officially designated as a 'New Town' under the 1946 Act, like Newton Aycliffe and Peterlee, its construction nevertheless embodied the 'Garden City' concepts of, open spaces, and community facilities (the Billingham Forum containing a theatre, ice rink, swimming pool and a number of sports halls was opened by the Queen in 1967), with walkways offering access to multi-level, car-free shopping. The walk took us past the children's play area and shops such as Dewhurst's, Lipton's, Freeman Hardy Willis and the Chain Library towards the bird-cage like spiral walkway that gave prams, push-chairs and wheelchairs access to the shops on another level. But we don't stop. On past Woolworths, we decide not to go into Finlay's for a cup of coffee but instead turn right and go into Stott's the butchers for a pie and a hot pasty. Pasty and pie in hand we then walk past the real bird cages in the main square - one containing budgerigars, the other canaries and some more exotics - towards the newly opened Brunswick Bowl, on top of which stands a huge bowling pin. We sit on a low wall opposite Sparks cake shop and begin to nibble at our lunch.

"Did you see Sabrina[122] when she opened the bowling alley?" I ask Roy.

---

[122] Wikipedia writes: " Norma Ann Sykes (born 19 May 1936), better known as Sabrina, was a 1950s English glamour model who progressed to a minor movie career. Her main claim to fame was her hourglass figure of prodigious 41-inch (100 cm) breasts

CHAPTER 9

"No, don't be a tit, we were playing that night."

"I'm certainly not as big a tit as Sabrina's! Wish I'd seen them, er... I mean her."

"Me too," leered Roy " but we have more on our minds than Sabrina's chest. We have to take some decisions about the group. I think we should try and go back to France. We have already built up a good reputation amongst the GIs. I'm sure we can get another tour over there and who knows even a recording contract. I think we have a greater chance of getting that in France than here in good old Blighty. We're from an unfashionable part of the country: Stockton/Billingham is no Liverpool and Teesside doesn't have the same attraction to agents and record companies as Merseyside. Maybe we can start to make it big in France and then that might open the door here."

"But we don't have Sam Curtis anymore and, anyway, would you want to have someone like Sam, Starlite Artistes in London and Carl Friedrich in Chateauroux all creaming money off us again?" I protested.

"Yeah, I agree; that's why we need to go directly to an agent in France. And, you know, I have the name and address of an agent based in Paris that one of the club managers back in France recommended to me last year, which I had forgotten about."

"Who is he?"

"He's an ex US soldier, a black man, whose name is Jimmy English."

---

coupled with a tiny 19-inch (48 cm) waist and 36-inch (91 cm) hips .." http://en.wikipedia.org/wiki/Sabrina_(actress)

"A black American who's called English! You must be joking?"

But Roy wasn't joking. Three weeks later after a letter and a couple of 'phone calls, Jimmy had offered us a one month contract at Fontainebleau, which, if we were any good, he would extend for a further five months. A US base at Fontainebleau was to be our first venue, and we had to be there by the first of September. But first we had to travel to Paris to meet Jimmy and sign a contract. Goodbye Billingham, bonjour La France!

CHAPTER 9

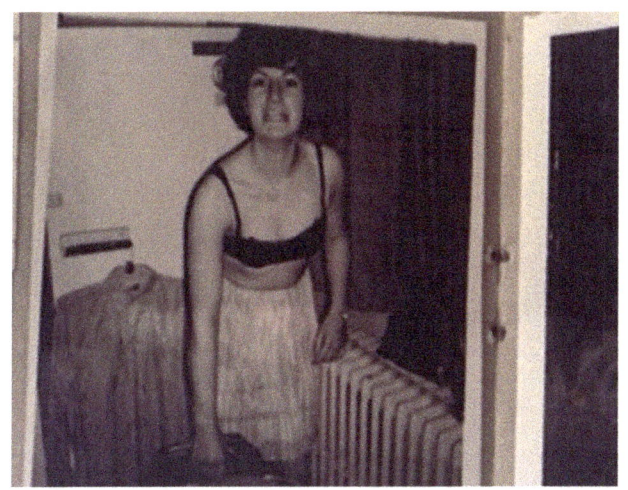

Jenny, Fontainebleau – 'That photo'

The Standard Atlas

Recording at Polydor Studios, Paris

Recording at Polydor Studios, Paris

CHAPTER 9

Recording at Polydor Studios, Paris

Recording at Polydor Studios, Paris

Back home in Billingham, March 1964

The Denvers, US Army General Depot, Ingrandes, April 1964

CHAPTER 9

LP_Front Cover

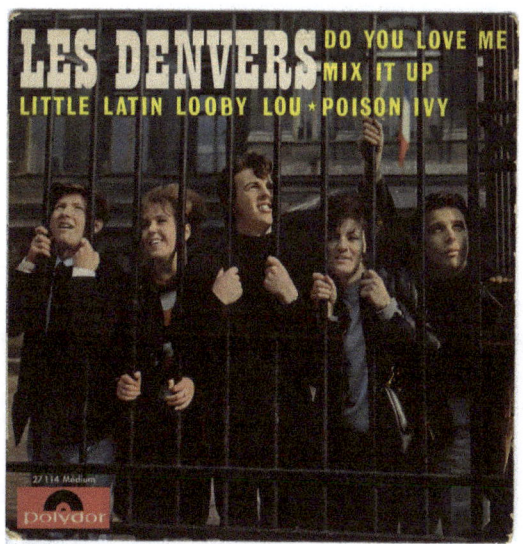

EP Front Cover

B – side of first single

LP on sale in Orleans shop window

CHAPTER 9

Recording for Europe No 1 radio station

Pauline aka Jackie Peters

Jenny and Mal at Prey

BKA, Mal and 'Tilly', US Army General Depot, Chinon, September 1964

CHAPTER 9

The Denvers, US Army General Depot, Chinon, September 1964

CHAPTER 10

ENTER JIMMY ENGLISH

Roy nosed the Standard Atlas through the lunchtime traffic on the Boulevard de Clichy and made a right turn into Rue Blanche and then left into Rue Bruyère. It was a typically late-summer day in Paris and the hot, dusty Paris streets seemed a world away from the weather we had left behind on Teesside. It was 28 August 1963. Nearly, three weeks had passed since the Great Train Robbery had shocked Britain when £2.6 million (around £46 million at today's prices) was stolen from a Royal Mail train travelling between Glasgow and London at the Bridego Railway Bridge, Ledburn near Mentmore in Buckinghamshire[123].

Our journey to Paris had involved a detour to Brussels for a brief vacation capped by a visit to the Atomium[124] built for Expo '58 the 1958 Brussels World Fair - see Chapter 5. Now as we approached Paris our excitement began to build as we wondered where this journey would take us. We dreamed our dreams, but nearly four thousand miles away in Washington DC that day, Martin

---

[123] http://en.wikipedia.org/wiki/Great_Train_Robbery_(1963)
[124] http://en.wikipedia.org/wiki/Atomium

CHAPTER 10

Luther King Jr was articulating a much more profound dream in a speech to over 250,000 civil rights supporters from the steps of the Lincoln Memorial. At the head of the March on Washington he called for an end to racism in the United States and he dreamed a dream where "my four little children will one day live in a nation where they will not be judged by the color of their skin but by the content of their character." And as if to underline Martin Luther King's message out through the door of his office at 29 Rue Bruyère strode Jimmy English, a black American who had been able to build without suffering prejudice or discrimination a successful variety and music agency in France, not in the USA.

"Roy, good to meet you. Why don't you introduce me to the boys and girls in the band."

"Sure," said Roy, and after he had introduced each of us he turned and pointing to Jimmy he said "And, this is Arthur English!" [125]

Our eyes dropped to the pavement, but Jimmy was quick to retrieve the situation:

"Roy, I may wear wide neckties but I ceased to be a 'spiv' and lost my cockney accent years ago. Let's go get some lunch. Do you like Chinese?"

We all nodded; and Roy, suitably chastened as his attempt at being a 'big-shot' evaporated, could only mutter:

"Yes, Jimmy. Sorry, Jimmy."

---

[125] In the post-war years he was considered to be " One of Britain's great variety comedians Arthur English was known as 'The Prince of the Wide Boys', a cockney 'spiv' character outrageously dressed on stage and wearing a huge kipper tie." http://www.imdb.com/name/nm0257583/

Within half an hour we were seated in a very smart Chinese restaurant quite close to Rue Bruyère and Jimmy's French wife had joined us. This of course meant that we had to polish up even more our 'please' and 'thank you's' and try not to wolf the food down too quickly despite the waves of hunger that began to wash over us as soon as the aroma of Chinese food wafted into our nostrils as we entered the restaurant. In Stockton and Billingham in 1963 there were I believe one or two Chinese restaurants, but for most of us our exposure to 'Chinese' food was via the packets of dehydrated Vesta Chicken curry that my mother would occasionally cook as she sought to induce a more cosmopolitan outlook in my father and I. But here was a meal that included egg rolls, dim sum, and banana fritters served by ostensibly authentic Chinese waiters. Needless to say we were impressed. And we were meant to be!

Jimmy said that we would begin our engagement at the EM Club on the US army base in Fontainebleau on September 1st. This would give us enough time to get ourselves settled in to an inexpensive hotel - he gave us some suggestions - and then get over to the base, report to the EM Club manager and move our gear into the club. Jimmy would come down and listen to us play once we had settled in and if we were good enough, which he was sure we were we would be offered a contract for a further five months.

"And guys," he continued "if you are good, there is the possibility of a record deal. Polydor France has noted the success of the Beatles and other Liverpool bands and would like to have a similar band or bands on their books. They are all the more keen to do this

CHAPTER 10

since the company originally recorded the Beatles in Germany as a backing group to Tony Sheridan." We all shuffled in our seats and started to kick each other under the table. "It's in your hands boys and girls." He concluded.

Fifty-five kilometres to the south of central Paris and set within a large forest lies the attractive town of Fontainebleau. It is famous for its elegant Château de Fontainebleau, a palace that was built for Louis XIII (1610-43) by Androuet du Cerceau. It was here at the front of the Chateau that Napoleon in 1814, shortly before his first abdication and exile to Elba, took a final salute from his Old Guard: hand selected veteran soldiers who had served Napoleon since his earliest campaigns. But the history and aesthetic beauty of Fontainebleau were far from our minds as we turned off the Ave Marechal de Villars into the US army base at the Caserne Lariboisiere, which was within easy walking distance of the town centre.

The buildings that formed the core of the base were originally a French military barracks dating back to Napoleonic times and they still exist in much the same configuration today as an Ecole de Gendarmerie. Single Enlisted Men lived in the four floors of the barracks, while married personal lived off post, or "on the economy" to use the GI terminology. In September 1963 there were four military detachments based on the site: HQ personnel, medics, military police (67th M.P. Company) and signals (the 293rd Signal Company). Once through the base security the Headquarters and barracks block lay directly ahead of us and directly behind this imposing building stood the single storey

EM Club[126], which was to be our place of work for the next month.

Once we had found an hotel in the rural outskirts of the town, we soon settled into a similar work routine to the one we had adopted the previous year in north east France: a lie-in to mid-morning, or later(!), coffee and light breakfast at the hotel, then a drive to the base early to mid afternoon , practise until around 4-5pm, a break followed by dinner at the Club, get changed in cramped dressing room diagonally opposite the stage, then on stage at 7.30pm and back to the hotel around midnight. Monday's continued to be our day off, and we would take advantage of the warm, sunny September days and sunbathe on the first floor veranda at the front of the hotel.

We certainly needed to practise. While we had built a reasonable repertoire after Pauline and Adrian had joined the group for a one to two hour gig on Teesside this was far from enough to fill a three to four hour session, six days a week! Inevitably, we would often repeat numbers particularly some of those performed in the early evening when the Club would be nearly empty and there would be just a few tired and sometimes home-sick faces peering into their bottles of Budweiser, Millers or Schlitz. But we also had to keep up with a music scene that was introducing a lot of interesting new songs to add to those by Frank Ifield, Kathy Kirby and the Batchelors that were still popular but which didn't light our fire and we guessed wouldn't do much for the GIs.

---

[126] Actually named the Lower Four Club, presumably because only the Specialist ranks of Spec 4 and below could use the club. Spec 5's were classed as NCOs.

CHAPTER 10

We had mastered most of the tracks of the Beatles *Please Please Me* album released in March and the single *From Me to You* that was released in April. Their next single *She Loves You* was released in August went straight into the UK charts and was at number 1 for much of the month of September. Also in September there was the Searchers' *Sweets For My Sweet*, *By the Way* by the Big Three, *Da Doo Ron Ron* and *Then He Kissed Me* by the Crystals, Brian Poole and the Tremeloes versions of *Twist and Shout* and *Do You Love Me*, and *I Like It* by Gerry and the Pacemakers. We would learn all of them and then try them out on the GIs. Many of these songs would be new to the GIs even though some such as *Twist and Shout*, *Do You Love Me*, and *Sweets for My Sweet*, were actually British covers of usually African American songs. But others such as *By The Way*, *I Like It*, and *I'm Telling You Now*, riding high in the charts that month by Freddie and the Dreamers, were written by the prolific English composer of pop songs: Mitch Murray.[127]

For the most part the GIs loved the songs and our versions of them and having two females vocalising the melody and harmonies gave the songs a special twist, which seemed to be appreciated. This would often lead to enquiries about where they might get hold of the record and so we would direct them to the version by the specific Liverpool or other UK bands and also draw their attention to some of the original US versions. And would we be recording any of them? They often asked. "Maybe" was our usual answer!

---

[127] http://en.wikipedia.org/wiki/Mitch_Murray

A step in that direction was made when Jimmy came down to Fontainebleau to see us play and liked what he heard and saw. So, on 16 September we were offered a contract for the next 5 months: 1st October to 29 February 1964. The contract stated that we were to play for the US Armed Forces in Europe at "various installations as directed by PARTY A" i.e. Jimmy English. So, we didn't know where we would be going when the contract was signed. Not that we were much bothered about that: getting a contract was the key issue. And the fee? $1250 dollars per month and that for the whole band, which for an equal division meant $250 each, or at the dollar sterling exchange rate at the time[128] £90 per month or about £21 per week. This was higher than the average weekly wage in the UK of around £16 per week[129], but it could not be described as big money. Still, we had a contract as professional musicians and Jimmy had made noises that he would try and get an A&R[130] man from the Polydor Paris record label to come and listen to us. But it might not be for a couple of months.

As summer rolled into autumn Fontainebleau and its surrounding forest became more striking as the leaves

---

[128] £1 = 2.79 dollars http://fxtop.com/en/currency-converter-past.php?A=250&C1=USD&C2=GBP&DD=16&MM=09&YYYY=1963&B=1&P=&I=1&btnOK=Go%21

[129] UK goverment figures released on 21 January 1964, see http://en.wikipedia.org/wiki/1964_in_the_United_Kingdom

[130] Artists and repertoire: " the division of a record label or music publishing company that is responsible for talent scouting and overseeing the artistic development of recording artists and/or songwriters." http://en.wikipedia.org/wiki/Artists_and_repertoire

CHAPTER 10

on the trees displayed a complex mixture of deepening hues of gold, brown and red. Occasionally, on our day off, or at weekends, we would drive over to Barbizon admiring the beauty of the autumn forest on the way. Barbizon, is famous for its named school of painters, particularly Jean-Baptiste-Camille Corot, Théodore Rousseau, and Jean-François Millet, who were attracted to paint the natural beauty of the landscape in Barbizon and surrounding area. Millet developed the focus on landscape to embrace scenes of peasant life, as in his famous painting *The Gleaners (1857)*, which portrays three peasant women working at the harvest.[131] Of course, at the time we had only a hazy awareness of the cultural significance of Barbizon. For us, a visit to Barbizon was a pleasant afternoon trip out. However, some of the GIs told us that close to Barbizon were some high-class nightspots where top American stars such as Frank Sinatra would go to chill out, or live it up, when they were visiting France. We never did find out if this was true, or whether our legs were being pulled.

Back in our own nightspot we were about to meet some American stars who were, at that time, as famous as Frank Sinatra. A GI friend told us that the Everly Brothers were to appear at the base NCO club the next night and he could via his contacts at the club, arrange for us to meet them after we had both finished our shows at the EM and NCO clubs, respectively. Moreover, he would bring along his camera, he was a photographer on the base, and take a photo of us together. Naturally, we jumped at the chance. We learned that the Everlys

---

[131] See http://en.wikipedia.org/wiki/Barbizon_school

had arrived in France to play the Paris Olympia on 23 September, after which they were doing some shows for US forces at bases around Paris before travelling to England to begin a tour of the UK on the 29th. The Everlys were to top the bill, Bo Diddley and Little Richard were to support and the show would be opened by the Rolling Stones, which was to be their first UK concert tour after their foray to the Outlook in Middlesbrough in July. By the end of the tour in November, the Stones had recorded their second single, *I Wanna Be Your Man*[132] and were on their way to a position in the rock and pop pantheon that would eclipse even the Everlys.

We, meanwhile, were standing outside the NCO club slightly shivering in a light drizzle when the doors to the kitchen and storeroom were pushed open and out walked Don and Phil. A Citroen DS car simultaneously pulled up alongside. We were introduced. They were charming, especially Don, while Phil although not unfriendly was taciturn. We spoke about music and the Beatles in particular in whom they showed a keen interest, with Phil smiling when I told him that his hairstyle was now closer to a Beatle cut, if a little shorter, than the swept back quiff that he had traditionally sported. The photo was then taken: me in the middle, Jenny, Don and Adrian to my right, Pauline, Phil and Roy to my left. The light from the flashbulbs had hardly faded before they jumped into the back of the Citroen, which then sped smoothly and quickly on its hydro pneumatic suspension towards the main gate of the base and out into the damp night.

---

[132] Written by Lennon and McCartney, and reaching No 12 in the UK charts.

CHAPTER 10

On October 4th, the *Billingham Express* ran a short article in its inside pages with the headline "Denvers provide backing for the Everly Brothers" above the photo of us with Don and Phil. This was clearly the product of an over-enthusiastic Denvers PR department, in the form of a letter written by Roy to the paper. Many more of these letters were to be written to the *Express* with the paper duly and less than critically reporting the contents. For example, on February 14, 1964 a piece appeared in the *Express* - next to an advert for Gerry and the Pacemakers forthcoming 21st February appearances at Stockton's Globe, "Now Booking - 10/6, 8/6, 6/6" - with the headline " 'Tres Bon' is verdict on Les Denvers". The paper had received a letter from The Denvers, Central Publicity Office, 39 Rue Bruyere, Paris, and reports, slightly tongue in cheek:

"The contents of the letter were even more surprising. According to the writer a certain Jacques Belfort, the Denvers are very much in the limelight over there. And how! M. Belfort says many inquiries about the Denvers have been received from Teesside. He claims differing newspaper reports have confused the facts, and asks me to make them clear ..." There then follows a listing of the personnel in the group ending with ".... and Adrian Tilbrook , 15 year-old drummer, from West Hartlepool."

The article continues:

"M. Belfort says the Everly Brothers like Adrian's work so much they wanted to retain him as permanent drummer. Adrian decided to honour his Denvers' contract and refused their offer. The last two paragraphs of the letter make interesting reading: 'They (the Denvers) are all very English, and all name fish and chips as their favourite dish. Black pudding, steak-and-kidney-pud and pear drops are also favourite eats. They like the Beatles ('cos of the 'air), Eddie Cochran, Bo Diddley and Chuck Berry, and, of course, the Muddy Waters, the Contours and Johnny Horton. They are well liked over here, because they are just like a normal bunch of kids. They joke about and are not stiff-collared like so many bands. There was an article in a Paris paper about them throwing threepenny bits off the Eiffel Tower. "Asked by a reporter why, they answered: 'Because we have run out of pound notes!" ' That's show business!"

Close inspection of M. Belfort's syntax shows an unusual degree of symmetry with the syntax of a certain M. Roy Smith, although I think the use of the word 'the' - think Les - in front of Muddy Waters may have been designed to throw the intrepid *Billingham Express* reporter off the scent!

By March 1964 the hyperbole had got worse. We had recorded our LP in Paris in February, of which more later, and had returned to Teesside for a month's vacation in March. On 13 March the *Express* ran an article with a banner headline on page 5: "Teesside beat group's disc tops 200,000 before issue." Accompanying the article at the foot of the page was a photograph of the four Teesside members of the band - Jenny being on holiday in London - strolling arm in arm through Billingham Town

CHAPTER 10

Centre with winning smiles on our faces. Next to the photograph of us was a photograph of the equally smiling, and more winning, Frank Ifield who was advertised to appear at Stockton's Globe for a week commencing April 6th. However, Ifield's star must by then have been on the wane because in contrast to Gerry and the Pacemakers the seat prices to see him were a mere 7/6d, 6/- and 4/6d. Indeed, in a further low blow to Ifield, the advert above his in the paper for the Hippodrome Stockton offered at 8/6d, 6/6d and 4/6d seat prices the following fare:

ON THE STAGE

JOHN COLLIN

and TV's DELIGHTFUL PERSONALITY - THE WIGGLE-GIRL
from 'DOUBLE YOUR MONEY'
NANCY ROBERTS

in the UPROARIOUS COMEDY by CHARLES DYER
RATTLE OF A SIMPLE MAN
with BRIAN CULLIS

Commencing Monday, March 9 Week.

Nancy is pictured by the *Express* above the advert in tight black sweater, with flowing blonde locks, head cocked and another winning, 'Double Your Money' smile.

Meanwhile, adjacent to these adverts the *Express* appeared to have belatedly begun to smell a rat with the Denvers' proclaimed progress towards superstardom.

Referring to the two hundred thousand advance orders for "Les Denvers first E.P." the paper notes:

> "This is the shock claim of 18-year-old Roy Smith, leader of the group who are now enjoying a month's vacation in Billingham after playing in France since last September."

But clearly not wishing to spoil a Billingham success story the *Express* reported the band as " . . riding the crest of a wave." Roy and Pauline a.k.a. Jackie are then allowed to tell *Express* readers what the Denvers' success is really all about.

First Roy:

> "We have got ourselves a good reputation on the Continent. There are too many groups all trying to do the same thing in England. If we did exactly the same over here *we would be earning a good deal less*" (Italics added)

Then Pauline/Jackie:

> "We wouldn't give it up for anything. *Where else could I earn so much money* at the age of 17?" (Italics added)

Let me remember what that contract said: $1,250 dollars per month for the whole band, about £21 per week if shared equally. If the *Express* was not completely fooled by our claims of success then we certainly were, or at least we desperately wanted to believe in that success. We had to buy into the myth of financial

CHAPTER 10

and popular success otherwise what we had given up in terms of schooling and normal career prospects would have been hard to justify.

Back in Fontainebleau another photograph, less auspicious than the one with the Everlys, began to cause us problems and for Jenny in particular.

A band on tour spends most of the day together and so becomes a family. The caution, reserve and inhibitions that govern most human relationships fall away. We were no different. We became as brothers and sisters, less concerned about personal space and privacy and more likely to argue with one another which, given our youth, occasionally led to blows. There was no separate dressing room for the girls. We all mucked in together. So, one day when Roy took a photograph of Jenny in her bra and waist slip as she was getting ready to go on stage little was thought or said about it. A couple of days later Roy passed the roll of exposed film to our Everly photographing GI friend asking him if he wouldn't mind developing the film and making some prints. The prints were duly returned to Roy. We all had a little giggle at some of the snaps and then thought no more about them. That is until we drove into the base one day, entered the EM Club and found ourselves confronting two large Military Policy men intimidating in their white caps with black peaks, well-pressed light khaki fatigues, black and white MP armbands, shiny black boots and black belt with holster and gun attached on one side and baton or nightstick on the other.

"We'd like you to accompany us ma'am."
"Why, what's happened?"

"It's nothing to worry about, we and some colleagues from the British Military Police just want to ask you a few routine questions." And with that they walked out of the club with Jenny between them.

The rest of us just looked at each other as we fumbled for cigarettes and lighters muttering things like "What the fuck's going on?" But all we could do was get on with our rehearsal and wait. Meanwhile, over at the HQ building Jenny was being given the third degree - well, almost. They showed her a print of Roy's photo in her bra and slip.

"Can you confirm that this is you?"

"Yes, but ......"

"Do you know that many copies of this photo are circulating around the base?"

"No, this is just a snap taken of me in the dressing room by Roy the leader of our band."

"And what about this photo?" A black and white picture of a dark haired nude woman with her back to the camera is pushed across the table towards Jenny.

"Is that you?"

"No, I am fairly certain it isn't me."

"Are you sure it isn't you?"

"Well her hair's longer and her bum's smaller for a start; lucky cow!"

"This is no time for jokes ma'am. We believe you may have been offering services other than music to the GIs."

"What, you're accusing me of being on the game?"

"Have you any convictions for soliciting back in the UK?" At which point, the British MP, small, slightly seedy looking and much less smartly dressed than the

CHAPTER 10

Americans, leaned across the table towards Jenny and said:

"We can check you know!"

"You can check as much as you bloody well like. I have no convictions for anything. Now let me out of here."

But the questioning continued for some time before a tired and angry Jenny was allowed to return to the Club a little more than half an hour before the start of the evening's show.

Nothing came of it because it was purely the fantasy of the Military Police. Perhaps it is understandable that the MPs had to investigate when it came to their attention that several copies of the photo were in circulation at the base. A prostitute plying her trade on the base under the cover of a female singer would clearly be a problem for the military authorities who had to manage the hundreds of young, horny and relatively rich GIs in their charge. But the photo was innocuous enough. The incident put a great strain on Jenny. There was clearly the risk that some of the GIs would conclude that there was no smoke without fire and try to proposition her, or think she was an easy lay. It tainted the remainder of our stay in Fontainebleau that month. Yet, Jenny being the trooper that she was did not name the GI who had printed Roy's snaps.

In October we moved to a US base at Ingrandes near Chatellerault in the Poitou-Charentes region. The accident with our Atlas van - see Chapter 5 - was not an auspicious start as we nursed our sore heads and cuts and bruises for a few days afterwards. The base at Ingrandes was quite different from Fontainebleau. While the Fontainebleau base was small and compact using old

French army barracks close to the city centre, Ingrandes was about five kilometres outside Chatellerault and the base itself was large, well spread out in rural surroundings with purpose built, but very functional, buildings. The EM Club was basic but had lots of atmosphere with the GIs' tables close to the stage. This was in stark contrast to some of the later clubs such as Chinon where the stage was set well back from the tables with a large dance floor acting like a sea between the audience and us. What made it worse was that the sea was usually empty because there were little or no women for the GIs to dance with on weekdays and only a few more at weekends. But the open dance floor did have one advantage. It allowed Jenny and Pauline to come down from the stage and do a floorshow type act on the dance floor. Jenny's rendition of the song *Fever*, in the version made famous by Peggy Lee's 1958 recording, was particularly popular, as was *Shakin' all over*, at least in part because she was almost lying on the floor by the time the song ended. And all this was usually performed in a tight black sexy shift dress. And we thought the GIs came to hear our music!

Black shift dress notwithstanding, we continued to take our music seriously by rehearsing new songs and seeking to improve our existing repertoire. This meant that we even went into the Ingrandes EM Club to rehearse on Saturday mornings! On the first Saturday of our stay in Ingrandes, 5 October, we paused our rehearsal to listen to *Saturday Club* which went out on the BBC Radio Light Programme, which we had little difficulty in getting in the middle of France. As noted in Chapter 4, the programme, hosted by Brian Matthew, went out from 10am to 12pm UK time every Saturday

CHAPTER 10

morning and if I was out of bed it became essential listening in my early teenage years. The programme offered live performances, sometimes pre-recorded, of the top pop stars of the day and so was much different from the packaged playlist of singles that formed most pop music radio programmes. This meant from a musical standpoint you could get a better idea how the band or singer actually sounded since the BBC would not play around with the music and add effects in the way that recording studios, even then, were want to do. In addition, while Brian Matthew was intrinsically "old school' he was intelligent and usually sympathetic to the bands and their music, in stark contrast to the inane, self-obsessed chatter from the DJs that soon was to dominate the airwaves on BBC Radio 1 and the commercial radio stations. October 5th was a special day too: it was the fifth anniversary show. The Beatles were billed to be on it doing a pre-recorded 'Happy Birthday' for the show as well as host of other top acts[133]: The Rolling Stones, The Everly Brothers, Frank Ifield, Joe Brown & The Bruvvers, Clinton Ford, Kathy Kirby, Arthur Greenslade & The Gee Men, Tommy Roe, and Kenny Ball's Jazzmen. While we were happy to continue our practising while Frank Ifield and Kathy Kirby were on we had our ears glued to the radio when the Beatles and the Everly's appeared.

---

[133] There is some confusion in the sources about who exactly appeared on the show, particularly whether the Rolling Stones actually appeared – see http://en.wikipedia.org/wiki/Saturday_Club_(BBC_radio) and http://epguides.com/SaturdayClub/. My memory fails me unfortunately.

The interview with the Everly's and their subsequent performance of two songs[134]: *Walk Right back* and *Wake Up Little Susie* was especially interesting to us because we had met them a little over a week before in Fontainebleau. Listening to the one-minute, thirty-second interview with them before they played their two songs we basked in a form of reflected glory, as if a little bit of their fame had attached to us following our meeting and brief conversation with them. Then just before the interview ended Matthew asked Don and Phil about their then current home in Southern California and whether they were surfers. They replied that they were not but the surfers had their own language and distinctive hairstyle with Phil responding to Matthew's question "What's it like?" with "It's sort of similar, I guess, to what would be called a Beatle haircut here, you know." I shouted to the rest of the group: "I told him that!" Which was sort of true because in our brief conversation I mentioned to Phil that his own hair, which had lost its quiff, was like a Beatle haircut and he replied " …is that what you would call it?" Whether he did get it from me or not it certainly made my day: Brian Ashcroft, aspiring pop star/bass player and now cultural adviser to the Everly Brothers!

Paradoxically an opportunity for possible fame and fortune would be given to Roy that very same day and it would pass him by. The Billingham Express of Friday October 11th, 1963 under the headline *Roy misses a big*

---

[134] The interview and songs can be heard on You Tube here: https://www.youtube.com/watch?v=y61YZLsSO3c

CHAPTER 10

chance outlined, more or less accurately, for once, what happened:

> "Roy Smith, 17-year-old leader of the Billingham rhythm group, the Denvers, was this week offered a first-class ticket to hit parade success. But he was unable to take it.
>
> The offer was made on Saturday by Mr. Sam Curtis, London agent and manager for many recording artists. It was: 'Do you want Jet Harris's job in the guitar-drums duo with Tony Meehan?'
>
> Jet Harris pale, blonde (sic) ex-member of the Shadows announced last week, 'I'm quitting show business.'
>
> Immediately Mr. Curtis had to search frantically for a good lead guitarist to team up with drummer Meehan in a provincial tour which was to start at the week-end.
>
> So on Saturday a telegram was sent to Roy Smith's home in Finchale Avenue, Billingham, asking him to take Harris's place. Unfortunately, Roy was not there.
>
> His father, Mr. Jack Smith told the 'Express': 'Roy is still in France with the Denvers. There was a bit of a mix-up over the telegram and I was not able to contact him until Sunday afternoon. By then Mr Curtis had got someone else.
>
> He added: 'If Roy hadn't been in France he could have taken the job. It was quite a chance.'
> ....

The *Express* article while accurately relating the events surrounding the telegram to Roy, left a couple of questions unanswered: Why had Jet said he was quitting show business? And, why did Sam try and replace Jet, a bass player, with a lead guitarist such as Roy? As to the first question, while Jet Harris did have drink problems when he was in the Shadows and afterwards, giving up alcohol completely later on, he was not a loony who would suddenly walk out on his successful new partnership with Meehan. What happened according to his obituary by Spencer Leigh in the *Independent*[135] was that Jet had been involved in a serious car accident with his girlfriend, the singer Billie Davis, in late September in which he had been quite badly hurt. Spencer Leigh suggests that his manager (Sam) insisted that he do the *Thank Your Lucky Stars* TV show where Harris and Meehan were due to appear not long after the accident. Harris refused, leaving Meehan to mime to the record on the programme alone, and walked out. He was found by the press three months later living with his girlfriend in digs in Brighton. And the reason why Sam wanted to replace Jet with a normal lead guitarist was that Jet's work with Meehan was closer to lead guitar work than normal bass guitar. For example, on their first hit record *Diamonds* recorded in late 1962 with a young Jimmy Page of future Led Zeppelin fame on rhythm guitar, Jet had used a standard six string Fender Stratocaster detuned one whole tone to produce a more bassy sound while still retaining the range of the six string guitar. However, in later recordings and in his stage performances he frequently used a Fender VI, an electric six string bass guitar.

---

[135] See http://www.independent.co.uk/news/obituaries/jet-harris-bassist-who-enjoyed-solo-success-after-being-sacked-by-the-shadows-2246304.html

CHAPTER 10

So had Roy missed a big chance? I doubt Roy would have taken it even if he could have been contacted on the Saturday. The offer from someone whom we knew well and who knew Roy well was clearly flattering and an indicator of how Roy's talents were viewed favourably by people at the top of the music business. But it would have seemed likely that the offer if real, and not one offered to many, would not have led anywhere. It could only have been a stopgap appointment for some or all of the tour. He was being asked to replace a member of a famous duo! A duo that had effectively broken up and would not reform. There was clearly no future in the arrangement. However, Roy would have moved into a circle of musicians that might have led to greater future opportunities than he had with the Denvers. In addition, to the Harris-Meehan link to Jimmy Page, John Paul Jones – later bass player for Led Zeppelin – was starting out his career as the bass player in the supporting band to Harris and Meehan on the tour that Roy had been asked to join. So maybe this was, as the *Express* said, a big chance missed.

However, playing lead guitar for the Denvers at a US base in Ingrandes in October 1963 did offer some consolations. One of these was Yana! Yana was, in the words of this biography:

"b. Pamela Guard, 16 February 1932, Romford, Essex, England, d. 21 November 1989, London, England. A popular singer in the UK during the 50s and 60s ……. In the 50s her single releases included sultry renderings of 'Small Talk', 'Something Happened To My Heart', 'Climb Up The Wall', 'If You Don't Love Me', 'I Miss You, Mama', 'I Need

You Now' and 'Mr Wonderful'. Her glamorous image made her a natural for television, and she was given her own BBC series in 1956. Later, following the advent of ITV, she appeared regularly on Sunday Night At The London Palladium. In 1958, Yana starred in Richard Rodgers and Oscar Hammerstein II's Cinderella at the London Coliseum ...... Two years later she was back in the West End with Norman Wisdom in the London Palladium's longest-running pantomime, Turn Again Whittington. She was something of a pantomime 'specialist', and throughout the 60s and into the 70s, was one of Britain's leading principal boys. ...... In her heyday Yana toured abroad, including the Middle East, and she appeared on several US variety shows hosted by Bob Hope and Ed Sullivan. She also played small roles in the British films Zarak, with Victor Mature and Michael Wilding, and The Cockleshell Heroes, an early Anthony Newley feature. Her last performance is said to have been as the 'Good Fairy' in The Wizard Of Oz at an English provincial theatre in 1983. She died of throat cancer six years later."[136]

Yana *was* glamorous, a classy Sabrina – see Chaper 9 - with talent![137] And because of the entertainment successes she had in America, noted in the biography above, as well as her voluptuous looks she was considered

---

[136] From http://www.allmusic.com/artist/yana-mn0000587834/biography

[137] A fan web page devoted to Yana can be found here http://yanaguard.webs.com

CHAPTER 10

suitable by the USO as an entertainer for US troops. So imagine the sense of anticipation and excitement experienced by three teenage male musicians when we heard that she was coming to perform a so-called "floorshow" – USO term – at the EM Club in Ingrandes. On the appointed day, we went on stage and performed the opening set and then it was Yana's turn. The GIs, as the saying goes, "went wild" as Yana with true professionalism wrapped them around her little finger. Her show over, we returned to the stage to finish off the evening's entertainment. Then while we were playing Yana appears at the side of the club with her manager and watches and applauds our set. When we finish and the club empties she comes over to us and praises our performance, buys us all drinks, shows genuine interest in us by asking where we come from in England, how long had we played in France and so on, and in the process adds three teenage boys, at least, to her list of lifelong fans.

During our time working the US military bases there were of course many USO floorshows visiting and performing at the clubs where we were in monthly residence. For some of these shows Adrian and myself were asked to play drums and bass respectively in support of the act who might have brought no more than a supporting keyboard player to back his or her performance. Understandably, this could be quite a nerve racking experience when they stuck sheet music in front of us just before they were about to go on stage with often no rehearsal or sound check. We just had to get on with it. Adrian being the brilliant musician that he was took this in his stride. I managed to get by, but only just.

Of course being in such a position had its compensations. A popular act with the GIs was the belly-dancer shows. Occasionally, the dancers would let one of the GIs get up and dance with them, producing a battery of howls and wolf-whistles from his buddies in the club. So I, if providing rhythmic support to the dancers, would find my eyes drifting away from the blur of notes on the bass clef, often in compound time signatures such as 9/8, to the twisting and gyrating, sparsely clad, backside only a few inches – the stages were usually quite small! – away from me. The distraction would became almost unbearable and the beat from the rhythm section would frequently falter if the dancer turned her backside to the audience and while still shaking her buttocks ever so slowly leaned forward towards us!

Of course very few of the floorshows were as exotic as Turkish belly dancers but the variety was huge, with conjurors, magicians, an occasional trick-cyclist, fire-eaters, sword swallowers, knife and tomahawk throwers, plate spinners and more, all parading their talents in front of the GIs. The common thread, if there was one, was that usually the act featured a sparsely clad and very attractive female, who helped salve temporarily the homesickness and military tedium borne by the young GIs.

But not all the floorshows were run-of-the-mill variety acts; there were occasional shows by top US artists such as the Everly Brothers performance at Fontainebleau mentioned earlier. We were fortunate to play, at the humble EM Club at the US Army Signal headquarters in Orleans in May 1964, on the same bill as Billy Eckstine, one of the greats of popular music in the twentieth century. A former big band leader in the 1940s with an array of future jazz names playing in the band including Dizzy Gillespie, Dexter Gordon, Miles Davis, Art Blakey, Charlie Parker, and Fats Navarro, with Sarah Vaughan as female vocalist, he would subsequently become one of the greatest singers of jazz and popular songs[138]. Lionel Hampton[139] said of him

> "He was one of the greatest singers of all time.... We were proud of him because he was the first Black popular singer singing popular songs in our race. We, the whole music profession, were so happy to see him achieve what he was doing. He was one of the greatest singers of that era ... He was our singer."[140]

The Orleans EM Club comprised a small L shaped room with a small stage at the apex of the L. The dressing room for the band and visiting artistes was in fact a small storeroom containing largely crates of beer at the foot of the L. Each evening the longer arm of the L was populated by white GIs while in the shorter arm sat the black GIs. During the time we played there in 1964 racial tensions were running quite high. This was brought home to us starkly when on our first evening playing the club Pauline/Jackie accepted an invitation from one of the black GIs to sit at his table and have a drink during the band's break. We thought nothing of it, until next day when we entered the club we were told in no uncertain terms by the white GI EM Club manager that our 'girls' must not fraternise with the black GIs. Our response was to say that if our 'girls' could not fraternise with the black GIs then the whole band would not 'fraternise'

---

[138] Source http://en.wikipedia.org/wiki/Billy_Eckstine
[139] See http://en.wikipedia.org/wiki/Lionel_Hampton
[140] Source http://en.wikipedia.org/wiki/Billy_Eckstine

with anyone, white or black. We asked for a table next to the stage and in our breaks that is where we sat. The GIs, white or black could come over and talk to us but we didn't and wouldn't go to them. It made life difficult but we didn't want to provoke a race riot. Moreover, while we had experienced some of the racial tensions that existed between the black and white GIs when we played at Vassincourt in 1962, we found it difficult to comprehend racial prejudice it was simply beyond our ken. We took people as we found them and made friends irrespective of their colour. Added to this were our positive feelings about so-called 'black' music such as the blues, soul and jazz to a lesser extent. Many of the black GIs were more into such music than the white GIs and therefore had a lot in common with our musical tastes and so were interesting to talk to. We were also interested in country music and rockabilly, which was more a 'white' preserve and so we would often compare notes with white GIs about such music. The key point was that our musical and other interests were not exclusive and it irritated us that we were being implicitly asked by the club management to make choices based on race.

It was into this atmosphere that Billy Eckstine, Mr. B, an icon of black music, stepped one spring evening in 1964. Still trim and handsome in his fiftieth year and past the highpoint of his career he, nevertheless, played a set to the GIs that was of such quality, playing trumpet as well as singing, that it simply transcended the racial tensions in the Club. The white GIs seemed just as enthusiastic about his performance. Moreover, it seemed to us, and I suspect to all of the audience as well, that he was such a good guy. Despite his stardom he uncomplainingly shared the 'dressing room' of beer crates with us, although we were discreet enough to get out of the room when he and his small supporting trio arrived to change for their act. As usual with visiting acts, we went on first then returned to the stage once the 'star' had performed to play the last hour or so of the evening. He stayed awhile, applauded our music then walked out waving to us on stage as he left leaving behind a warm glow in all parts of the club. Billy Eckstine was one of the nicest entertainers I have ever met, he was courteous, considerate and displayed great humility: a star and a true gentleman. I mourned his passing in 1993.

Back in October 1963, seven months before we were to meet up with Billy Eckstine, our thoughts were turning to our next residence. Jimmy had been curiously quiet and we had heard little from him during the month. Roy would occasionally speak to him on the 'phone, usually to complain about our pay and the cost of hotel bills, food, drink and cigarettes. Without the US bases where we had access to cheap food, booze, clothes and ciggies we would really have struggled, since our hotel costs consumed such a large part of our income. Jimmy's response was usually to plead poverty in his inimitable way: "No money, man! No more money. I got you the best deal I could." And if Roy pressed too hard Jimmy's ultimate weapon was to remind Roy about "Mah heart Roy, mah heart." So, for fear of Jimmy's ample frame being found lifeless sprawled across his expensive Parisian desk, Roy backed off. Then, just as we were beginning to wonder if he had abandoned us, he'd come walking in through the door of the EM Club, immaculately dressed in a medium brown wool suit, shiny brown brogues, a beige shirt with button down collar, topped by a fawn knitted tie and a smile beaming from his round dark brown face. "Hey, so you guys are up!" It was two o'clock in the afternoon! "Practising, that's what I like to see. Keep the tunes fresh and the boys wanting more."

"So, where do we go next Jimmy?" we asked.
"Camp des Loges."
"Where's that?" Roy asked.
"Paris, Roy. Gay Paree dear boy. Gay Paree."

CHAPTER 11

A TASTE OF PARIS

"If you are lucky enough to have lived in Paris as a young man, then wherever you go for the rest of your life, it stays with you, for Paris is a moveable feast." — Ernest Hemingway, A Moveable Feast

Well, not Paris exactly! We were to stay at Saint-Germain-en-Laye about 12 miles or 20 kilometres to the west of Paris. And the US base we were scheduled to be resident at was not just any base it was Camp des Loges, the headquarters of the US European Command (EUCOM). EUCOM headquarters had in 1954 relocated to Camp-de-Loges, a French Army base west of Paris near to Supreme Headquarters Allied Powers Europe (SHAPE). Previously the headquarters had operated for two years in the I.G. Farben Hochhaus (renamed the C. W. Abrams Building) in Frankfurt[141]. EUCOM had been under the leadership of the distinguished US General, Lyman Lemnitzer[142], since January 1963. His

---

[141] Source: The History of EUCOM http://www.eucom.mil/mission/background/history-of-eucom
[142] Source: http://en.wikipedia.org/wiki/Lyman_Lemnitzer

appointment[143] was actually a demotion from his role as Chairman of the Joint Chiefs of Staff in the US at the end of his term of office because of his strong anti-communist and ant-Cuban views. Indeed, it has been somewhat improbably suggested that Lemnitzer had a key role in both the 1944 reintroduction of the Mafia into Sicily and in the Kennedy assassination, which was to dominate our lives just three weeks after we started at Camp des Loges, out of revenge for the demotion and for Kennedy being soft on communism[144]! Anyway, in Lemnitzer's day job EUCOM's task was to prepare plans for the defence of Western Europe within the NATO framework against the Soviet Union and Warsaw Pact[145].

So that was the big picture and a million miles from our concerns as we set up our gear in the EM Club after the long, cramped drive from Ingrandes. The club was a simple rectangle, adjacent and connected to the NCO Club. At the two narrower ends of the rectangle were the stage and the bar respectively. In fact the bar, being the main reason most of the GIs would enter the club, was large and spread across the corner and part way up the right long side of the rectangle. The GIs entering the club would be confronted by the bar on their right, several tables and chairs and at the end running across the full length of the top of the rectangle stood the stage.

---

[143] Lemnitzer was both commander of U.S. European Command (EUCOM), and Supreme Allied Commander Europe of the North Atlantic Treaty Organisation (NATO), so not such a terrible demotion!
[144] Source: http://www.progressivepress.com/book-listing/gladio-natos-dagger-heart-europe
[145] Source: http://en.wikipedia.org/wiki/United_States_European_Command

CHAPTER 11

It was a high stage, about 3 to 4 feet off the ground and had to be entered by steps at the side. Needless to say the high stage promoted much swearing and cursing from us as we struggled to lug amplifiers, drums, guitar cases, microphones and stands and our own PA system up the stairs and onto stage.

"If you guys were in the army then you wouldn't be puffing and panting so much!"

These words from a medium-sized guy as he walked towards the stage dressed in civies wearing a black blazer, grey slacks and a white open-necked shirt. A pair of black horn-rimmed spectacles and a smart hairstyle set off his tanned Italian features, a hairstyle which was longer and more civilian than the almost cropped regulation cuts imposed on the GIs.

"I'm Howard DeSilva, the manager of this club and you'll be working for me while you're here. You will behave properly while you are in the club, you will start on time at 19.00 hours prompt, take only short breaks, you will not drink too much, and you will respect the clientele." Then his gaze settled on Jenny and Pauline: "And for you lovely ladies, the number one rule is you don't fraternize with the GIs, accepting a drink is ok but no more and I guess you know what I mean by that?" He smiled, turned away then with a flick of his coiffured head back in our direction he shouted: "And, welcome to Camp des Loges!"

Needless to say we waited until we were sure he was out of earshot before mumbling to each other choice phrases such "wop prick". "Who the fuck does he think he is?" "Bet he just wants to try and get Jenny and Pauline for himself." And Jenny responding with "you must be joking that speccy-eyed bastard has no chance, he wouldn't get a job as the doorman at the Ealing Cinema back home never mind bloody entertainments manager." In fact, Howard DeSilva's bark was much worse than his bite. He ran a professional club and never bothered us since we did as we were told. Indeed, on one occasion during our stay at Camp des Loges he invited the whole group to his home for a barbecue. We ate on a first floor terrace at the back of his home - it was November! This I believe was our first exposure to New York strip steaks cooked on charcoal: an exquisite taste which neither I nor Roy – he tells me - have been able to emulate in any steak that we have cooked since.

A much bigger human shadow than Howard DeSilva fell across our lives during the next two months in the form of a Mrs Benson!

Jimmy English, as always concerned about the welfare of the young souls in his charge, arranged for us to stay with a US army family in Saint-Germain-en-Laye. The father was a US army Master Sergeant who stayed with his wife and daughter in a large house they rented near to the base. Their home more a chateau than a house was called Le Couleau a name, which did not seem to have an English translation, although some said the name meant running water. We turned up on the doorstep that first day to be greeted by a less than friendly Mrs Benson complaining that we were too late for dinner, which was always eaten at 6pm and we had better not forget it. Mrs Benson was a German woman who had married her US husband during an earlier tour of his in Germany. She looked formidable and was! Her German accented English prompted us to giggle behind her back that we "mustn't talk about the war!" – and this was long before *Faulty Towers*. Mrs Benson – we

CHAPTER 11

knew no other name and did not dare ask if we could be on first name terms – mirrored almost exactly any stereotyped image we might have of a German *hausfrau*. She ran the house like a military operation. We were not the only guests and we shared our meals with Bob an affable Spec 4 US serviceman from SHAPE. Cooking was Mrs Benson's pride and joy as she served us classic German meals heavy on cabbage and sausage, which in our vocabulary were best described as stews. Mind you, these hot substantial meals were necessary because the winter of 1963-64 was cold and inside the house was little warmer than the outside.

Jenny and Pauline were banished to a room at the top of the house and despite the laws of physics their room seemed to be the coldest place. So in recognition of this and in an act of international goodwill Mrs Benson allowed Jenny and Pauline to have a heater, which she would switch on for them and then, when quite reasonably they left it on through the night, Mrs. B. would creep into their room and turn it off – heating costs were included in our rent!

However, Mrs. Benson's international goodwill was heavily circumscribed. She clearly did not like the British or the English. She used the terms interchangeably lumping the English, Scots and Welsh together. And over dinner we were often treated to a diatribe about Britain being full of homosexuals, how the English were lazy and not as industrious as the Germans, how we depended on the Americans – no acknowledgement of how West Germany had benefited from the Marshal Plan - and so on. I felt the urge to shout "so who won the war then?" But usually a large mouthful of sauerkraut and German sausage prevented me from airing my prejudices in response, fortunately for me. Her husband was only infrequently present for the evening meal because of his duties on the base and we did wonder whether the rigours of his domestic life were proving more onerous than the military discipline on the base.

After a couple of weeks Roy could take Mrs Benson no more and lost it with her over some attempted restriction she had tried to impose on us. So she threw him out and he ended up for a while sleeping on the floor of a British army corporal, Jake, whom we had befriended and who with his wife was stationed at Camp Voluceau a British base attached to SHAPE. I'd like to say I was made of sterner stuff but I stayed on at the Bensons not because I was less troubled by Mrs Benson but because I was more attracted to her daughter Gisela!

Gisela was about two years older than me and was attending the US High School at SHAPE for the dependants of US service personnel. She was particularly interested in English literature and while I had left school before my O Levels I had read enough to be able to talk to her about what she was studying. We became friends. I was a young male going on seventeen and the hormones were racing so I was keen for our friendship to become more than platonic. Unfortunately for me, we got no further than cuddles and the occasional kiss. Maybe this was for the best. If Mrs Benson had found out that I had been rogering her daughter I fear the meat cleaver that she wielded so expertly on joints of lamb and beef might have been put to another use!

By this stage the lives of the band members had drifted apart somewhat. Roy was living elsewhere, I was obsessed with Gisela, Jenny and Pauline would sometimes go on their own to Paris, while Tilly would often go to the base early and practice on his own. We could go our separate ways because there was an excellent army bus service both to the base and to the centre of Paris. We still practiced together but not every day. Our music was well received by the GIs and we still all retained a strong yearning to make records and become famous – whatever that meant. Indeed, Jimmy English had promised that through his links with Polydor he would try and get an A&R[146] person from the label to come down to Camp des Loges to hear us play live. But by mid November there was no sign of him – it was invariably a 'him'. We were also still feeling the pinch financially and a record contract might allow us to make more money from appearances and even record sales. The Paris region was more expensive than most other areas of northern and central France. Petrol in particular was very expensive and while we could use army buses to travel across the Paris region, we still needed to run the Atlas van. In this context Roy got an offer he could not refuse.

US servicemen and women had access to cheap booze, cigarettes and petrol or gasoline. With prices much higher in the French economy, there were clearly opportunities for arbitrage. A GI could make quite a bit of extra money selling alcohol, cigarettes and gasoline on the French economy, while French citizens who had the opportunity to purchase such items would also gain. The main loser would be the US government who

---

[146] Stands for 'artists and repertoire'. An A&R manager makes the decision on whether to sign an artist and negotiate the deal. It is his, or her, job to get the rest of the label interested in the artist, such as the PR and promotions department.

effectively subsidized the goods by charging the servicemen the lower US prices even though the products had to be purchased at European prices or shipped at high cost from the States. So, quite reasonably, it was illegal for US service personnel to service this 'black' market, and a court martial would invariably follow if a GI was caught. However, if somebody, say a civilian with access to the base, acted on the GI's behalf then it became less risky for the GI because the activity would be deniable. Civilian band members such as ourselves who entered and exited the base daily were therefore ideal targets for any GI wishing to run a bootleg operation. Roy agreed to make frequent runs of alcohol contained in the boot of a car to locations in central Paris where he would leave the car. The alcohol would be removed a short time later and someone else would pick up the car and drive it back to the base. So there was a chain of deniability, which would make it harder for the authorities to wind up the operation. In return the GI gave Roy gas coupons, which were issued by the US Quartermaster and which were accepted (sometimes grudgingly) at gas stations in the French economy. This allowed the holder to have cheap petrol while the US army would reimburse the gas station when the coupons were cashed in.

Clearly, this was not a riskless activity for Roy and for the whole band because if he had been caught doing this he would at best have been sent home to the UK and at worst tried and possibly jailed by the French authorities. All went well from Roy's standpoint until late one rainy Paris evening he was driving a black VW Beetle into the centre along Rue de Batignolles, towards Place Clichy and thence Pigalle when a traffic light changed suddenly to red. Roy hit the brakes, the VW's

CHAPTER 11

wheels locked and he skidded into the back of a Citroen 2CV or Deux-Cheveau. The 2CV in Roy's words: "ping ponged through the red lights across Place Clichy." The French driver was clearly not amused, although fortunately there was little damage to either vehicle, the car bumpers having done their job. A bottle of bourbon from the amazingly still intact cargo in the boot at the front of the VW was lifted surreptitiously from it and offered in compensation to the Frenchman who, to Roy's relief, accepted graciously. Roy was thus able to drive off before the incident could come to the attention of the French police!

The Beatles phenomenon was by mid-November getting bigger and we were receiving mail from back home, which indicated the excitement felt at the prospect of the Beatles appearing at the Globe Stockton on the 22nd of November. Even with tickets priced at 6/6d, 8/6d and 10/6d, - average earnings were around £15 to £16 per week and less for manual workers - the five thousand seats for the two performances that evening were soon sold out. The Beatles had had major hits with *Please Please Me, From Me to You* and *She Loves You*, which had been at number one in the charts for four weeks, was currently third in the charts and would rise back to number one for two further weeks at the end of November. In addition, their album *With the Beatles* was to be released on the same day as their Stockton appearance and the songs were eagerly awaited, with the LP enjoying advance orders of 270,000.[147] We were no different except that we wished to learn the new songs

---

[147] Source: http://en.wikipedia.org/wiki/The_Beatles

quickly so we could cover them for our GI audiences. The Beatles had appeared at the Astoria Ballroom Middlesbrough, just five months earlier on the 25th of June. The Astoria was a venue that we enjoyed playing at and we were envious that one of our local rivals the Johnny Taylor 5 had provided the support[148]. Worse, we missed the show because we had to fulfill a booking at another venue ourselves. Now, in November, the impact of the Beatles and their popularity had grown apace in those five months, making us even more envious that we could not be there to see them.

So it was with such thoughts that we took to the stage at the Camp des Loges EM Club at around 7pm (CET)[149] on the evening of Friday, 22nd November 1963. Fifteen minutes later at 6.15pm (GMT[150]) or 7.15 (CET) the first of the Beatles two shows that evening at the Stockton Globe commenced. The show, compared by Frank Berry, was opened by the Rhythm and Blues Quartet, later to become the Spencer Davis Group[151]. The Vernons Girls provided an interlude before the Brooks Brothers – a fellow Starlite Artistes' act back in 1962 - took the stage, followed by Peter Jay and the Jaywalkers, which took the show to the interval. As the excitement began to develop into a frenzy at the Globe, with the Beatles thirty-minute set due to end the show after performances by the Rhythm and Blues Quartet and the Kestrels[152], we were playing to a much less excited and half-empty EM Club.

---

[148] Source: http://www.stanlaundon.com/beatles.html
[149] Central European Time
[150] Greenwich Mean Time
[151] Source: http://www.stanlaundon.com/beatles.html
[152] A vocal harmony group from Bristol.

CHAPTER 11

With about 15 minutes to go until our first scheduled break at 8pm, I noticed that Howard DeSilva had appeared at the front of the stage. He motioned to us that he would like to make an announcement when we had finished the number we were playing. We finished the song. He walked up the steps at the right of the stage and approached one of the microphones. He paused and then said very quietly into the microphone that AFN had just interrupted their programmes with a special news bulletin to announce that President Kennedy on a visit to Dallas Texas had reportedly been seriously wounded, perhaps fatally[153]. DeSilva said that he would give more news as soon as he had it. Many of the GIs had continued to drink and talk through DeSilva's announcement and the sound level in the club dropped only slightly. Roy and I and the rest of the band shot looks at each other, which clearly could be read as: "what do we do?" Roy said let's replace the next number with a ballad.

Forty five minutes later at around 8.30pm CET and 7.30pm GMT as the Beatles took to the stage at the Stockton Globe for their first show that evening, DeSilva walked to the front of the stage and indicated that we must stop playing. He again took the steps up to the stage, approached the microphone and in a voice faltering with emotion he announced:

"AFN have just announced that the President of the United States John Fitzgerald Kennedy died this evening

---

[153] See http://afrts.dodmedia.osd.mil/heritage/first50/Chapter%2019_Armed%20Forces%20Radio%20Begins%20Television%20Service.pdf This announcement was about 10 minutes after the shooting.

in Dallas Texas. The band will cease playing as a mark of respect."

The GIs at first continued their talking and drinking. But I could see several mouthing to their colleagues: "What did he say?" The hubbub began to subside. Somebody shouted "Kennedy's dead!" The noise diminished further. As we turned to switch off our amplifiers, the first thought that came into my mind was: "Why did he say the President's full name?" My second thought was "I'd better put my bass away in its case." Everyone seemed to be behaving like directionless zombies. To say we were all stunned would be to understate what was happening in that room. Then suddenly loud American voices could be heard through the large speaker in the corner of the room near to the stage. DeSilva had decided to route the AFN radio broadcast through the house PA. This gave the whole room a focal point and these young, mainly 19-year old to 25-year old, GIs gradually drifted over in silence to gather round the speaker. Chairs were pulled up. They all stared bewildered at the speaker. Some were fighting hard to hold back tears. Some didn't bother to try.

For the first time, the enormity of what had happened and what was happening began to dawn on me. I thought of my mother and whether she had heard the news back in Stockton where, unbeknown to me, the audience was leaving the Globe to be confronted with talk of Kennedy's assassination from passing strangers as they walked or boarded their buses home. The Beatles now back in their Globe dressing room were told about President Kennedy. On hearing the news, John Lennon reportedly asked if the second show that evening should

CHAPTER 11

still go ahead.[154] But go ahead it did. The likely riot that would have occurred if they had pulled out was too much to risk even in the face of such a momentous event as Kennedy's assassination. Nevertheless, the audience at the second house were much more subdued. Shocked by the news about Kennedy's assassination, Lynda Richardson, a fan travelling back to Redcar by coach, remembered: "It really made me feel guilty for enjoying a great wonderful evening when he was assassinated. No one spoke a word all the way home."[155]

Some GIs started to drift away from the club and we thought we should do the same. DeSilva said we should report for work as usual the next day Saturday, usually a big night at the Club, but he doubted we would have to play. He would let us know when we arrived at the club after he had consulted his superiors. As we walked towards the van Roy said: "Bloody strange that Jenny was singing *End of the World* when DeSilva stopped us playing to make his announcement about Kennedy's death!"

I recited the last verse of Skeeter Davis' hit song to myself:

> *Why does my heart go on beating?*
> *Why do these eyes of mine cry?*
> *Don't they know it's the end of the world.*
> *It ended when you said goodbye.*

---

[154] http://www.stanlaundon.com/beatles.html
[155] Source: http://www.gazettelive.co.uk/news/nostalgia/50-years-beatlemania-hit-teesside-6327515

"Yes, Roy, bloody strange!"

And we drove off into the cold November night.

The next few days passed in something of a blur. Breakfast at the Benson's next morning was understandably full of talk about the assassination. Bob the GI lodger told us how an NCO upon hearing the news that Kennedy was dead got up and shouted "good!" He then walked out of the NCO Club. But that wasn't the end of the story because word came back to the club that he had been followed out of the club and beaten up. Nobody was saying who had done it. Mrs Benson's husband, a man of few words, blamed the Soviets for Kennedy's assassination. He said Khrushchev had never forgiven Kennedy for besting him over the Cuban missile crisis a year ago. " It's just been on AFN that they have charged a guy named Oswald or something, he's a commie sympathizer and they say he has lived in Russia. We could be at war within the week." I shivered as memories of the stress and worry we had experienced over Cuba flooded back into my mind. Thankfully Mrs. Benson kept her own counsel. I supposed she was finding it hard to link those lazy, English, homosexuals to Kennedy's death!

US forces were put on alert after the assassination and all had to report to base that Saturday morning. But despite Oswald's link to Russia the murder did not seem to have been the result of a Soviet plot. At the base DeSilva told us the EM Club would be closed that night and almost certainly for longer. On Sunday we were told that the club would be closed until the funeral and for a period of mourning after that. Jimmy English came round to inform us that we would start playing again at Camp des Loges two weeks later on Monday, 9th December and play there over Christmas until the end of the month

CHAPTER 11

before moving to Fontainebleau. We were to fly home from Paris Orly on the Tuesday. Later that Sunday we heard and saw on the Benson's TV set the shooting and murder of Lee Harvey Oswald in the basement of Dallas Police headquarters by a local nightclub owner Jack Ruby. On Monday 25th, we sat with Bob and the rest of the Benson family, with me covertly holding Gisela's hand, and watched the State funeral procession and interment at Arlington of President Kennedy.

Two memories stick in my mind from that day. One is of the towering figure of President of France Charles DeGaulle and the other is of little John F. Kennedy junior, 3 years old that very day, saluting his father's flag-draped coffin as it was carried out from St. Matthew's Cathedral.

On Tuesday evening, I walked into my parents' living room and hugged my mum. My dad appeared shortly afterwards having cut short his nightly visit to the Kings Arms. Needless to say there was only one topic that dominated the discussion. Although my father did mention that there was a new television programme that I might be interested in that had started on Saturday evening, which he urged me to watch the following Saturday.

"What is it called?" I asked.
"Dr. Who!"
"Dr. Who?"
"Yes, Dr Who!" my dad replied.
"Oh, dad, I think you've had too many pints of Newcastle Exhibition Ale, again. Goodnight!"

But he was right and little did I know then that 50 years later it would still be going strong and that I would become a life-long fan.

My bedroom at the front of the house was as I had left it in August, except perhaps a little tidier! I looked out of the window down into Matlock Gardens. Lights were blazing in the Woolley's house at number 24 opposite. Mr. Thompson at number 26 was going back into his house with a bucket of coal shoveled from his coalbunker at the back of the house. Mrs. Turnbull at number 22 was opening her living room curtains ready for the morning and having a last look out before going to bed. I smiled, ducking down before she noticed me, and crawled into bed pulling the blankets around me and hugging the hot water bottle that mum had placed in my bed. I felt like a rabbit that had returned to the safety of its warren and slept like a log until the following afternoon.

The days in Stockton passed quickly. Talk in the town was of the Kennedy assassination and the Beatles visit. Billy J Kramer and the Dakotas part of Brian Epstein's Liverpool stable, played in the town at the Odeon on Wednesday 27th, the day after I got home. The show was billed as "The Billy J. Kramer Pop Parade" and included a large support: Johnny Kidd & The Pirates, The Caravelles, The Fourmost, Houston Wells, Tommy Quickly, The Marauders and compered by Ted King. All the shows in those days had to have a comedian compere. I didn't much care for Billy J. Kramer, even though we would later record one of his numbers, *Little Children*. But I was keen to see Johnny Kidd & The Pirates whose hit *Shakin' All Over* was a particular favourite, especially the insistent guitar riff at the start running down an E minor pentatonic scale. Unfortunately, it was too late to try and get tickets and I am not sure I could have spared the cash to pay for a ticket, so I missed them.

CHAPTER 11

There were trips to Stockton via the 24 United Bus from Hillcrest at the bottom of Matlock Gardens to Stockton High Street, thence to Burdon's in Yarm Lane. The ostensible purpose was to buy spare strings for my bass guitar but, it must be admitted, I also went to impress the girls behind the counter in the shop with our exploits and hopefully to meet and also seek to impress members of other local bands. Beatlemania had not passed Burdons by for as I walked in I noticed a poster in the window declaring: "JUST ARRIVED! Beatles electric guitars, only 6gns." Now 6gns was £6 and 6 shillings, so that was pretty cheap even for those days and clearly the guitars which were probably cheap Hofners were a million miles from the Gibsons, Epiphones and Rickenbackers actually used by the Beatles. Although it is true that Paul McCartney did use a violin shaped Hofner bass. So you can imagine that I was rather sniffy about the poster thinking about my £129 Gibson EB3 bass sitting at that moment in its case at the back of the Camp des Loges stage.

Visit to Burdon's over and I was off back into the High Street to drop in at Leslie Brown the main record shop in Stockton to look through and hear some of the latest releases in the listening booths. Brown's was fairly popular in the local youth scene but the shop was also keen to market its wares widely and so hit on the marketing wheeze of capitalizing on the frequent shows at the Globe with the advertising strap line: "Always in Stock: Records from all the 'GLOBE' Stage and Film Presentations."[156] Brown's also advertised itself as a

---

[156] Source: http://www.stanlaundon.com/bands/globe/lesliebrown.jpg

recording studio, although I am not aware of any local band that took advantage, or could afford to take advantage, of their facilities.

These trips were made on my own because I had already begun to lose touch with school friends and indeed most were still actually sitting at their desks while I rummaged through the singles and LPs in Leslie Brown's. But I did meet up with Peter (Pedro) Thompson who by then was playing with the local band the Whirlwinds and was later to join the Bluecaps, a band that was to become something of a local legend[157]. I excited Pedro with stories – no doubt exaggerated - of our exploits in Paris and he promised to come over and see me next year and sample the life there himself, but before he could do so he would have to get the money together for the trip. In addition, my mum said that her, dad and Adrian's and Pauline's mums planned to come and see us in France for Christmas. I said "Great!" But I had mixed feelings. It would be fun showing them around Paris and the base but the thought of negotiating with Mrs Benson to fix up their accommodation filled me with fear!

So with some old connections re-established and Dr. Who viewed – the first episode was reshown just before the second episode on Saturday November 30th because it was felt by the BBC that some may have missed it due to the events surrounding Kennedy's assassination[158] – I met up with some of the other group members and we returned to France.

---

[157] See: http://www.stanlaundon.com/globe.html
[158] See: http://en.wikipedia.org/wiki/Doctor_Who

CHAPTER 11

A short while after we got back a strange thing happened: Adrian lost his drums! On our Monday night off we had agreed with Jimmy English that we would play at a 'Showcase' event to let other agents/venue managers and the like see lots of different bands and entertainers for future bookings. At the end of the night Adrian's Sonor drum kit was loaded on top of the van (in fibre drum cases) and we set off back to St. Germain en Laye and the Bensons. During the journey we stopped the van for a 'comfort' break and it was then that we discovered that the drums, apart from the accessory case (snare drum stands and cymbals), had gone missing. We backtracked for a number of miles and searched the side of the road but to no avail! Roy suggested that maybe one of the other bands following us from the event had seen the drums lying by the side of the road and had taken a fancy to them. "Maybe they will recognise the drums from the event and contact Jimmy to let him know that they'd found Tilly's drums." I ventured. "Well, if you believe that Brian you'll believe anything!" was Roy's sardonic reply. And of course he was correct, we never did see those drums again.

That left us with a problem. Jimmy English's promise to us that he would arrange for a Polydor A&R man to come and hear us, was about to be kept. He had arranged the visit the following week, the week before Christmas. Adrian was reduced to playing with only a snare drum, hi hat and cymbals. We could get by without bass drum and tom toms at a pinch but we couldn't put at risk a possible future recording contract because of it. As luck would have it Adrian had struck up a good relationship with the drummer from a German jazz band at the Officers Club, which was also attached to the EM club by way of the kitchens? When they found out that we were auditioning for Polydor – a German record label - the drummer asked his German bandleader if he could loan Adrian his kit when the Polydor visit occurred. He agreed and so Adrian was able to use his kit on the night of the Polydor visit.

On the night in question, we were well into our set at Camp des Loges nervously peering at the entrance to the club, which was directly opposite the stage at the end of the room next to the bar, when I saw the large frame of Jimmy English, as usual dressed in a smart brown suit with matching accessories, coming into the club. Behind him walked a short Frenchman, wearing spectacles and sporting a small moustache. They stood for a while near the bar watching us and then took a table and ordered some drinks. By then the rest of the band Roy, Jenny, Pauline and even Adrian, whose view was restricted by being behind us, had also noticed Jimmy come in and we began to exchange furtive glances. We had rehearsed for this moment and so we began to play the songs that we thought we did best, even though we had played a couple of them earlier in the evening – the GIs didn't seem to notice, or perhaps even care! After about 45 minutes Jimmy and the Frenchman got up and started to walk towards the exit to the club. Jimmy waved to us then they both disappeared through the door. And that was it. Had we blown it? We couldn't tell. Roy rang Jimmy the next day but all Jimmy would say was that M. Faladeau had kept his counsel.

The drums returned to their rightful owner in the Officers Club, we soldiered on, with Howard DeSilva

CHAPTER 11

being very understanding about our absent drums. Upon relaying this story over dinner next day at the Bensons, before we departed for the club, Mrs Benson reminded us rather cryptically that we all had a lot to be thankful to Germans for! I then had to trade even more on German goodwill by requesting her to put up my parents over Christmas. This she agreed. But it looked as if Adrian and Pauline's mums would have to stay in St. Germain itself. Moreover, Mrs Benson said that the local community usually put on an excellent Christmas lunch and for a small sum we all could go including our parents. The sum was larger than I had anticipated. But, hey! It was Christmas.

Our parents duly arrived at Orly airport on Christmas Eve and were taken to their respective accommodation. Mrs Benson was friendly and civil to my parents. I had of course schooled my father that he "mustn't, under any circumstances, mention the war!" On the next day, Christmaas Day, we all assembled at 1pm outside the community hall then trooped in, along with about thirty other mostly French locals, the Bensons and ourselves. We soon realized that this wasn't going to be 'haute cuisine' or a fine example of 'cordon bleu' cooking. There was plenty of salad and one medium-sized chicken to share between 30 people! My mother kept whispering things to me like "Where's the crackers?" And I would respond with comments like "Never mind the crackers, where's the food?" And of course, no Christmas pud! The Bensons didn't at all seemed phased by what was set before them, which I found difficult to comprehend given the meaty fare that was the staple element in Mrs. Benson's dinners. So, that was my one and only French Christmas lunch and it was the most memorable for all the wrong reasons. And for my mother, worse was to come because there was no Queen's speech to comfort her when we got back to the Benson's house!

With Christmas over and New Year on the horizon we had to begin preparations for our move to Fontainebleau. Accommodation was arranged for our parents who we put on a train at Paris for Fontainebleau. I cannot remember playing New Years Eve at Camp des Loges but it was a Tuesday and not our day off so we must have played. We travelled by van to Fontainbleau on a quiet New Year's Day, while Adrian travelled back to London where he met up with his dad. Next day they bought a Ludwig Classic drum kit (Silver Sparkle) from CE Footes in Soho. He then flew back to France with the kit and was met at Orly by Rawlins Spivey, Jimmy English's driver and general factotum. Rawlins then drove Adrian to Fontainebleau arriving just in time for him to set up the new kit and play that evening, the first night of our Fontainebleau engagement on 2nd January 1964. And the bass drum was so loud compared to the previous kit that it had to be filled with newspapers to control the sound!

What would this New Year bring?

We were soon to find out. Next day Roy rang Jimmy to ask for news. After a pause he said

"Wait a minute" and pretended to fumble for a paper on his desk. "Yes, I've got it here. Let me see. Ah yes Roy, it looks as if the Denvers have been offered a recording contract. You will make your first record at the Polydor studios here in Paris before the end of this

CHAPTER 11

month at a date to be arranged. A very Happy New Year Roy to you and the rest of the band! And Roy."

"Yes, Jimmy."

"Don't ask me for more money, mah heart you know won't stand it."

"Ok, Jimmy. Happy New Year!"

CHAPTER 12

LIVERPOOL PARTY

The Fender Bassman amplifier hummed quietly as I checked the tuning of my Gibson EB3 bass. I was sat half facing a movable soundproof partition, an empty music stand in front of me and close to my right knee stood a metal ashtray fixed to a two-foot metal stand in which lay 2 crushed cigarette butts, while a third burned slowly at the side of the ashtray. Jenny and Pauline stood talking in front of two microphones almost directly in front of me about 6 feet away. At the other side of the partition Adrian could be heard tinkering with his drum kit while the deeper timbre of Roy's voice in conversation with Rawlins Spivey, Jimmy English's driver and factotum, drifted across from his supposedly soundproof 'booth' next to Adrian.

We were having a break after spending most of the morning recording tracks for our album in a recording studio used both by Polydor and Phillips situated at 44 Rue des Dames, in the Batignolles area of Paris. The large room in which we stood and sat displayed bulbous sound dampeners on its walls yet looked more like a cinema than one's expectation of what a recording studio should look like. Indeed, that was its provenance:

CHAPTER 12

built in 1938 and renamed Cinema Meteore in 1939, it continued in that role until it closed in 1957. Fortunately, the cinema avoided the traditional British fate of ex cinemas in becoming a bingo hall and became a recording studio instead[159]. Many famous French stars, such as Johnny Hallyday, had recorded there for the Phillips label but we were one of the earliest non-French rock bands that Polydor France had had on their books.[160]

The day before we had travelled up by van from Fontainebleau and suffered the agonies of a flat tyre as we struggled to change it with cars and lorries thundering past only inches away. Eventually, we reached our hotel in the Batignolles area and crawled into our beds to be woken early next morning by a bright-eyed and bushy-tailed Jimmy accompanied by Rawlins. Thirty minutes later we all walked into the studio and were met by M. Faladeau our producer. The whole day had been set aside for the recording and it was made clear to us that studio time was precious and so we shouldn't mess about. In case our new status as recording 'stars' had gone to our head Jimmy reminded us that we still had to bring in our gear from the van and set it up. This we did suitably chastened but with Rawlins providing a helping hand.

We had recorded about 20 songs by the late evening of that day, with each song re-recorded several times before M. Faladeau and ourselves were happy. Added to this, the singers Jenny, Pauline and Roy recorded

---

[159] https://www.flickr.com/photos/56556694@N04/9314799310/in/photostream/
[160] Dave Dacosta and the Strollers preceded us.

harmonies by double tracking as they sang over some of the recordings we had made earlier. As the day dragged on Jenny and Pauline's voices began to suffer through frequent use but Rawlins came to the rescue with hot drinks containing honey and lemon, which kept them going. By 9.30pm we had recorded covers of pop rhythm and blues songs by US female and male singers or vocal groups, such as the Shirelles (*Love is a swinging thing; Boys*), nascent Motown groups such as the Marvelettes (*Mix it up*), the Contours (*Do you love me*), the Righteous Brothers (*Little latin lupe lu (or looby loo*), the Isley Brothers (*Twist and shout*), the Coasters (*Poison Ivy*), and Ray Charles (*Sticks and stones*). Several of these songs had already been, or would be, covered by the Beatles (*Twist and shout; Boys*) and the Rolling Stones (*Poison Ivy*). In addition, we also covered songs recently written for, or simply recorded by, Liverpool groups such as the Merseybeats (*I think of you*); the Big Three (*By the way; Some other guy*) and Billy J. Kramer and the Dakotas (*Little children*).

Sadly, no Denvers penned originals. However, the record company clearly perceived correctly that we were strongly influenced by the then booming 'Liverpool Sound' and their American R&B influences. So, we learnt some weeks later that they had selected 14 of the songs and would be calling our album *Liverpool Party*! We understood why Polydor had done this in an attempt to cash in on the Liverpool Sound boom but it depressed us given that we believed we'd added our own style to the music. However, Roy's comment to the *Billingham Express* that *Billingham Booze-up* was our preferred title was just a little wide of the mark! Yet, a look at the back of the LP cover of our album reveals both the limits of the imagination of Polydor's marketing department and the

CHAPTER 12

company's desire to cash in on the growing Beatlemania and the booming popularity of the Liverpool Sound. Of the 10 LPs and EPs presented in the lower half of the cover two have 'party' or 'partie' in the title and two featured the (Les) Beatles!

Polydor had been fortunate to record Tony Sheridan in Germany backed by the original members of the Beatles from their Hamburg days, one of several backing bands that Sheridan used. In 1962 the label had released Sheridan's album *My Bonnie* in which the Beatles were his backing group but for various reasons renamed the band as Tony Sheridan and the Beat Brothers[161]. Their strong belief was that Tony Sheridan was the star material and not the Beatles. However, when the Beatles began to gain international acclaim Polydor decided to re-release the material including two songs – *Cry for a shadow* and *Ain't she sweet* – the Beatles had recorded on their own. The *Les Beatles* EP featured on the back cover of our LP includes the Sheridan songs *My Bonnie* and *When the saints* but makes no mention of poor Tony Sheridan. Such is the fickle behaviour of the moguls of the pop music business!

We finally got to see for ourselves what was driving Beatlemania when on 16 January, 1964, the Beatles arrived at the Paris Olympia to undertake 18 days of concerts, on a nine-act bill, playing two and sometimes three sets each day.[162] Bill Harry, founder of the *Mersey Beat* music paper notes that Bruno Coquatrix the impresario who owned the Olympia booked the Beatles on 17th July

---

[161] https://en.wikipedia.org/wiki/Tony_Sheridan
[162] http://www.beatlesbible.com/1964/01/16/live-olympia-theatre-paris/

1963 when they were not yet big stars and Brian Epstein accepted a very small fee of £3,000 which meant £75 a performance. Rather than seeking to cancel the contract Epstein insisted that the group fulfill their earlier commitments and so they arrived in Paris for the 18-day stint, something which they had not done since their Hamburg days and which they would never do again[163].

We managed to get tickets for the first matinee performance on 16 January. It's a cliché but we were 'blown away' by them. Musically and rhythmically they were clearly special. All those gigs at the Star Club in Hamburg had turned them into an exceptionally tight musically outfit of talented players and clearly John, Paul and later George, were immensely gifted songwriters. Bill Harry writes that

> "The quality of the Beatles' concerts in Paris were among the best they ever gave because there was no Beatlemania in Paris. They could hear themselves and their vocal harmonies were perfect. The crowd usually reacted quietly and very often with only a few clapping."[164]

This is true but only part of the story. That first concert was a joy to hear and watch because the group could be clearly seen and heard.[165] But incipient

---

[163] http://www.triumphpc.com/mersey-beat/beatles/beatles-paris2.shtml
[164] http://www.triumphpc.com/mersey-beat/beatles/beatles-paris2.shtml
[165] Unlike a Rolling Stones concert I attended at the Globe Stockton about a year or so later when I neither heard nor hardly saw any

CHAPTER 12

Beatlemania was present that afternoon. The first show was a matinee and there were many more young people present than in the first evening show. Some of the young girls present in the audience did have an emotional response to the group that could be described as Beatlemania. Nevertheless, British TV viewers were shown news clips of masses of young girls screaming at the Beatles and most of that was contrived, whipped up by the UK press and television media who were there filming the crowd as much as the Beatles. In order to film the proceedings lights had to be switched on while the TV producers urged the audience to shake their heads and scream, which many did while the lights were on but then subsided as soon as they went off; my first experience of how the presence of the media, particularly the electronic media, serves to affect events as well as report them. The TV producers wanted to report that the Beatles were taking France by storm just as they had done in Britain and were so keen to ensure that the reality matched their expectations. However, 24 days later on February 9th the Beatles, with *I Want to Hold Your Hand* at No. 1 in the US charts and remaining in that position for 7 weeks, made their first appearance on the Ed Sullivan show in the US, watched by 73.7 million people[166]. The storm of Beatlemania had reached the shores of America.

Enthused by the Beatles we went back to our 6 nightly shows at the EM Club in Fontainebleau hoping that our record would set us on the road to comparable

---

of the proceedings because of the screams and other antics of the mainly young female audience.

[166] http://www.onthisday.com/events/date/1964

stardom, but knowing in our hearts that we could never hope to match the Beatles.

Apart from the week spent back home following President Kennedy's assassination, we had now been away from home for nearly 5 months and the strains were beginning to show. Roy and I had had a few 'punch ups' but for the most part we got on very well together. However, Adrian was starting to get on my nerves. This was purely irrational on my part but I felt that he was repeatedly needling me unnecessarily for reasons I couldn't understand. It came to a head one evening in the cramped dressing across from the EM Club stage just before we were about to start the evening show. Adrian said something and as defendants sometimes say to the judge 'something in me snapped'. The next thing I remember I was battering Adrian mercilessly with Roy and Jenny, soon to be joined by the Club manager who had been alerted by the sound of the fracas from the dressing room, trying and ultimately succeeding in pulling me off him.

This was clearly serious. I felt ashamed. No amount of taunting from Adrian could possibly justify the scale of the assault I had launched on him. Roy and the Club manager made me apologise and I/we were let off because for one brief moment I feared I was going to be responsible for the band being sacked from the club. After all, no club manager wants a nascent homicidal maniac entertaining his customers! Thankfully that did not happen. But it was a warning that I had to heed. Living cheek by jowl with four others for 15 hours a day was not healthy, certainly for me. I feared our relationship was becoming a marriage from hell and resolved to spend more time away from the others especially on our day off.

CHAPTER 12

It was at this time that I began to have the first regrets about leaving school early and started to worry what my future might hold. There was still the record and anything was possible but seeing the Beatles underlined, if only sub-consciously, how good we had to be to enjoy great success. I became more withdrawn and took to reading George Orwell in my spare moments while worrying what 1984 would have in store for me.

My parents had been back at home for nearly four weeks after their Christmas trip to see us, and my mother had resumed sending letters with news of home and the wider world. Telephone calls were too expensive for routine communications and were only used for exceptional circumstances and emergencies. So, it was from these letters that I learnt what my mother was doing at work, who my father had been chatting to, who had inquired about me, how my grandparents were, what Grandma Hardwick had been giving my mam for lunch, when she dropped by in her lunch break - I salivated at the thought of Grandma's pies, Yorkshire puddings with mint sauce and gravy, and her steamed egg puddings! And her delicious cups of tea: first tea leaves were mashed with a little boiling water and then after a few minutes more boiling water was added to fill the teapot. The Great Train Robbers had been caught and were to go on trial, the Rolling Stones were coming to Stockton in February (19th) and there was a new pop TV programme that had just started on the BBC which she thought I might like: Top of the Pops!

Reminders of home such as these made me feel homesick – the opposite of my mother's intentions – and increased my alienation from the band. Maybe this was the anticlimax after the adrenalin rush of recording at

Polydor. The audience at Fontainebleau EM Club was kind to us but this was our second month at the club and frankly I was becoming bored. Yet, we were soon to move to a US Air Force base at Evreux in Normandy for a month then back home to Stockton for March. Perhaps things would get better.

Evreux, or to give it its correct name, Evreux-Fauville, was certainly different. Being a US Air Force base the routines and rhythms of the place seemed to differ from the US Army bases. As Wikipedia[167] reports the 322nd Air Division (Combat Cargo) was the main host unit at Évreux airforce base. It was established on 12 August 1955 and remained at Evreux until 1 April 1964. The 322nd directed the three Troop Carrier Wings in Europe - the 317th and 465th at Évreux as well as the 60th at Dreux-Louvillier Air Base, which was located about 35 miles away to the south of Evreux.

The servicemen on the base either operated or maintained the squadrons of C130 Lockheed Hercules cargo/troop carrier planes stationed there. The C130 four-engine turbo-props were a sight to behold: looking like oversized, pregnant albatrosses as they lumbered along the runways and aprons they nevertheless demonstrated surprising agility with short take off and landings. Chatting to aircrew in the airbase club we would be regaled with stories of missions accomplished: of rafts, tents, and emergency food supplies airlifted to flood victims in the Netherlands, of aid given to earthquake victims in Italy, Greece, Pakistan and Yugoslavia, and of trips to Wheelus Air Base in Libya in support of fighter weapons training.

---

[167] https://en.wikipedia.org/wiki/Évreux-Fauville_Air_Base

CHAPTER 12

Nine months later in November, when I had returned to Evreux with the Jaybeats after the Denvers broke up at the end of September, an even more exciting event took place that involved all on the base in one way or another.

In the former Belgian Congo, purported communist Simba rebels took American consular officials and other resident civilians of the city of Stanleyville hostage. The US government agreed with Belgium to put together a joint rescue mission known as Operation *Dragon Rouge*. So, on 24 November 1964, American C-130E Hercules planes flying from Evreux dropped 350 Belgian paratroopers onto the airfield at Stanleyville against heavy opposition. The paratroopers then took the airfield, cleared the runway to allow the C130s and other aircraft to land, then made their way to the Victoria Hotel, in the centre of the city, and prevented the Simbas from killing most of the hostages. The freed hostages were then evacuated on the C130s from the airfield. It is reported that during the next two days more than 1,800 American, Belgian and other European civilians were evacuated as well as around 400 Congolese civilians. But sadly, around 200 foreigners and thousands of Congolese were executed by the Simbas before and after the raid.[168] [169]

Expecting at worst small-arms fire as the planes went in to drop the paratroopers they were greeted instead by tracers fired from Chinese-made 12.7mm anti-aircraft machine guns as well as from hand-held weapons.[170]

---

[168] https://en.wikipedia.org/wiki/Lockheed_C-130_Hercules#Military
[169] https://en.wikipedia.org/wiki/Operation_Dragon_Rouge
[170] http://www.historynet.com/congo-crisis-operation-dragon-rouge.htm

Some of the planes were hit but not fatally and the pilots nevertheless managed to maintain their course and successfully complete the drop. The evidence of these hits was clearly visible when the planes returned to Evreux with, for example, small pieces of rudder and tail plane seen to be missing and bullet holes in wings and fuselage.

Not unnaturally, there was something of a holiday atmosphere at the base after the planes returned, even though the planes from the 464th Troop Carrier Wing that flew the mission were soon to rotate back to their home Airforce base at Pope in North Carolina. Shortly afterwards, and while I was there, the base received an official visit from General Lyman Lemnitzer, Supreme Allied Commander of NATO and, as noted in Chapter 11, also head of US European Command (EUCOM), to honour the aircrews. Sometime later the aircrew that participated in the Congo missions were all awarded Air Medals for their role, while the 1964 McKay Trophy, an annual award for the most meritorious flight of the year by U.S. Air Force planes, was awarded to the *Dragon Rouge* force.[171]

Meanwhile back in early February 1964 the Denvers had settled into their hotel in the centre of Evreux, which was about 2 miles to the west of the base. We soon got into the routine of sleep, lie-in, travel to the base, eat, practise, eat, play, drink, travel to the hotel, sleep ...... There were occasional highlights such as supporting the famous Platters on a 'floor-show' evening with their singing of *My Prayer* taking me back to my nine-year old self at Wolviston Primary school participating in country

---

[171] *ibid*

CHAPTER 12

dancing sessions! In between, practicing *Strip the willow* and the *Dashing white sergeant* Mr. Fleming or Mrs. Pottage would put a modern 78rpm record on the Dansette record player and one of those occasions was the first time I heard *My Prayer*.

Our effective confinement to the base meant that we saw little of the town of Evreux itself. I have no recollection of visiting the cathedral. Despite my membership of a rock band I was unaware until years later that Evreux became host to an internationally known annual rock festival *Le Rock dans tous ses états* from 1983, which continues today. Moreover, given my later profession as an economist I was unaware that Evreux was the birthplace of the famous economist and founder of general equilibrium theory Leon Walras. We became very familiar with the base, the inside of our hotel and a little of night time Evreux but that was it. Indeed, my strongest memory of Evreux is listening to the Beatles song *All my loving* on the jukebox in the bar of the hotel, which Pauline and Jenny kept playing on those evenings when we passed through and stopped for a drink after finishing playing at the base. This is so strongly printed in my mind that whenever I do hear that song I am immediately taken back to that dark hotel bar in Evreux. I remember little else of the place!

US Army personnel will hate me for saying this but the aircrew, medics, fitters, mechanics, drivers and other airforce specialists that we entertained each evening were on average a more sophisticated bunch than the young soldiers that had been the mainstay of our audiences over the previous 5 months. They seemed to be more knowledgeable about music and had broader interests. One such was Tom Kalk.

Tom was mature, intelligent, tall, bespectacled, and drove a green Sunbeam Alpine sports car, which we envied immensely. I can't remember his specific role in the US Airforce at Evreux: he certainly wasn't flight crew but he did make frequent trips to Wheelus Airbase in Libya. Tom became a good friend to the band and was non-threatening because he didn't seem to be angling to get into the knickers of Pauline or Jenny or, heaven forbid, Roy, Adrian or myself! Tom gave us access to the PX so we could buy good quality US made clothes such as *Fruit of the Loom* underwear and T-shirts, button down shirts, gas coupons and of course cheap cigarettes. While we were earning better money than in 1962 we still didn't feel rich so access to the subsidised PX was a great help to our personal economy. Moreover, since we hardly ever went shopping on the local French economy, largely because we were either at the base or sleeping, access to the PX was a lifeline for basic necessities.

As February drew to a close with little event, Tom said to Roy that he would like to travel back to England with us and also visit some relatives of his in southern England. Roy contacted his parents and they agreed to put him up at their home in Billingham. And so on March 1st we set off in our Standard Atlas van with Tom following in his Sunbeam Alpine, or more accurately Tom driving ahead and then waiting for us to catch up. This made travelling in 'Charlie'[172], stuffed as it was with our band gear, suitcases and *bric a brac* collected over the past 6 months, more comfortable because each of us took turns in

---

[172] After Charles Atlas the then famous bodybuilder.

CHAPTER 12

travelling with Tom in the Sunbeam. Soon we were at Calais, on the cross-channel ferry and watching with lumps in our throats as the white cliffs of Dover and England came into view.

Our time back in Stockton and Billingham seemed to pass quickly. Much time was spent in preparing to go back to France and the US Army General Depot at Ingrandes near Chatellerault. As related in Chapter 5, 'Charlie' was sold and replaced by a brand new white Commer van, a marked improvement in comfort and drivability on the Standard Atlas.

I started driving lessons on 5 March, my seventeenth birthday, passing my test, amazingly, on 20 March. Each day between the 5th and the 20th I had a driving lesson and sometimes a double lesson with BSM. My mother had scheduled these for 1pm or thereabouts so she would come into my room before she went to work, wake me with a cup of tea, and urge me not to sleep in and miss my lesson! Sure enough, I would quickly slip back into the land of nod then wake with a judder and feeling of horror as bleary eyes focused on the clock that read 12.10pm. Out of bed like a shot, jump into clothes, rush downstairs, grab the now cold bacon sandwich that my mother had left me and dash out of the house, running down Matlock Gardens to the Hillcrest bus stop to catch the number 24 United bus into Stockton. Interestingly, BSM's offices were in Yarm Lane a few doors down from Burdon's. So, after an hour of clutch-slipping hill starts, kerb-clipping reversing, failed emergency stops and dodgy three-point turns, I would leave my exasperated instructor and sally forth into Burdon's, the now recording 'star' returning to his musical roots. A smiling Maureen soon takes the gilt off my gingerbread by reporting that Roy had been in earlier in the day and had clearly managed to appropriate all the kudos we were likely to get from our new status. Worse, Tom had been in with him and Maureen couldn't stop talking about him. The rare presence of a tall, handsome American in the shop was clearly more significant than anything Roy and I might have achieved on the music front. So, no stars falling on Stockton for us and unfortunately for Tom his star in Stockton was also about to wane.

On March 10 a US Air Force RB-66 reconnaissance, plane based at Toul-Rosieres France, was shot down over East Germany by Soviet MiG fighter jets after straying out of one of the Berlin air corridors. The three-crew members parachuted to safety and were released several days later. This followed the 24 January shooting down of a US Air Force T-39 Sabreliner, by a Soviet fighter over Thuringia, about 60 miles inside East Germany while on a training flight. The crew of three was killed. The leave of US Air Force personnel in EUCOM was cancelled and Tom had to return to Evreux.

Despite my earlier homesickness I soon began to feel the urge to get away again. I found it hard to return to the nest despite my mother's best efforts to make me comfortable. And my father too was particularly solicitous, taking me to St James' Park on Saturday March 14th to see Newcastle beat Sunderland 1- 0 (a McGarry penalty). Sadly, Newcastle were now in the Second Division and a 27,341 crowd was well short of the 50,000 plus crowds that would regularly grace the terraces in the days of Jackie Milburn.[173] Yet, we would

---

[173] http://www.nufc.com/html/1963-64.html

CHAPTER 12

gain promotion back to the First Division next year after finishing 8th in the Second in 1963-64. The walk from Newcastle Central Station, up Pink Lane, past overflowing pubs and bars through a sea of hopeful faces atop black and white shirts, into Bath Lane, the Gallowgate, Barrack Road and then the looming stadium still fills me with excitement and anticipation. But even here back in March 1964 I couldn't escape echoes of my American and musical connections. On March 14th we heard that Jack Ruby had been found guilty by a Dallas jury of the murder of Lee Harvey Oswald, the alleged assassin of President Kennedy.

The following Saturday I manage – with hindsight, heartlessly – to escape my mother's entreaties to stay in that evening and watch the Eurovision song contest on television. So, with *nul points* from her I escape for an evening with Pedro and the Whirlwinds. I learn the next day, Sunday morning, that, much to my mother's chagrin, the UK entry, Matt Monro singing *I love the little things*, had been beaten into second place by, in my mam's words, 'some Italian song'. The UK was to win it 5 times during the rest of my mother's life, in fact winning in the year my mother died, 1997, and never winning it since. At least that Sunday lunchtime my mother still had the *Billy Cotton Band Show* and *Family Favourites* radio shows to keep the music flowing and offer some lift to her depressed spirits and no doubt much of the rest of the British population.

On Sunday, 29 March we say goodbye to our parents and head our new Commer van down the A1 to London, Dover and thence to Ingrandes. The first (pirate) commercial radio station Radio Caroline begins broadcasting outside British territorial waters. To us a welcome addition to the singular Radio Luxembourg in contrast to the sterility of BBC radio – Saturday Club excepted of course! Maybe this is a good omen for us of a new dawn once our album comes out. But before that could happen we had to return to Paris for photographs to be taken for the album and EP covers. With these completed on a sunny April Monday, our day off work at Ingrandes, we wait with some trepidation for the album to be released. May comes and we move for the first time to Orleans and the EM Club at the US Army Signal headquarters. The nature of the club and our support for Billy Eckstine's floorshow were covered in Chapter 10.

It was at Orleans that we had regular contact with the *Jaybeats*. They were a rock band and were playing at the other US EM Club across town having just come down from a month's engagement at Dreux-Louvillier Air Base. Its drummer Donnie, a Mancunian, ran the band. His wife Val was one of the singers, Jeff was the rhythm guitarist from Rhyl in North Wales, there was a bass player whose name escapes me, and Andy, from Shrewsbury, who played lead guitar. I became friendly with Andy and started to hang out with him and Jeff to a lesser extent when time permitted, remembering the pledge I made to myself not to spend as much time with the other members of the Denvers. In addition, there was Brenda, the band's other female singer. She was nineteen years old, dark haired, attractive in a sexy way and had a cutting sense of humour. I fell for her. One problem was that she was going out with a US airman from Dreux. And he drove a sports car! So, on the face of it, since I struggled to steer even the Commer, not much hope for me. Nevertheless, Brenda's presence

CHAPTER 12

made spending some of my leisure time with Andy and Jeff an even more rewarding possibility. It was on one of these get-togethers with me travelling in the Jaybeats' mini-van that the rest of the Denvers experienced the horrific accident on the N10 in the Commer van, which is related in Chapter 5. Rather irrationally, that accident instead of drawing me closer to my fellow band members seemed to put another psychological barrier between them and me. But then our record was released.

Polydor never gave us a date when it was to be released. We just found out about it: a random hearing of a snippet of *Mix it up* on the French radio station Europe No. 1, a chance sight of the album and EP cover in a record shop window in Orleans and an impromptu visit to a bar in Pigalle Paris where we were confronted with one of our songs blaring out of the jukebox as we walked in. Eventually, Jimmy contacted us to say that after we had worked at Camp de Loges again in June we would do promotional work the following month: some radio work and some one night stands to US bases in France and Germany. We were to be based in Paris again for the next two months.

CHAPTER 13

COMING OF AGE

Hotel Monnier is today a 2 star hotel located at 14 Rue Henry Monnier in the 9th Arrondissement. The hotel's website[174] tells us that it is

> "… less than a 7-minute walk to the Moulin Rouge in the famous Montmartre district. …. located near a variety of restaurants and less than a 10-minute walk to the Lafayette and Haussman department stores. Monnier hotel is 200 yards from Metro Saint George (line 12) and a 10-minute walk to the RER A station, Haussman-Saint Lazare. … 9th arr. is a great choice for travellers interested in shopping, museums and architecture."

It was also a great choice for us in June 1964. Our Commer van had been written off in the accident on the N10 outside Orleans and we were unlikely to get another one until the insurance claims had been sorted out and we knew that would take ages. Rawlins Spivey

---

[174] http://www.hotelmonnier.com

CHAPTER 13

had driven us and our instruments and amplifiers in Jimmy's Volkswagen camper van to Camp des Loges. With no transport we couldn't stay at the Benson's again, which required a vehicle to get to the base and in any event the thought of Mrs. Benson's heavy Germanic stews and her hectoring ways meant that we didn't wish to repeat the experience. So we chose to live in the centre of Paris instead!

This wasn't so daft as it seems. Granted it was quite a way from the base but all throughout the day and late into the night US Army buses commuted between the base and central Paris. This service allowed the GIs to visit the bars and fleshpots of Paris in the evening and still be back on base for reveille and work in the morning. As musicians playing on the base there was no objection to us travelling on US Army transport and so we could play out the rest of the month at the base without calling on Jimmy and Rawlins to help us out with transport. The following month, July, we had a tour planned to promote our record and Jimmy had agreed we could use the services of Rawlins and the camper van to do the one-night stands.

The bus would cover the 14 miles or so between the base and the centre of Paris in less than 45 minutes and would drop us off close to the Etoile on the Champs-Elysees. Most nights we would hail a taxi back to the hotel and the two or three of us would share the 5Fr cost. But on some of the warm May evenings we would walk the two and a half miles back to the hotel. First down the Avenue de Wagram, then right into the Boulevard de Courcelles, then Boulevard des Batignolles, around Place de Clichy into Boulevard de Clichy to Place Pigalle, Rue Frochot and then Rue Henry Monnier.

As we walked towards Pigalle a feeling of excitement and anticipation would get stronger and stronger. The offices, hotels and the odd quiet bar or restaurant began to be replaced by busy and more brightly lit cafes, bars, and brasseries many with whicker chairs and tables on the pavement. The aroma of Gauloise, Gitanes, grilling steaks and garlic began to envelop us. Beautiful young women gazed intently across red check tablecloths, glass of wine in one hand and a half-smoked cigarette in the other, at their boy or girl friends. From some café bars the drifting sound of live jazz or blues intermingled with the aromas of cooking food and tobacco. Across the Boulevard de Clichy through the two lines of trees defining the central pathway and beyond the parked Deux Chevauxs, Peugeots and Citroens, could be glimpsed the glittering and flashing neon of the Moulin Rouge. And between the trees, walking casually up and down the boulevard, their high-heels clicking on the cobblestones, tripped transvestite prostitutes. At least that was what our GI friends told us, because from thirty paces and probably closer they were indistinguishable from females. Then at Place Pigalle a glance up Rue Andre Antoine or Rue Houdon would reveal other ladies of the night plying their trade and bringing back memories of our first trip to Paris with Sam Curtis at the end of May 1962 – see Chapter 6.

On most nights, despite the temptation to linger and stare at the cascade of exotic sights that flowed before our eyes, we would turn off Place Pigalle and hurry to Hotel Monnier and our beds after a tiring evening's work. But on some evenings and often on our day off we would immerse ourselves more in the life of the Pigalle and Montmartre areas. Close to Rue Henry Monnier

CHAPTER 13

was Rue Pigalle – officially called Rue jean-Baptiste Pigalle, but nobody we knew used the full name and indeed when the GIs spoke of "Pigalle" they usually meant Rue Pigalle. Rue Pigalle was a magnet for the GIs seeking a good time. This was principally because of the many bars specifically catering to GIs that lined the street. The most popular were the *Canada Bar, Nebraska Bar, A Bar* and *Blue Train*. There were other famous GI bars in Paris at that time but not on Rue Pigalle including the *Sun Club, 2Ks, Hotel Fontaine, American Legion,* and *La Boheme*. The latter became *Buttercup's Chicken Shack*, behind which lay an interesting tale.

Buttercup came from Altevia 'Buttercup' Edwards who was Bud Powell's 'wife'. Powell[175] a brilliant modern jazz, bebop, pianist who had suffered severe mental illness and hospitalization for many years in the 1940s moved to Paris in 1959, in the company of Buttercup, whom he had met in 1954. While in Paris, Powell was helped by Buttercup to get his life somewhat back on track and he recorded again in Paris with among others the well-known jazz drummer Kenny Clarke[176]. Clarke, one of the four members of *Dizzy Gillespie's Big Band* who founded a quartet that became the *Modern Jazz Quartet* in 1952, moved to Paris in 1956 and remained in France until his death in 1985. Powell was diagnosed with tuberculosis in 1965 and moved back to the US, where he died on July 31, 1966, after suffering from the effects of tuberculosis, malnutrition, and alcoholism. Buttercup stayed behind in Paris

---

[175] https://en.wikipedia.org/wiki/Bud_Powell#cite_note-Pullman_2012_chapt.3D10-12
[176] https://en.wikipedia.org/wiki/Kenny_Clarke

opening her *Chicken Shack* in 1966 and continuing to be a fixture in the American jazz social milieu that existed at that time in Paris centred on the *Le Blue Note* and *Living Room* jazz clubs. Sadly, just as the *Chicken Shack* was opening *Le Blue Note* was closing and reopening as a discotheque, finally closing altogether in 1968[177].

A personal coda to this story occurred one evening when Roy, Adrian and myself went out for a drink with Rawlins. Searching for a suitable bar that would admit a seventeen-year old (me) and a sixteen-year old (Adrian), we 'bumped into' Kenny Clarke and Buttercup having a drink at a pavement table of a bar off Pigalle. Rawlins a jazz aficiando and an ex US marine to boot was part of this American jazz milieu and so knew both Buttercup and Clarke well. We spent part of the evening with them listening to both regale us with stories about the jazz world in Paris. Throughout all this Adrian sat mostly open-mouth finding it difficult to take in that he was drinking with, and chatting to, one of the greatest drummers in the world!

Our contact with American jazz musicians didn't end there. In our conversation with Kenny Clarke and Buttercup the name Benny Waters was mentioned and Clarke suggested that since he was playing almost at the top of the street where we were staying we should drop by and hear him play with his band. Waters was an accomplished saxophonist, clarinetist, vocalist, and arranger[178]. He played and recorded with many of the

---

[177] https://fr.wikipedia.org/wiki/Blue_Note_(Paris)
[178] http://www.encyclopedia.com/topic/Benny_Waters.aspx and https://en.wikipedia.org/wiki/Benny_Waters

CHAPTER 13

jazz greats of the 1920s, 1930s, and 1940s, including Ella Fitzgerald. In 1952 he embarked on a European tour with a Dixieland band led by Jimmy Archey. Impressed with Paris he decided to stay and did so for forty years only travelling to the US in 1992 at the age of ninety for cataract surgery, which failed to cure his blindness. Yet he continued to play, perform and record until his ninety-fifth birthday and died in 1998 aged ninety-six. His fifteen-year stint playing at the *La Cigale Café* on the corner of Boulevard de Rochechouart and Rue des Martyrs in Pigalle was very popular. So much so, in fact, that in 1996 he was awarded the *Légion d'honneur* by the French Ministry of Culture.

So, one evening, we – that is the band including Jenny and Pauline - dropped into the café and caught the end of his set. He was wonderful and seemed able to play with great flair anything from the blues to Dixieland. He was also charming. When we were introduced to him after his show he ordered us all drinks and made quite a fuss of us. I realized later, perhaps cynically, that the presence of Jenny and Pauline might have been the reason for the attention he lavished on us. I read later that he had a reputation for carousing, and ".... a career punctuated with drunken episodes, myriad girlfriends, the occasional brawl, two volatile marriages and divorces."[179] After telling him about the type of music we played and what was on our just released album, he interrupted and said that he loved the blues as any brother of Muddy Waters should! Even then

---

[179] Paula Span's review of his memoir published in 1985 *The Key to a Jazzy Life*; cited in http://www.encyclopedia.com/topic/Benny_Waters.aspx

I knew that Muddy Waters, the so called "father of modern Chicago blues" was not his real name - McKinley Morganfield in fact – and so I assumed that he was either joking, perhaps even making fun of our perceived ignorance, or seeking to impress us, especially Jenny and Pauline, with something that he thought would be likely to do so. I suspect it was a bit of each. We left the café certainly impressed but there was a slightly sour taste.

On most evenings but especially at weekends Pigalle was flooded with GIs seeking a good time. Most GI bars did not have live music – although some of the bigger clubs did - but instead had jukeboxes offering 45rpm singles of singers and bands that would appeal to American ears. Some of the larger bars/clubs had 'bouncers' or doormen who would vet the GI clientele excluding any who were stoned or drunk. Some of these clubs were permissive of soft drugs such as marijuana being smoked, easily purchased from the Algerian pedlars that prowled Pigalle selling – as noted in Chapter 6 – anything from carpets to drugs and I suspect some clubs also offered under-counter sales as well. The US authorities were clearly keen to stamp out the habit and so would send plain clothed CID military policemen to the bars and clubs to try and catch GIs in the act. The doormen at some of these clubs would get wise to which Americans were the undercover military police and when the CID were present the doormen would often refuse entry to those GIs that they knew liked to smoke and/or seek to buy the weed.

These bigger clubs were no-go areas for us due to our age: we wouldn't have got past the doorman, so when we did go for a night out in Pigalle we would choose

CHAPTER 13

one of the smaller bars. Our favourite haunt was the *Blue Train*. Situated half way down Rue Pigalle, we often dropped in early evenings for a jambon and a Coca Cola. By now we were drinking alcohol but it was still only the occasional beer, although some experimental drinking of Pernod had produced near oblivion!

The *Blue Train* was actually shaped like a train. When you walked through the door from the street you were in the corridor of a train with fake windows and views of countryside on your left and the bar on your right. Passing through the corridor/bar past the one or two hard-core drinkers perched on bar stools, the bar opened up to what was the café/restaurant. This was shaped like the inside of a passenger railway carriage with fake windows and views and tables and chairs lining each side of a central walkway where right at the end, between the final two tables, sat a large jukebox. The bar would usually be fairly quiet in the early evening so we could eat our jambons and feed money into the jukebox eating and listening without interruption. As the evening wore on a couple of young women would come in to the café area with a drink put money in the jukebox and start dancing. They would often smile at us but Roy and I knew that the girls were on the lookout for bigger fish, they were scouting for GIs. And sure enough soon GIs – young faced, clean shaven with closed cropped hair, dressed in smartly pressed US army uniforms of light khaki trousers, open-necked khaki shirts from which the top of a white *Fruit of the Loom* t-shirt would be visible - started to drift through from the bar area looking to dance with the young women. At this point, as they say, we would make our excuses and leave.

Once we were out on the street the 'buzz' of Rue Pigalle soon hit us. Music drifted out of the bars, young women, some Sylvie Vartan lookalikes in boots, short skirts, leather coats and long blonde hair, hurried by usually in twos but frequently on the arm of a GI. Everybody seemed to be smoking. Groups of GIs spilled out onto the pavement drinking bottles of Kronenborg or Heineken beer. There was tension in the air. Gendarmerie police cars cruised slowly down the street, the grim-faced officers inside scanning the pavement looking for trouble. And trouble there was when the alcohol began to make itself felt.

Scuffles would occur between GIs, between GIs and the few British soldiers that had ventured up from SHAPE, and occasionally between GIs and French boys: possibly Johnny Hallyday[180] lookalikes searching for their Sylvie resulting in the inevitable clashes with Sylvie's GI suitors. On rare occasions there would also be fights between women usually over some GI prize. I witnessed one that occurred at the junction between Rue Pigalle and Rue de la Rochefoucauld. The fight between two young French women was not pretty to watch and the GI calls of 'cat fight' soon resulted in a large crowd of mainly GIs egging the combatants on.

---

[180] Rock musician Johnny Hallyday met Sylvie in 1962, during her second concert in Paris Olympia Hall; they were married on April 12, 1965. Wikipedia reports that they " .... were their generation's "golden couple" in France, and their marriage was among the most carefully watched relationships for the nation's publicity ." They divorced in November 1980. Hallyday died in December 2017. The French nation mourned him with his funeral attended by President Macron and two of his predecessors.

CHAPTER 13

But as the crowd, in an echo of a Roman crowd at gladiatorial contests at the Forum, bayed for blood the gendarmerie arrived and escorted the fighters away. The GIs drifted back to their bars and I rather shamefacedly returned to the Hotel Monnier.

Then late one evening Adrian and I decided to go for a walk across place Pigalle and along Boulevard Clichy past the Moulin Rouge and into Montmartre. We strolled casually looking into shop windows and ignoring the invitations of the touts standing outside clip joints and sex shops when suddenly a hand roughly grabbed my left shoulder. A shorty stocky man in a leather coat pushed me up against the wall and started to frisk me while shouting 'police' into my face. Another presumed cop held on tight to Adrian. After the first cop had finished with me he turned to frisk Adrian. Still not satisfied he ordered us to turn out our pockets. I had a few coins, a wallet with some notes, a lighter and a packet of American cigarettes. Adrian had much the same minus the lighter and cigarettes – he didn't smoke – but as a final gesture he reached inside his leather jacket and said to the glowering plain-clothes policeman "… and I have this!" There, nestled in the palm of his hand was a black-handled flick knife! At the sight of this the cop half whistled, turned and began to wave his arm in a furious beckoning motion to someone further down the street. Within seconds an unmarked police car pulled up alongside the pavement and we were bundled – and that is the right word for it – into the back seat of the car. I was pushed in first and found myself sitting next to a gaunt, pasty-faced, handcuffed man who refused to even acknowledge our presence as he stared in zombie fashion straight ahead.

As we were being driven away I tried in my imperfect French to explain who we were and asked them to contact Roy or Jimmy. At first my pleading seemed to have no effect, until I realized that rather than being driven to a police station the car was moving along Rue Henry Monnier and then stopped at our hotel. The leather-coated cop got out of the car and disappeared into the hotel. About fifteen minutes later the car door was pulled open, we were told to get out and effectively released into Roy's custody, with the cop indicating that he was confiscating the flick knife.

As the car pulled away both Adrian and I simultaneously began to question Roy how he had got us off. Roy explained that the cop had phoned Jimmy from the hotel who had vouched for us, and then Roy had explained that Adrian was young and very impressionable. But what appeared to Roy to clinch our release was when he had hit on the idea of suggesting that it was a US soldier who had given the flick knife to the impressionable Adrian and that we all could agree what bastards *les soldats Americain* were. At that, the cop's eyes had brightened and it was then that Roy thought he had made the decision not to charge us and let us go. We had been very lucky and could have been prosecuted and deported.

As I got ready for bed thinking that Roy was the hero of the day, I opened the drawer of the bedside cabinet and took out my own black-handled flick knife that I had bought from a shop in Montmartre at the same time as Adrian had bought his. We had both had the foolish notion that possessing such a weapon would afford us some protection if somebody attacked us. Thankfully, I had not bothered, or had forgotten, to take mine with me on our late night jaunt. I slowly

CHAPTER 13

wrapped the knife in a cloth and got rid of it the next day in a refuse bin off the Boulevard de Clichy. So ended the only period in my life that I ever possessed, or carried, a personal weapon.

Unfortunately, that incident wasn't our only brush with the forces of law and order in France. And both subsequent incidents involved Andy Wheeldon the lead guitarist of the *Jaybeats*.

The first occurred when Andy came up to visit us at Camp des Loges for a couple of days. It must have been our day off too because we met him at the base and then Andy, Adrian and I took the US Army bus to the Etoile in mid afternoon. It being a nice June day we decided to walk back to Pigalle. We hadn't gone far along the Avenue Wagram before Andy intimated that he wanted to go for a piss. There being no pissoirs in evidence I suggested that he use a building site, which was about 20 or 30 yards up the Avenue. The entrance to the site was a door that was held to a wooden hoarding by a loose nail. So I pulled on the door, it came open and I suggested to Andy that he push it to as he left when he'd done what he had to do. Adrian and I then walked on a little way, turned a corner and paused to look into some shop windows. After about 5 minutes or longer I began to worry and I said to Adrian: " Where the fuck is he?" Adrian shrugged and made some rude comment about Andy being unable to find his dick. So, exasperated, we moved away from the shops, turned back round the corner, walked a few yards and then noticed Andy with his hands in the air and his back pressed against the hoarding of the building site. Standing in front of him were three gendarmes, one, dressed in royal blue trousers, black tunic and a kepi sporting the white braid of a senior officer, was waving a revolver attached to a white lanyard, while his two companions, with less braid on their kepi's, were brandishing sub-machine guns that clearly had been pulled out from under the black capes that both sported. As we approached I could see that all colour had drained from Andy's face and that he was quite reasonably almost 'crapping himself'. I hailed the officer with a polite *bonjour* and pointing to Andy said that he was *mon bon ami*, at which the officer and one of sub machine gun toting gendarmes turned their guns on me! The officer eventually made clear that they thought Andy had broken into the building site to steal lead or copper but I finally convinced them why Andy had really gone into the site. Rather grudgingly they let us go on our way leaving us to ponder again how easily it was in France to fall foul of the law.

The second incident occurred funnily enough when I made a reciprocal visit to Andy and the other *Jaybeats* who were then playing in Fontainebleau. This trip also provided me with another opportunity to try and progress my hoped for relationship with Brenda. We'd enjoyed a great evening, had eaten well, drank much wine and finally returned to the boarding house where they were staying. After a couple more beers the others retired to their beds leaving Andy and I to continue our conversation over more beers. The cumulative effect of the alcohol had clearly loosened our inhibitions because the conversation turned into a singsong, in which we were both thoroughly absorbed when the door of the little kitchen in which we were sat burst open and a man rushed in. The man dressed in a nightshirt tucked into trousers with braces hanging down either side started to shout angrily 'whisky beatniks…. whisky beatniks … '. With my brain sufficiently anaesthetized by alcohol

CHAPTER 13

I picked up a butter knife from the table and started to wave it at the man only to realise that he was holding a gun! And he was angry! Sobering up fast, I put the knife back on the table as gently as I could and both Andy and I offered our apologies. He grunted a couple more 'whisky beatniks ...' then did an about face and walked out of the kitchen. We both started to snigger primarily in relief before the significance of what had happened dawned on us again and we crept quietly to our beds. The next day, mid afternoon, we thought we should go and look for the man to offer more sober apologies. But he had gone. The landlady of the boarding house eventually told us later that day that he was a gendarme who was staying over night before leaving very early to travel to a new posting further south. Hence his anger at having his sleep interrupted by the 'whisky beatniks.'

During this time we also came to realize that Adrian, Pauline and myself were also in breach of British law! Under the *Children and Young Persons Act 1933* a licence must be obtained before a child/young person under the age of 18 can go abroad for the purpose of: singing, playing (a musical instrument), performing or being exhibited 'for profit', including any broadcast performance. In June 1964 all three of us were under eighteen and Roy had been under eighteen until 11 November 1963. We were completely ignorant of this requirement. No previous manager or agent had mentioned this to us, while Jimmy claimed to be in the dark about the vagaries of British law. We would have sailed on blissfully unaware of this requirement if it had not been for the actions of a certain English booking agent whose name thankfully escapes me.

This agent began turning up at the EM Clubs in Orleans and then Camp des Loges to watch us perform. He was charm personified. Dressed in a long, black open overcoat, covering a white scarf, smart grey suit and tie, over shiny black patent leather shoes, with a thin face sporting a thin moustache and dark, wavy hair, he had the look of a slightly louche Spitfire pilot. The car he drove further reinforced this impression, which was a sporty Mark II Jaguar Sedan in British racing green. He let it be known that he could do better for us than Jimmy if we were to switch to him at the end of our current contract. But we were not sure that his intentions were sincere. He had an eye for the ladies, which rested squarely on Pauline, whom he would invite out for drinks and a meal. Pauline was not at all taken with him and quite frankly considered him to be a 'creep'. So taken all things into account and given our felt loyalty to Jimmy, we politely but firmly rebuffed his advances and never saw him again.

A little later Jimmy got in touch to say that the British Embassy in Paris had been on the 'phone to inquire about certain under-age British subjects who were working illegally for him in France. Jimmy was almost literally 'wetting himself':

> "... mah heart Roy it can't stand another shock like this: first, the French police and young Adrian and now the British Embassy. Ah've a reputation in Paris to protect. Why did you boys and girls come over without your licences?"

We still found it hard to believe that Jimmy didn't know about the British requirement that young persons

CHAPTER 13

working abroad required a licence given the large number of British acts he had represented in the past. But perhaps he really didn't know; any sub-eighteen year old from Britain who had worked for him in the past probably didn't have a licence either. The issue now was not to dish out blame – although we had a good idea who had tipped off the British Embassy and we hoped his ears burnt with our imprecations as he motored along in his Jag! We had to get a licence and fast. Our parents were contacted and Adrian's father in particular set the wheels in motion for the three of us to secure the licence. This wasn't as easy as it might sound. A magistrate at Bow Street Magistrates Court in Covent Garden London could only grant the licence. An application form had to be completed for each of us under the guidance of a local solicitor on Teesside and we needed to hire a London barrister to present our case to a magistrate in chambers at Bow Street Magistrates Court.

The three of us flew back home while Roy and Jenny held the fort at Camp des Loges, helped by a couple of extra days off. A date had been set for the hearing in front of the magistrate and a few days later we, with one parent from each family in tow, took the train to London. Upon arrival we met up with the barrister, had coffee with him at a Lyons Corner House to discuss the application and critically to explain why we had been performing abroad without a licence. That done we presented ourselves at the allotted time at the Bow Street Court. Only the three of us plus the barrister were allowed to appear before the magistrate, although we understood that a parent could be called in if there were matters that required clarification.

So we sat in a narrow corridor waiting our turn, for there were others there too in similar circumstances. As the time passed I began to feel uncomfortable in my ill-fitting suit and began to fidget in my seat. As I looked down I noticed a pair of stockinged legs belonging to someone sitting next to me. Surreptitiously, I began to turn my head and lean back to determine what this female sitting next to me looked like. My eyes gradually moved up her body past her skirt and cardigan until I could see her face and lo and behold it was Helen Shapiro![181]

I tried a smile but she responded with only a faint, facial flicker, seemed reluctant to engage and appeared just as nervous as myself. Helen had had massive hits in 1961 with the songs *Don't Treat Me Like a Child,* which rose to number 3 in the charts followed by *You Don't Know,* a chart topper, and biggest of all *Walking back to happiness* which stayed at number 1 in the charts for three weeks in October/November 1961. These were followed in early 1962 with *Tell me what he said* which rose to number 2 in the charts. After that her recording successes diminished. She had turned fifteen in September 1961 and by the time she was sixteen she had been voted Top Female Vocalist in the UK and was the headline act with the Beatles supporting in their first UK tour in 1963. When we sat next to each other in Bow Street she would have still been seventeen turning eighteen in September 1964. By then she had travelled extensively including making an album in Nashville in the US the previous year. So she was probably at the

---

[181] https://en.wikipedia.org/wiki/Helen_Shapiro http://www.billboard.com/artist/303417/helen-shapiro/biography

CHAPTER 13

court to renew her licence. Unless …….. Had she too been a victim of her management's ignorance and fallen foul of a louche looking agent frequently seen behind the wheel of a racing green Jaguar?! Within a few minutes her name was called and she got up and went unaccompanied it appeared into a magistrate's chambers. Then we too were called.

The magistrate appeared old but kindly. Dressed in a dark jacket, white handkerchief loosely placed in his breast pocket, grey waistcoat, white shirt and blue tie, he leaned back in his chair revealing pinstriped trousers and invited our barrister to make the application. We remained standing trying hard to concentrate but my eyes couldn't help wandering round the room noting the legal books on the shelves, the coat stand in a corner and a copy of the *Times* half folded on the magistrates desk.

"Are you having fun in France?"
Caught in mid-daydream I realised that the magistrate was speaking to me.
" err … Yes, ….. Sir!"
"What is it you play?"
"Pop …. popular …. music, sir." Interjected the barrister.
"Pop …. music? I see …. Does this find favour with your American audiences?"
"err … Yes, ….. Sir!" I stuttered.
There was a brief pause, and then he said
"Well, enjoy your adventure."

At that we were ushered from the room, our barrister continuing to converse with the magistrate as the door closed behind us. A couple of minutes later as we squirmed on our seats back in the corridor the barrister emerged a half-smile on his face and when he got close to us he whispered:

"You're legal!"

A big cheer rose as the full band took the stage at Camp des Loges a couple of nights later. Roy joked with the GI audience at how strange it was that some of us had to be licensed "just to play to you guys." Some wit in the audience shouted
"A licence to thrill, not a licence to kill!"
Roy shouted "Nice, one." And Pauline and Jenny shimmied in their shift dresses to great whoops from the GIs as we went into the first number of the evening's set.

The licence fiasco had served to bring the group together. We had overcome an external threat and this had clearly served to reinforce the bonds between us. Moreover, our prospects seemed to be picking up. Our record was being played on the radio, and could be heard in several jukeboxes across Paris and beyond. The Europe No.1 commercial radio station (now known as Europe 1) wanted us to record some numbers for broadcast on their popular *Salut les Copains* music programme. We had some one-night stands scheduled to begin in July and Jimmy had written to Adrian's father intimating that he might receive offers for us to play to US forces in Germany during November, December and January next year, 1965. In recognition of our new licensed world he also requested that the parents of the three under-age band members sign the new

CHAPTER 13

three-month contract that would take us to end-September[182]. After July, where we would continue to be based in Paris to undertake the occasional one-night stand, we were to travel south to the Loire for a two-month stint at the US Army base in Chinon.

We recorded two numbers for Europe No 1: Peggy Lee's *Fever* in which Jenny excelled, which was not on our album, and *Poison Ivy*, which was. After that we started working on the set that we would play on the one-night stands that were to begin in July. During these rehearsals Roy began to mention that he thought after listening to our album several times that out sound was "a bit thin." He had a point. After Johnny Maunder had left the band, we had dispensed with a rhythm guitarist and added another female singer Pauline. This meant that Adrian and I as the rhythm section behind the vocalists and Roy's lead guitar had to work hard to drive the beat and fill in the music. Little more was said until one day as we were getting ready to travel out to Camp des Loges to practise and do the evening show, Roy walked into the hotel accompanied by a tall, thin, guy with shortish blond hair and a reddish nose.

"Hi everyone, I'd like you to meet Malcolm."

"Call me Mal..." Malcolm interjected in a strong Brummie accent.

"Yes, Mal a great keyboard player and our new band member!"

---

[182] A photocopy of this letter can be found on Adrian's *Just Drumming* website: http://www.justdrumming.co.uk/page6.html

CHAPTER 14

MOVING ON

Mal was and remains an enigmatic figure. We were never clear where he came from, how Roy found out about him, and when he contacted him. We could understand the reason behind Roy employing him, for we had discussed the need to fill out the band's sound earlier. What we, that is the entire band except Roy, found difficult to stomach was that his appointment underlined the fact that the Denvers was Roy's band. We had felt the band was a co-operative where decisions were jointly made when in fact that was clearly not the case. Roy had simply been managing us with a light touch. And, if I am honest, I guess I was particularly miffed because while ultimately accepting that this was Roy's band I felt that he and I had for the past couple of years run the band together and at the very least I had participated in the key decisions. Clearly, there was some hypocrisy on my part: it was ok if I felt Roy and I were running the show, never mind the others, but as soon as I had been cut out of the decision making loop I started worrying with the others about being excluded! Nevertheless, even allowing for my own hurt pride, I do believe that Roy had unwittingly created a 'cuckoo in

CHAPTER 14

the nest' situation that subconsciously began to loosen the ties holding the band together and weaken our loyalty to him.

None of this was raised with Roy at the time. Our conscious concerns about the process underlying the appointment were soon put aside. Mal fitted in well with us, was a talented player and a good guy. His playing certainly gave us a more rounded sound on stage and the versatility of the keyboard meant that he could add something to almost all our repertoire. He also brought a little spice into our lives. There was no doubting that Mal liked to party and a can or a bottle of beer was never far from his hand. He also had an exotic taste in women!

His current girlfriend could be politely described as a 'lady of the night', so having little to do during the daytime apart from sleeping she would often turn up at Hotel Monnier looking for Mal. She was good fun and we would often find her knocking on our bedroom door – I shared with Adrian and Mal – asking to see Mal. Frequently, Mal wouldn't be in but Adrian and I being younger and inveterate sleepers-in would often still be in our beds. So she would simply march in and sit on the end of one of our beds and chat to us. She was quite attractive and you can imagine the effect she could have on two young heterosexual males still in bed as she kept crossing and uncrossing her stockinged legs her short skirt riding up while she conversed with us. But she resisted our less than subtle suggestions that she might climb into bed and give one of us a cuddle and remained clearly loyal to Mal in her own way. I became a little infatuated with her and looked forward to her visits. At least that was until one visit when sitting on the end of my bed she noticed a photograph I had on the bedside table of Brenda my unrequited love in the *Jaybeats*. When she suggested that the photo reminded her of a transvestite she knew who worked the Boulevard de Clichy my ardour began to cool – not for Brenda I hasten to add!

Mal's propensity to party and his success with the ladies came together one evening when my good friend Peter 'Pedro' Thompson – see Chapter 4 – from Norton was visiting me in Paris for a couple of days. On the evening before Pedro was due to travel back to Teesside we all went out for a meal and afterwards ended up in the *Blue Train*. Mal and Pedro had got along famously and both were very drunk. Pedro had quite longish, frizzy hair at the time and Mal's girl friend started to play with his hair and began backcombing it. Pedro was 'away with the birds' and before I could intervene Mal's girlfriend and one of her girlfriends had pulled Pedro's trousers up to reveal his bare legs, put a blouse – where did that come from? – over his shirt, some lipstick on him and marched him outside the bar into the street. They then propped him up against a wall and encouraged him to proposition passers-by, male or female! This was potentially very dangerous and I wanted to intervene but the girls kept insisting that this was harmless fun and that I shouldn't be so stuffy. Before long two equally inebriated GIs were to be seen with their arms round Pedro while Mal's girls giggled in the background. At this point Adrian and I intervened and with Pedro's arms around our shoulders we half dragged/carried him back to his room at the hotel and put him to bed. Next morning we walked with him to the Gare de Nord to catch his train back to England as he nursed a very thick head. And he was apparently oblivious of

CHAPTER 14

much that had happened the previous night because as he was about leave us he said:

"Oh, by the way I found a girl's blouse in my room. I'm not sure how it got there so I handed it into reception!"

Pedro's visit brought a little bit of Stockton – well Norton! – back into my life, which served to ratchet up the homesickness feelings I had intermittently been having for the previous couple of months. I suspected that Pauline, Adrian and even perhaps Roy, were also affected. But as the bonds between band members gradually weakened and the draw of home increased a new challenge emerged on the horizon. June 1964 was drawing to a close and with it our residency at Camp de Loges EM club. The 'tour' that Jimmy had arranged for the band to promote our album to US troops was looming.

However, a *Beatles World Tour*[183] this was not. We were still to be based in Paris and would make two, three day or four day trips to US bases in France and some in Germany. Jimmy was keen to introduce us to US troops in Germany and had hopes of getting us some monthly residencies at US bases there at the end of the year and in 1965. Moreover, while the numbers of the US military were falling in France[184] several of the soldiers leaving were going on to Vietnam where the number of US military personnel was rising rapidly.[185]

---

[183] The Beatles had begun their '*World Tour*' on June 4th in Copenhagen, Denmark.

[184] Around 33,000 in 1964 compared to the peak of more than 71,000 in 1957.

[185] The number rose from a little more that 17,000 in 1964 to more that 129,000 in 1965 peaking at 537,000 in 1968 as US blood and treasure were sucked into the disaster that became known as the Vietnam War.

"Hey Jimmy are you going to open an office in Saigon?" Mal irreverently asked Jimmy one day. "Maybe, mah boy. Maybe!" was Jimmy's laconic reply. But the prospect of further months away in Germany, never mind in France, in 1965, appealed much less to me than it would have done six, even three, months previously, and as for Vietnam!

Of course, after the accident in Orleans we still had no van, so Jimmy drafted in Rawlins to drive us in the VW camper van to the gigs, with most of the gear strapped precariously on top of the van. Our forays out of Paris usually began with Rawlins and the VW van arriving early at the Hotel Monnier. Of course being teenagers we wouldn't necessarily all be up and Rawlins would be forced to cajole and threaten – " It's a long walk to Orleans!" - before we would all slide sleepily into the van and then doze for most of the journey to our destination. Some of the bases we played at during this session of one-nighters represented a return visit to old friends in, for example, Fontainebleau and Ingrandes. The GI audiences were enthusiastic and the evenings post gig were often spent in nicotine and alcohol fuelled reminiscences with the club manager, club staff and GI mates. Then it is was back on the road as the sober and much put upon Rawlins - our guardian angel – drove us as we slept back to Paris.

But not all trips required us to travel back to Paris the same day. Our visits to Germany obviously required at least a one-night stop over. Germany - or West Germany as it then was – was literally completely new territory to us. The country seemed cleaner, busier, and more dynamic than France. The US bases seemed bigger and better than their French counterparts, which was

CHAPTER 14

maybe because we were now on the front line of the Cold War. Whatever the reason, the US authorities were clearly putting much more resources into their German military outposts and that even went as far as the fees paid for visiting bands, although Jimmy wasn't prepared to admit it!

One evening we pulled into Baden-Baden a spa town, located in the state of Baden-Württemberg in southwestern Germany. I can't remember which base we had played at but we all slunk off to our rooms and were soon fast asleep. Next morning, Rawlins decided that we should do some sightseeing before we returned to Paris. As he entered the room Roy and I shared, Roy moved across to the window threw open the curtains and declaimed "Let's go see what the niggers are like in this town." Then "Gulp" as the black, ex US marine Rawlins Spivey shot him a quizzical look, smiled, turned towards the door and quietly whispered "Ok, boss." Needless to say Roy, the most non-racist person you could meet, was mortified.

That incident apart, little of import happened during our one-night stands to promote our LP. The excitement of travelling to different bases to perform soon began to pall and we longed both for our days off and for the quieter pace of a monthly residency, which we were to begin again in August at Chinon, which was located on the banks of the Vienne river about 6 miles from where it joins the Loire. Our days off from touring were mainly spent in bed trying to catch up on our sleep, followed by furtive trips to the *Blue Train* for food and drink. The new Beatles album *A Hard Day's Night* was released in the UK in early July and from what we could gauge from friends back in Stockton our own album paled in comparison to their catchy self-penned songs. Moreover, the Beatles were coming to Stockton to play again in October. We didn't know where we would be but Stockton and other parts of the UK seemed to be developing a thriving music scene both in terms of local bands and performances by some of the top British and US singers and bands.[186] Paris for all its glories could not compete with that.

Maybe we would be better off back in Stockton, or if not Stockton why not try our luck in Britain again, or move on and do something else? Yet, we did have a recording contract, something that would be difficult to obtain in the UK where the quality of the competition was clearly intense. Moreover, Jimmy had been very successful at not only getting us a recording contract with Polydor France but also in getting work for us in the past and probably in the near future. The possibility of playing the US military bases of Wiesbaden, Stuttgart and Frankfurt, or perhaps Saigon, seemed a tad more enticing than drawing the dole in Billingham!

Roy and I had struggled to find work in London before stumbling on Sam Curtis. And, yet, as a band the bonds of our relationship were less strong than they used to be. We were growing up and therefore perhaps growing apart as our interests and passions began to

---

[186] The list of concerts at the Stockton Globe and Odeon during 1964 as well as events such as the Redcar Jazz Festival contains most of the top acts of the time including *inter alia*: the Beatles, Rolling Stones, Animals, Gerry & the Pacemakers, Searchers, Billy J. Kramer, Swinging Blue Jeans, Roy Orbison, Chuck Berry, Carl Perkins, Joe Brown, Dusty Springfield, Adam Faith, Rod Stewart, Long John Baldry, Gene Vincent and more.

CHAPTER 14

diverge. Might there be better opportunities for each of us individually?

Adrian was a young and superbly talented drummer; did he not see that the Denvers was almost certainly only the beginning of his career? Jenny and Pauline were good singers and surely would prosper in other bands back in Britain, or develop solo careers. Roy, it seemed to me would always have success no matter what he turned his hand to. And me? Well, I knew that I wasn't in Adrian's class as a musician and I couldn't sing as well as Jenny and Pauline. Nor did I have Roy's entrepreneurial abilities musically or otherwise. In moments of clarity I could not see a successful musical career ahead of me. But what should I do?

These thoughts and questions swirled around in my head all through July and into August as our touring ceased and we left Paris for Chinon, or more specifically Chinon Engineer Depot, Saint-Benoît-la-Forêt. We chose to stay at Azay Le Rideau in the Loire valley. Azay is famous for its château. Wikipedia writes: "(b)uilt between 1518 and 1527, this château is considered one of the foremost examples of early French renaissance architecture. Set on an island in the middle of the Indre river, this picturesque château has become one of the most popular of the châteaux of the Loire valley." And typically despite our residence for two months in a hotel in the centre of this small town – around 2,500 people - we never sought to visit the château!

What we did do, though, on our days off and during the day before we travelled to the base at Chinon, was swim in the Indre. The month was August, the weather was hot and we were in no hurry to rush to the base and practise. The hotel also had a decent restaurant, which offered local wines that we occasionally sampled and which meant that we didn't have to rush up to the base to get food. Our tastes in food and drink were also beginning to become a little more sophisticated so that the diet of burgers, pizzas and steaks at the base snack bars held less attraction than it once did. However, when sat in the hotel restaurant Roy would more often demand *Le Champagne Etats Unis* to the bemusement of the waitress who would then offer a disdainful smile when informed that what Roy was seeking to order was Coca Cola!

Yet, these pleasant summer days and our well-received performances each evening at the Chinon EM club, failed to halt the creeping malaise that was spreading through the band. Jenny was clearly yearning to get back to her family in London. Adrian was clearly homesick but did his best to hide it. I was homesick too but also increasingly drawn to my friends in the Jaybeats, especially Brenda, who were still working at US bases in the Paris region. Roy, Pauline and Mal, perhaps sensing the disaffection amongst the others in the band began to talk about forming a trio and playing together on their own[187]. Matters came to a head in September, our second consecutive month at the Chinon base, when Adrian's mother and my mother visited us at Azay for a holiday. Adrian and I picked them up in a GI friend's car and drove them back to our hotel.

Both mothers were shocked at our appearance. My mother insisted again that I looked too thin and pasty and Adrian's mum seemed even more concerned about

---

[187] They would eventually become the bizarrely named *B.O. Trio* staying on in France and Germany playing one-night cabaret shows largely for US forces.

CHAPTER 14

the condition of her own son. By the end of the week relations between Adrian's mum and Roy had deteriorated because it was evident that she was pushing to take Adrian back to Hartlepool with her. My mother didn't go that far with me but she was not happy either. Yet it was clear that even if Adrian did not return to Britain with his mum, he would leave the band by the end of the month.

Moreover, our parents had not signed the contract that Jimmy had offered us for the final three months of the year, so we were under no legal obligation to continue in France. Roy made it clear that Jimmy had indicated to him that while he wished the Denvers to stay together if we broke up he would try and get work for the trio that Roy had in mind. I had made several contacts with the Jaybeats during the month and it appeared that they were keen for me to join them if the Denvers split up. Their current bass player could play rhythm guitar and would be prepared to do so to allow me to join the band. But they whispered that they were not sure how committed he was to the band anyway. The Denvers were set to break up.

My eyes scan the stage of the Chinon EM club where amplifiers are sheathed in their covers, guitars are in their cases and drums and PA equipment are all boxed and ready to transport. As I look over at the dying embers of the Denvers images flash through my mind: Roy stepping out of the Bedford van in Matlock Gardens inviting me to join the band; Johnny Maunder picking up an Elvis Presley song as Johnny Rocco lays into thugs at the Hartburn Tennis Club; Johnny Rocco receiving a kicking in return at that Grangefield Grammar School dance; Johnny Rocco's voice bringing tears to the eyes of the diners below us as we play Middlesbrough's Empire Continental; the excitement of playing alongside Liverpool bands at the Outlook Middlesbrough; Roy and I meeting Hank and the rest of the Shadows; the mid-morning call from Sam Curtis; the first sight of France and those 'ladies of the night' lining the streets of Pigalle; screaming GIs as Jenny sings and dances *Shakin' All Over*; Louis smiling while playing his drums and then smashing up his room at the Hotel de Metz, Bar le Duc; the cold fear of nuclear war as we listen to AFN through the night at Nancy at a critical point in the Cuban Missile Crisis; meeting Jimmy English; standing shoulder to shoulder with the Everly Brothers at Fontainebleau; watching the anguished faces of the young GIs at the Camp des Loges EM club as they gather round a speaker listening to AFN reporting the ghastly news of President Kennedy's assassination; marvelling at the Beatles at the Paris Olympia; Pauline dancing innocently with a black GI at Orleans EM club as spurned white GIs look on with murderous faces; recording in the Polydor studios in Paris; listening to our single on a juke box in a Paris bar; hearing one of our songs played on the Europe No 1 radio station; the fights between Roy and Adrian and I; the brushes with the French police; the electric atmosphere of Pigalle .... ; my reveries are interrupted by the honking of a car horn.

It is time.

Adrian has already left for Hartlepool and Jenny for London. Mal, Pauline and Roy stand by the door of the EM club. I cross the club's dance floor and hug Mal who offers some long-forgotten indecent comment. I kiss and hug Pauline and then embrace Roy. Few words

CHAPTER 14

are said. By now we are outside the club. Andy sits at the wheel of the Jaybeat's van. Brenda is in the front seat. I walk towards them, pause, then turn and look back at Roy who gives me a wink. Brenda beckons to me and I quicken my pace towards the van. I focus on her smile and, suddenly, the future looks interesting.

EPILOGUE

I began writing this book in 2005 as I was recuperating from an operation to remove a – fortunately benign – tumour from my lung. The book progressed at a slow pace over the next thirteen years, because I could only write it by taking infrequent, brief periods away from my daily life in order to create the space to transport my mind back to the 1950s and 1960s and to undertake the associated research. In writing the book I wanted to record my time with the Denvers because I thought very few people understood what it was like to be a band member in that era. Yes, there are plenty of memoirs and biographies of well-known pop bands and key music figures yet little has been written about the experiences of those bands that may have briefly soared but never really made it. And even for those that do 'make it' they rarely endure. Indeed, the experience of the Denvers and the vast majority of other rock groups could be seen as a metaphor for life itself: hesitant beginnings, learning and adaptation, dreams and hopes, confidence, self doubt, hard work, successes, failures, self-realization, decline and finally, dissolution.

As the book recounts, joining the band and letting it assume a central role in your life also offered a route out of your likely life prospects as evidenced by the lives of parents, relatives and friends. In earlier years, Military or

EPILOGUE

National Service gave many working class boys a chance to escape the boundaries of place and possibly enhance their social and economic prospects. But conscription ended in the UK in 1960 and while many young men were content thereafter to return to the path set by their former civilian lives, the main impact of National Service was to promote character, self respect and self discipline rather than social and economic mobility. A pattern that would be replicated for many of the GI's that formed the bulk of our audiences at the bases we played at in France. Although, one suspects that the opportunities for social and economic mobility available to the GIs were greater than those available to the average ex-British squaddie! Moreover, while it was possible to sign on for a term in the military in your late teens, membership of a band appeared to our young minds to offer immediate glamour and status with our peers as well as the prospect of the proverbial 'fame and fortune' and none of the discipline and rigour associated with military life. The fact that the probability of musical success was exceptionally low and even, if realized, would almost certainly not last for long, was heavily discounted and largely dismissed from our thoughts.

Yet, one of the band's members, Adrian Tillbrook, did have a successful and lifelong career as a musician. Adrian's website http://www.justdrumming.co.uk/index.html charts his career and current activities. Johnny Rocco (Ronald Orten Porter) passed away, age 62, in 2004.[188] John Maunder passed away, age 69, in 2010.

---

[188] See his son Dean Porter's comments about his father on the *Picture Stockton Archive* website https://picturestocktonarchive.wordpress.com/2006/05/13/local-teesside-band-of-the-50s60s/

Louis Johnson is, I believe, still alive and well in Stockton after playing for many years with his Lou Johnson trio. Jackie Peters (Pauline Riley) subsequently sang for the Johnny Taylor Five, a well known local Teesside band, and then married and moved to Canada, where she still lives to this day. Jenny Paul (Jenny Hutchins) is in her mid seventies, retired, travels often, and is still her sharp self, living now in Aylesbury, Buckinghamshire. Roy Smith, worked in a bank, got married to Sandy, emigrated to Canada, had two daughters, became an executive in a large department store chain, developed a successful photography business, is now age 72, retired and living in Hamilton, Ontario.

And me? Well, I can feel another book coming on! Suffice to say, that after a brief period with the Jaybeats, from North Wales, Manchester and Shrewsbury, in France I returned home to Stockton. I worked initially as a building labourer and transport manager's assistant. I then took the other path that so many working class children have followed to grow away from their roots: education. I went to night school and took day release from my company, at first unpaid, and then with the company's support. I secured a place at the University of Lancaster in 1970 to study economics and politics. I graduated in the summer of 1973 and then went on to do a Masters Degree in Regional Economics. I began teaching in Glasgow at the then College of Technology[189] in October 1974 and have lived in the Glasgow area ever since. In October 1976 I took up a post as Lecturer in Economics at the University of Strathclyde and spent the

---

[189] Now Glasgow Caledonian University.

EPILOGUE

rest of my career at that university as a teacher and researcher until my retirement in 2010.

My personal life has given me much joy and some pain, notably widowerhood. I am today blessed with an extended family of a lovely wife, three children, two stepchildren, four step-grand children and a border collie called Islay! I occasionally write, usually about the Scottish economy, and I also do the occasional seminar, talk and lecture. Then when I walk out to the podium and see the audience before me my mind often drifts back to those days when I took the stage, guitar in hand, and I am back in the Denvers again.

June 2018
Glasgow

ACKNOWLEDGEMENTS

Many people have helped me directly or indirectly, knowingly or unknowingly, to write this book. A special thanks should be given to my ex band colleagues, especially Roy Smith, Adrian Tillbrook and Jenny Hutchins, who all read several chapters, answered numerous questions from me about the events surrounding the Denvers sojourn in France and corrected and supplemented my fading memory. That they picked up the threads of our relationship so readily after an interval of 50 years says a lot about them. Thank you guys!

Tom Johnson gave me access to, and membership of, his Yahoo group of ex US Army Military Police based at Poitiers, France in the 1950s and 1960s. A successful author himself he gave me much encouragement in writing this memoir. Derek Raffaelli helped me with psychoanalysis during a difficult period in my life and encouraged the writing of the book. Brian Cunningham helped me relearn guitar, revisit the music of the 1960s and made me remember what it was like to play music with others in a band. Ten years later our lessons continue as I strive to improve my playing. The book benefited significantly from his musical insights.

I am also grateful to Donald Murray and Charlie Woods who both read early drafts of the book. Charlie, in our monthly guitar playing sessions helped also to

ACKNOWLEDGEMENTS

rekindle and sustain my interest in rock music that informed the writing of the book.

Finally, my wife Wendy read all the chapters and offered suggestions that improved the book considerably. I am forever grateful for her support and love.

This book is dedicated to my children Lucy Hancock, Michael and Caitlin Ashcroft and my stepchildren Jamie Mackay and Kate Binner. You have enriched my life in ways that I haven't the words to explain. My life is unimaginable without you.

www.ingramcontent.com/pod-product-compliance
Lightning Source LLC
Chambersburg PA
CBHW050929240426
43671CB00020B/2967